KT-498-435

London
Shortlist

timeout.com / london

62

86

183

Contents

Sky Garden p166

ABOUT THE GUIDE

The *Time Out London Shortlist* is one of a series of pocket guides to cities around the globe. Drawing on the expertise of local authors, it distils their knowledge into a handy, easy-to-use format that ensures you get the most from your trip, whether you're a first-time or a return visitor.

Time Out London Shortlist is divided into four sections:

Welcome to London introduces the city and provides inspiration for your visit.

London Day by Day helps you plan your trip with an events calendar and customised itineraries.

London by Area is the main visitor section of the guide. It includes detailed listings and reviews for the very best sights, museums, restaurants ⑩, pubs & bars ⑩, shops ⑩ and entertainment venues ⑩, all organised by area with a corresponding street map. To help navigation, each area of London has been assigned its own colour.

London Essentials provides practical visitor information, including accommodation options and details of public transport.

Shortlists & highlights

We have selected a Shortlist of stand-out venues in each area, which are marked with a heart ♥ in the text. The very best of these appear in the Highlights feature (*see p10*) and receive extended coverage in the guide.

Maps

There's an overview map on *p8* and individual street maps for each area of the city. Venues featured in the guide have been given a grid reference so that you can find them easily on the maps and on the ground.

Prices

All our **restaurant listings** are marked with a pound symbol category from budget to blow-out (£-££££), indicating the price you should expect to pay for an average three-course meal for two (or the equivalent in a café or sharing plates venue) with drinks and service: £ = under £60; ££ = £60-£100; £££ = £100-£140; ££££ = over £140.

A similar system is used in our **Accommodation** chapter based on the hotel's standard prices for one night in a double room: £ = under £130; ££ = £130-£250; £££ = £250-£350; ££££ = over £350.

Introduction

London was – in the 19th century – a wonder of the world. The first city since ancient times to top a million inhabitants, an industrial powerhouse at the heart of the world's largest empire, it drew Monet from Paris to paint the smoggy Thames from the Savoy, while bad-boy poet Arthur Rimbaud saw in the city's vast railway stations cathedrals to modernity. Immigrants still feel London's pull today, bringing not wonder but their own energy and new ideas. You might feel it too, in our out-there nightlife, our food – once an international joke, now a rich stew of global influences and creativity – and our nation-defining cultural edifices, whether museums or theatres. London lives life at two paces. Where there is most money, things are more sedate, with the whisper of history audible in fine buildings and heritage sites that in places date to Roman times. Elsewhere, increasingly in the neighbourhoods beyond central London, the city is young, rich in variety and always hurrying after the next new thing. This guide takes you to the best of both Londons. We hope you enjoy our city.

Welcome to London

St Paul's Cathedral *p162*

Highlights

From historic sights to elegant parks, world-class galleries to cutting-edge theatre, we count down the highlights of this endlessly diverting and diverse city. Other destinations may flit in and out of vogue but London will always fascinate and inspire: here's why.

01

Design Museum *p108*

The loved but often neglected Design Museum finally has a home worthy of its sense of adventure: the former Commonwealth Institute is a dramatic, pioneering building that now houses a superb history of high- and low-brow design, as well as temporary exhibitions that will doubtless be eye-opening, silly, cerebral and fun by turns.

07

St Paul's Cathedral *p162*

As architectural masterpieces go, St Paul's is at the frou-frou end of things, with its frothy Baroque exterior. But the grandeur of the interior is quite breathtaking – and no less so for Sir Christopher Wren's audacity in giving the authorities precisely the cathedral they didn't want.

08

British Museum *p126*

This is one of the world's greatest museums – and also one of its most popular. No wonder: it's a compendium of key artefacts from most of the significant cultures of the world, from Egyptian mummies and the Rosetta Stone to monumental Mesopotamian sculpture and even an Easter Island head. Every visit uncovers further revelations and, since entry is free, you can head back as often as you wish.

09

Tate Britain *p88*

Since its dramatic extension opened in 2016, Tate Modern (*see p74*) has been right back in the limelight. But as the architectural plaudits die down, we find ourselves drawn back to the original Tate: lovely premises, blockbuster shows every bit as good as those at its bombastic younger rival and the entire chronological span of British art since 1545 to walk through. It's not so busy, either.

10

Tower of London *p165*

Who doesn't love a castle? The beginnings of this one were built in 1078, when William the Conqueror wanted to point out he was the boss – not just of the city, though it was rebellious, but of the whole country. The Tower was witness to many of the key events in London's history and is now a fabulous showcase for the Crown Jewels, as well as home to the traditionally dressed 'Beefeaters' (Yeoman Warders) and their ravens.

11

St James's Park *p91*

One of the city's joys is its chain of incredibly central parks: you can walk from Kensington Gardens and Hyde Park through Green Park to St James's barely touching the tarmac. The last is our favourite. Why? It's the prettiest, with lovely lakes for waterfowl – not just ducks, but pelicans too – and has a delicious view of Buckingham Palace.

12

Maritime Greenwich *p188*

The grand colonnades of Wren's Old Royal Naval College (don't miss the restoration tours of the Painted Hall) draw you into historic Greenwich Park, a fine introduction to London's most expansive UNESCO World Heritage Site. It combines the National Maritime Museum, the Queen's House art gallery (reopened after 400th anniversary renovations), the gorgeous *Cutty Sark* sailing ship and, yes, the Prime Meridian.

13

Victoria & Albert Museum *p100*

Stroll into the V&A's main entrance – that grand hall with its dramatic glass chandelier – and the scale of this museum of art and design, with its combination of stately historical context and cutting-edge modern design, is already apparent. It's gallery after grand and gorgeous gallery, with the reopened Weston Cast Court our absolute favourite. The Science Museum (*see p98*) and Natural History Museum (*see p96*) are fabulous too – but the V&A is unforgettable.

14

Houses of Parliament *p86*

Eye-popping and of huge historic significance, the grand buildings around Parliament Square are mostly Victorian, but their core is ancient: at the heart of the Houses of Parliament is Westminster Hall, a grand medieval hall that survived the Great Fire of 1666. Overlooking it all, the Big Ben clocktower chimes out across the city.

15

Westminster Abbey *p85*

Gothic grandeur at its most splendid. Westminster Abbey is not only a beautiful place of worship but it embodies much of British history. Crammed with monuments and statues, more than 3,000 souls are honoured throughout its chapels and cloisters, from kings and queens to historical 'celebs' such as Darwin, Dickens and Hardy.

Sightseeing

The key to London's geography is that it is effectively two cities, not one. The City is the area originally walled by the Romans, which through its mercantile wealth and the weakness of English kings secured considerable independence from Westminster, where the monarchs and, latterly, Parliamentarians reside. Around these poles, the patchwork of districts grew up that are now central London. The problem with a visit to London is – as it always has been – how to fit it all in. The truth is, you can't... not in a single trip, not in a single lifetime. So relax and do whatever you most fancy. If you've only a couple of days at your disposal, consider following one of our itineraries (*see pp50-55*).

Best views
London Eye *p72*
The Shard *p73*
Sky Garden *p166*

Best architecture
Old Royal Naval College *p188*
St Paul's Cathedral *p162*

Best fine art
National Gallery *p87*
Tate Britain *p88*
Victoria & Albert Museum *p100*

Best quirky museums
Geffrye Museum *p178*
Sir John Soane's Museum *p157*
Wellcome Collection *p129*

Best outdoor attractions
Chelsea Physic Garden *p103*
Queen Elizabeth Olympic Park *p187*
Royal Botanic Gardens, Kew *p20*

Best for history
British Museum *p126*
Imperial War Museum *p69*
Museum of London *p164*
Tower of London *p165*

Best for kids
London Transport Museum *p145*
Natural History Museum *p96*
Science Museum *p98*
ZSL London Zoo *p171*

A whistle-stop tour

The **South Bank** (*see pp66-80*) remains London's key tourist destination. The principal attractions are well established: **Tate Modern**, **Shakespeare's Globe** and **Borough Market**, the **London Eye** and the lively **Southbank Centre**. The **Shard** looks down on all of them from **London Bridge**.

Across the river, **Westminster & St James's** (*see pp81-92*) are the focal point of UK politics, location of the **Houses of Parliament**, **Westminster Abbey** and **Buckingham Palace**. **Trafalgar Square**, has two brilliant art collections along its pedestrianised northern edge at the **National Gallery** and the **National Portrait Gallery**.

To the west **Kensington & Chelsea** (*see pp93-110*) has a cluster of unmissable Victorian museums – the **V&A**, the **Natural History Museum** and the **Science Museum** – famous Knightsbridge department stores, and the boutiques and eateries of the King's Road, not to mention the fabulous new **Design Museum**.

The **West End** (*see pp111-150*) includes most of what is now central London. We start north of Oxford Street, in the slightly raffish shopping district of Marylebone with elegant Fitzrovia to the east. South is Mayfair, as expensive as its reputation but less daunting, with fine mews and pubs. The squares and Georgian terraces of literary Bloomsbury, home of the unrivalled **British Museum**, are to the east, from where it's a short hop north to the **British Library** and redeveloped King's Cross. Head south for **Covent Garden**, so popular with tourists that locals often forget its many charms – including the excellent **London Transport Museum** – and Soho, notorious centre of fun.

Bordered by Holborn to the west, **The City** (*see pp151-168*) comprises the once-walled Square Mile of the original city. Much more than a place just for finance workers, it has numerous historic attractions, of which the **Tower of London** and **St Paul's Cathedral** are the best known –easily accessed from the South Bank over the Millennium Bridge. Visit the **Museum of London** to get a grip on the city's bewildering past.

Around these central areas is a doughnut of other districts you won't want to miss: **North London** (*see pp169-176*) includes Camden, Islington, Highgate and Hampstead, while trendier-than-thou **East London** (*see pp177-187*) encompasses the eating, shopping and nightlife of Spitalfields, Brick Lane, Hoxton and Shoreditch, with Dalston to the north; further east still are the **Olympics Park** and **London Docklands**. And finally, there's historic **Greenwich** (*see p188*), lovely **Kew Gardens** and grand **Hampton Court Palace** (*see p20*), all of which are worth a day trip in their own right.

Making the most of it

Don't be scared of London's public transport: it's by far the best way of getting around town. Invest in an **Oyster**

Worth the Trip

London is huge – but here are two must-sees on the edge of town that we couldn't leave out

Hampton Court Palace

East Molesey, Surrey, KT8 9AU (0844 482 7777, www.hrp.org.uk). Hampton Court rail, or riverboat to Hampton Court Pier (Apr-Oct). **Open** *Palace Apr-Oct 10am-6pm daily. Nov-Mar 10am-4.30pm daily. Grounds dawn-dusk daily.* **Admission** *Apr-Oct £17.50; £8.75-£14.50 reductions; £43.80 family. Nov-Mar £16.50; £8.25-£14 reductions; £42.50 family. Free under-5s.*

A half-hour train ride south-west of central London, this is a spectacular palace, once owned by Henry VIII. It was built in 1514 for Cardinal Wolsey and for 200 years was at the focal point of English history: Shakespeare performed in front of James I here in 1604; and, after the Civil War, Oliver Cromwell was so besotted by the building he moved in. Centuries later, the rosy walls of the palace still dazzle. Its vast size can be daunting, so take advantage of the costumed guided tours. The Tudor Kitchens are fun, with their giant cauldrons and fake pies; the Great Hall has beautiful tapestries and stained glass, and the landscaped gardens contain fine topiary and the famous maze.

Royal Botanic Gardens (Kew Gardens)

Kew, Richmond, Surrey, TW9 3AB (8332 5655, www.kew.org). Kew Gardens tube/Overground, Kew Bridge rail or riverboat to Kew Pier. **Open** *from 9.30am; check website for closing times.* **Admission** *£15; £14 reductions; free under-17s.*

This half square mile of horticultural wonders is a joy to amble around in – surely the finest botanic gardens anywhere in the world. The unparalleled collection of plants was begun by Queen Caroline, wife of George II, with exotic plants brought back by voyaging botanists (Charles Darwin among them). In 1759, 'Capability' Brown was employed by George III to improve on the work of his predecessors, setting the template for a garden that has long attracted thousands of visitors each year. Head straight for the 19th-century greenhouses, filled to the roof with tropical plants, and next door the Waterlily House's quiet and pretty indoor pond (closed in winter). Brown's Rhododendron Dell is at its best in spring, while the Xstrata Treetop Walkway, some 60 ft above the ground, is terrific fun in autumn.

Kew Gardens

travel smartcard (*p200*) on arrival or use a contactless debit/credit card to roam cashless through the city by bus, tube (underground trains) and train, especially the excellent London Overground – which is treated as part of the underground network. The opening of the much anticipated Crossrail from 2018 will transform travel to the south and east.

The tube is the easiest mode of transport for visitors (avoid rush hour: 8-9.30am, 4.30-7pm Mon-Fri), but buses are best to get a handle on the city's topography. Some good sightseeing routes are RV1 (riverside), 7, 8 and 12, and to a enjoy a classic red bus, hop on the **Routemaster Heritage bus** (*p200*) which runs from Tower Hill via Monument and St Paul's Cathedral to Trafalgar Square. Note that no London buses accept cash anymore – if you don't have an Oyster, you'll have to use a contactless debit or credit card.

In the centre, many attractions are surprisingly close to each other and can be easily reached on foot. The **Transport for London walking map** (http://content. tfl.gov.uk/walking-tube-map.pdf) reveals, to cite only the best-known example, that Covent Garden station is only a five-minute walk from Leicester Square station. It looks much further on the schematic Underground map. Alternatively, the **Santander Cycles** bike hire scheme (known as 'Boris Bikes') can be a lot of fun and an inexpensive way to get about (*see p203*).

To avoid the worst of the crowds, avoid big attractions at weekends and on late-opening nights, and aim to hit blockbuster exhibitions in the middle of a run; January to March are the quietest months for visiting attractions, July to September the busiest. Last entry can be up to an hour before closing time (we specify when it is more than an hour before), so don't turn up at the last minute and expect to get in. Ring ahead to confirm opening hours.

Changing the Guard

London is a past master when it comes to military pomp

On alternate days from 10.45am – or daily from 10.15am April-July – one of the five Foot Guards regiments lines up in scarlet coats and tall bearskin hats in the forecourt of Wellington Barracks; at exactly 11.27am (10.57am April-July),the soldiers start to march to **Buckingham Palace**, joined by their regimental band, to relieve the sentries there in a 45-minute ceremony for **Changing the Guard**. The Guards regiments are the Grenadier, Coldstream, Scots, Irish and Welsh. (For details, visit www.royal.gov.uk/ RoyalEventsandCeremonies/ ChangingtheGuard/Overview.aspx: do check in advance for weather cancellations or last-minute changes of schedule.)

Not far away, at **Horse Guards Parade** in Whitehall, the Household Cavalry regiments – the Life Guards and Blues and Royals – mount the guard daily at 11am (10am on Sunday). Although this ceremony isn't as famous as the one at Buckingham Palace, it's more visitor-friendly: the crowds aren't as thick as they are at the palace. After the old and new guard have stared each other out in the centre of the parade ground, you can nip through to the Whitehall side to catch the departing old guard perform their dismount choreography: a synchronised, firm slap of approbation to the neck of each horse before the gloved troopers swing off.

As well as these near-daily ceremonies, London sees other, less frequent parades on a far grander scale. The most famous is **Trooping the Colour**, which is staged to mark the Queen's official birthday on the Saturday closest to 13 June (her real birthday is in April). At 10.45am, the Queen rides in a carriage from Buckingham Palace to Horse Guards Parade to watch the soldiers, before heading back to Buckingham Palace for a midday RAF flypast and the impressive gun salute from Green Park.

Also at Horse Guards, for two successive evenings in June, a pageant of military music and precision marching begins at 8pm when the Queen (or another royal) takes the salute of the 300-strong drummers, pipers and musicians of the Massed Bands of the Household Division. This is known as **Beating Retreat** (www. householddivision.org.uk/beating-retreat, tickets 7839 5323).

Changing the Guard

Eating & Drinking

'Boiled beef and carrots,' sang Harry Champion, darling of the music hall, in 1909, 'that's the stuff for your derby kell, keeps you fit and keeps you well.' For decades that would indeed have been as good as stuff for your belly got in London. Not anymore: thanks to its voracious cosmopolitanism, our restaurant culture has become a thing of joy. Many cities claim you can eat your way round the world without setting foot outside their boundaries: well, in London it's just true. We've even embraced British food, albeit in a rather modern form. As for drinking, London may have learnt the art of the bar from the Big Apple – and learnt that lesson surprisingly well – but we continue to own the pub. You'll find a drinking culture with a conscience, too – with bars focused on sustainability and pubs supporting local brands and producers, especially with the current vogue for craft beer

Best of British
St John *p159*
Regency Café *p89*
J Sheekey *p147*

Best afternoon tea
Diamond Jubilee Tea Salon at
Fortnum & Mason *p92*
Wyld Tea at Dandelyan *p77*

Best walk-in restaurants
10 Greek Street *p132*
The Barbary *p146*
Padella *p76*

Best traditional pubs
Cross Keys *p148*
Jerusalem Tavern *p160*
Ye Olde Mitre *p160*

Best cocktails
69 Colebrooke Row *p173*
Connaught Bar *p121*
Dandelyan *p77*
Swift *p137*

Best for a blow-out
Social Eating House *p136*
Hutong *p76*

and small-batch gin. A combination of rich traditions and a long history of bohemian revelry with a real taste for innovation makes drinking in London a real pleasure.

Best of British

For a period in the 2010s, every new restaurant seemed to be claiming its 'modern British' culinary heritage. The idea was simple: take out-of-favour but flavour-packed cuts of animal (bone marrow, pig's trotters, hearts) and offer them in simple preparations that let the unique qualities of the ingredients shine. Added to this were a couple of key themes: localism (sourcing superb ingredients from as close to home as possible) and the new casual gourmet diner, who was willing to pay for fine food but didn't relish the flim-flam of Mayfair haute-cuisine. Despite the vogue of this stripped-back blackboard approach, there's still plenty of room for what visitors might consider 'British' without the 'modern' appendage: you might fancy fish and chips at **Poppies** (6-8 Hanbury Street, E1 6QR, 7247 0892, www.poppiesfishandchips. co.uk) or **Hook** (63-65 Parkway, NW1 7PP, 3808 5112, www. hookrestaurants.com), for instance, or to indulge in the post-colonial excess of a leisurely afternoon tea. There's also a handful of places, such as **M Manze** (*see p76*), serving what was, for a century, the staple diet of the London working man: eels – once yanked straight from the Thames – and pie and mash.

The world in one city

From the coffee houses that flooded London during the Ottoman Empire in the 17th century, to the mass immigration from Bangladesh in the 1970s, Londoners have welcomed wave after wave of global food. By the 2000s chicken tikka masala was hailed as Britain's national dish, yet before that there was Chinese, Italian, even French. Fusion cuisine, once all the rage, retains a strong presence with North African, Japanese, Middle Eastern, Peruvian and even Nordic cuisine continuing to influence. Most recently, however, London has returned closer to home and sharing plates are back on trend. What's notable is how food arrives in London from abroad as cheap national cuisine, becomes dramatically popular, consolidates and is then reinvented as a luxury.

**In the know
Price categories**

All our restaurant listings are marked with a pound-symbol category from budget to blow-out (£-££££), indicating the price you should expect to pay for an average three-course meal for two (or the equivalent for tapas, dim sum, street eats, in a café or at a small plates venue) with drinks and 12.5% service:

£ = under £60

££ = £60-£100

£££ = £100-£140

££££ = over £140

Ye Olde Mitre

The plurality of pricey Italians in Chelsea and Mayfair is one example. But one does not replace the other: there are terrific, affordable curry options in the centre of town, as well as a growing number of decent options in the east and south of London.

69 Colebrooke Row

Enduring pubs

The 'local' – the public house, with its colourful characters and cosy interiors – remains the symbolic heart of boozing culture in the capital. With property prices at a premium and many street-corner pubs converted into luxury flats, a handful of historic inns have stood the test of time, holding licences since the 1600s. These creaking London legends are the best places to soak up a spot of history, warmed by the fire, ducking under low ceilings to fetch a pint of lukewarm ale before settling for a Sunday roast with all the trimmings.

Trending tipples

London's front-running cocktail bars treat their craft with the same skill shown by the capital's best kitchens, some of them even using skills derived from so-called 'molecular gastronomy'. Increasingly there's wizardry to be found in the glasses of hotel bars: **Dandelyan** (*see p77*) is a leader, with cocktail maestro Ryan

In the know
Late lunch

As you'll need to book a long way ahead for dinner at many of London's coolest restaurants, it is worth checking out lunchtimes, especially late lunches.

Chetiyawardana fast becoming a household name (albeit under his pseudonym, Mr Lyan) thanks to his madcap ideas, techniques and ingredients. Tony Conigliaro is another well-established innovator: his key bar, **69 Colebrooke Row** (*see p173*) has a lab upstairs where he researches new confections, but his **Zetter Townhouse** (*see p161*) hotel bar is another winner. Wherever you end up, cocktails in the capital are more about quality than quantity – even when they come with a good dose of fun.

Where to eat and drink

The **South Bank** (*see p66*), close to foodie magnets Borough Market and Maltby Street, offers plenty of quality chain options strung along the riverside, but **Soho** (*see p118*) is still the bohemian centre of the capital with plenty of eating options, both cheap and chic, and an increasing number of cocktail bars cropping up alongside the character-filled pubs. East of Soho, **Covent Garden** (*see p144*) remains a busy tourist trap, but some very decent restaurants have emerged. Expense-account eats are concentrated in **Mayfair** (*see p119*), where celebrity chefs thrive in the dining rooms of posh hotels, and drinks are served with a side of sophistication. Further west, **Marylebone** is another foodie enclave with top-

The Barbary

notch delis and cafés, as well as terrific restaurants. **Kensington and Chelsea** (*see p93*) does expensive special occasion destinations, but runs to more affordable fair too. The **City** (*see p151*) remains relatively poor for evening and weekend eats but **Clerkenwell** (*see p153*), just beyond the City walls, is a culinary hotspot and the birthplace of many London restaurant trends. Nearby, **Shoreditch**, once the epitome of cool, is still a lively part of town packed with drinkers and a huge number of eating options, but in-the-know boozers seem to have drifted north into **Dalston** or south to **Peckham** and **Brixton** where fledgling and creative drinks scenes are beginning to flourish; thanks to steep rents in central London, the same is true of diners. The biggest change to the capital's restaurant scene has been the growth of exciting new options in the more outlying areas.

Leaving it late

Although the Night Tube launched in London in 2016, many have questioned the need for a 24-hour tube service for London drinkers. The liberalisation of the licensing laws means that any pub or bar can apply to open late, but noise-nuisance restrictions mean most still close their doors around midnight, with only a handful of places (mostly in the periphery where neighbours are fewer and more tolerant) opening until 3am. In all cases, you'll have to be over 18 to be served alcohol (or even admitted to many venues at night), while many bars embrace a Challenge 21 policy - if you're fresh-faced, expect to have to show ID.

In the know
Essentials

Most restaurants accept credit cards (although American Express is least popular), but some of the cheaper places still only accept cash; if you're anywhere informal, like a street food stall, you should expect to use money rather than plastic. Service charges are frequently included in café and restaurant bills, but not always. Check: if such a charge hasn't been added, paying a tip of 10%-15% is usual. If you can, tip in cash: it's most likely to go directly to your server that way.

Shopping

Bustling, street-smart, savvy – London is a city where creativity flourishes in every industry, none more so than fashion. The defining look of the city is experimental, just not necessarily avant-garde, with the late Alexander McQueen one perfect example: the critics' darling who created a viable commercial brand. Unlike the pristine, classical style of Paris, say, or the more nakedly commercial nous of New York, London is blessed with a fashion scene that thrives on invention. It is fed by a wealth of new talent arriving from the fashion colleges and across the planet, talent that's sustained by a busy mix of high-end boutiques, trashy chains, dignified department stores and anything-goes markets. Whatever else, it seems Londoners just won't stop shopping.

It's the fashion

We'd argue London is currently the fashion capital of the world. So it should be no surprise that some of the world's finest fashion retailers are here, from small independents – like Soho's **Machine-A** (*p139*), a tireless champion of the most exciting emerging designers – all the way up to the big department stores. Part of the secret is that the big guys who might be in danger of slowing down have learnt to collaborate with the little guys who are still quick on their feet.

Selfridges (*see p119*) is a fine example. Opened in 1909, it is one of a handful of central London department stores to have thrived ever since the Edwardian shopping boom – yet in 2017 it hosted a pop-up stocking exclusive clothes, gifts and accessories by Fashion East, a non-profit organisation founded explicitly to bring on new talent in the hipster homelands around Brick Lane.

Big brands use the capital as a testing ground, so Londoners are exposed to all the latest initiatives and launches. After years of perfecting everything from the cut of the silk shirts to the scribbly font on the carrier bags, it was here that the H&M family launched the first branch of **& Other Stories** in 2013 – and it looks like the Swedish retail behemoth is at it again, choosing London as the place to open its first concept store, **Arket**.

It's not all about the high street, either: Japanese designer Rei Kawakubo of Comme des Garçons could have opened her ground-breaking concept store **Dover Street Market** (*see p90*) in Tokyo's buzzy Ginza fashion district, but she placed it among the stuffy old cigars and suits of London's Mayfair.

Only in London

While the city's particular strength is fashion, London has more to offer than posh frocks and directional sweatshirts. There's a wealth of niche shops, specialising in traditional umbrellas (**James Smith & Sons**, *see p148*), cheese (**Neal's Yard Dairy**, *see p149*) and gourmet teas (**Postcard Teas**, *see p118*) – even, in the mustachioed heartlands of east London, cacti (**Prick**, 492 Kingsland Road, E8 4AE, www.prickldn.com) and hand-carved wooden spoons (**Barn the Spoon**, 260 Hackney Road, E2 7SJ, barnthespoon.com).

Market up

East London is also home to two of the city's best markets: **Columbia Road** (*see p183*) and **Broadway Market** (*see p182*). The source of their success is very different: Columbia Road kept true to its traditions, while Broadway Market underwent stunning reinvention in the 2000s. If you're really just after a stroll (and the jam-packed crowds are part of the fun), Columbia Road's the one: stop to smell the roses before investigating the dinky independent shops round the corner. Broadway Market is the nexus of dress-down

In the know
Opening hours

Shops are generally open 10am-6pm Monday to Saturday, with few closing on bank holidays (Christmas is the sole exception to that rule). Most don't open until around noon on Sundays, which gives you plenty of time to refuel for a day of pavement pounding with a good brunch. In general the shops in central London close later on Thursday nights, with the Oxford Street stores staying open until 10pm.

Shoredith High Street

catwalk and street eats, but it's still possible to pick up an intriguing little something from the accessory and apparel stalls, not to mention those selling something altogether more mouth-watering. For gifts to take back home, though, we say nip round the corner to **Netil Market**, a great little space dedicated to local designer-makers and the perfect spot to pick up locally made gifts.

The two other key markets are at opposite ends of town. At the far end of the tourist-magnet South Bank, **Borough Market** (*see p78*) rejuvenated its noble history of food wholesaling with street eats and gourmet snacking – a reinvention that worked so well the cognoscenti now sniffily head a little further east of London Bridge to **Maltby Street** (*see*

In the know
Practicalities

Don't forget your tote bag! If the store you're shopping in only has plastic bags, you will be charged 5p extra to use one.

If you're travelling from outside the EU you can claim back most of the VAT – the 20% 'value-added tax' that's included in the price of almost everything you buy – via a scheme called 'Tax Free Shopping' (*see p209*).

p78). Then, in west London, Notting Hill's **Portobello Road** (*see p110*) has stall after stall of vintage goodies – with admittedly few bargains, but great atmosphere. Up-and-coming designers come out in force on Fridays.

You're booked

The bookshop didn't die, it turns out. Like everywhere else, their survival in London comes down to creatively selected stock, helpful and informed sellers, fine events and, wherever possible, a café. At different ends of the spectrum, the **London Review Bookshop** (*see p127*) and **Foyles** (*see p138*) tick all these boxes. The former is a tiny place with stock that's all killer and no filler; the latter is a multi-storey book palace, pragmatically redeveloped a few years ago. To these can be added historic beauties, like **Daunt Marylebone** (*see p118*) and specialists like comics emporium **Gosh!** (*see p138*).

Columbia Road Market

SPOTLIGHT ON LONDON'S OFF WEST END SCENE

Discover the best theatre like a true Londoner...

BOLD
BUSH THEATRE, W12 8LJ
⊖ Shepherd's Bush,
Shepherd's Bush Market

NEW
**ROYAL COURT THEATRE,
SW1W 8AS**
⊖ Sloane Square

INNOVATIVE
**BATTERSEA ARTS CENTRE,
SW11 5TN**
⊖ Clapham Junction

London's teeming with intimate theatres that offer visitors
world-class entertainment at a fraction of West End prices.

bushtheatre.co.uk | royalcourttheatre.com | bac.org.uk

Entertainment

To say London has brilliant and diverse entertainment is an understatement. What other European city offers anything like such exciting live music, theatre, clubbing and comedy? With a spectacular array of venues dotted across the capital, from world-class stadiums and art nouveau concert halls to warehouse clubs and secret cinemas, there's energy and creativity at every turn. These days, big doesn't necessarily mean best with many of the smaller venues creating the biggest buzz. And while the West End has traditionally been the heart of London's cultural scene, there's plenty of offbeat, home-grown talent to be found in less central boroughs. Wherever you venture, one thing is certain: you won't be bored.

Best for gigs
Corsica Studios *p78*
O2 Arena *p187*

Best theatre
Donmar Warehouse *p150*
National Theatre *p79*
Shakespeare's Globe *p71*
Young Vic *p80*

Best dance clubs
Dalston Superstore *p185*
Fabric *p161*
XOYO *p186*

Best arthouse cinemas
BFI Southbank *p78*
Prince Charles *p143*

Best classical music
Barbican *p168*
Kings Place *p130*
Royal Festival Hall at the
Southbank Centre *p80*
Royal Opera House *p150*
Wigmore Hall *p119*

Best LBGT clubs and venues
Dalston Superstore *p185*
SHE Soho *p143*

Film

Londoners still have a feel for the romance of film that out-of-town multiplexes will never satisfy. Perhaps that's why there's such a lively and varied range of screenings in the capital. Leicester Square stages most of the big-budget premières – but it also has the biggest prices. By contrast, the cheap-as-chips **Prince Charles** (*see p143*) repertory cinema is right around the corner and shows films that wouldn't come within a million miles of a red carpet. Outside the mainstream, the **BFI Southbank** (*see p78*) gets top billing for its seasonal explorations of various genres of cinema and TV. After the BFI, the **Curzon** group is the favoured choice for most cineastes; the intimate **Mondrian** (*see p194*) screening room is inexpensive for its South Bank location. For refurbished art deco gems try the gorgeous, historic **Phoenix** (52 High Road, East Finchley, N2 9PJ) or the **Rio** (107 Kingsland High Street, Dalston, E8 2PB) in Dalston. Add to that the vogue for summer screenings in unusual outdoor settings, an enthusiasm for experimental ciné clubs and a world-class film festival, and all you need to do is to get some popcorn and sit yourself down.

Classical music and opera

London's classical scene has never looked or sounded more current, with the **Southbank Centre** (*see p80*), the **Barbican Centre** (*see p168*) and **Kings Place** (*see p130*) all working with strong programmes. Even the once-stuffy **Royal Opera House** (*see p150*) now leavens its programme with occasional commissions, such as Mark Anthony Turnage's daring opera *Anna Nicole* (2011), the tragic tale of a Playboy model and her ancient sugar-daddy. And despite recent troubled times at **English National Opera** (*see p150*), the company has commissioned and produced top-class work from British composers, such as Ryan Wigglesworth's *The Winter's Tale* (2017) and Tansy Davies' *Between Worlds*, an opera about the events of 9/11 that debuted at the Barbican in 2015. Much of the city's classical music action happens in superb venues on an intimate scale. **Wigmore Hall** (*see p119*), **Cadogan Hall** (*see p106*) and **LSO St Luke's** (*see p168*) are all atmospheric places, and several churches make use of their acoustical design to host fine concerts.

Dance

London is the home of two long-established classical dance companies. The **Royal Ballet**, resident at the **Royal Opera House**, is a company of global stature, which managed to lure star Russian ballerina Natalia Osipova into its ranks. Contemporary premières have included Christopher Wheeldon's *The Winter's Tale* and

In the know
Tickets and planning

Always book ahead if there's a specific show that you want to see, and use the theatre or show's own website where possible. If you're flexible or are happy to queue, consider buying from the **tkts booth** (The Lodge, Leicester Square, Soho, WC2H 7NA, www.tkts.co.uk), which sells tickets for big shows at much-reduced rates, either on the day or up to a week in advance. Many West End theatres hold back a selection of day-seats for each performance, available at a knock-down price on a first-come first-served basis when the box office opens (usually 10am – but get there much earlier for anything popular).

Liam Scarlett's *Frankenstein*, while Wayne McGregor continues to choreograph extraordinary contemporary ballet. The Royal's (friendly) rival is **English National Ballet**, a touring company that performs most often at the Coliseum (*see p150*) and, for the regular *Swan Lake* 'in the round', at the **Royal Albert Hall** (*see p101*), but has recently expanded into venues more suitable to contemporary dance such as the **Barbican** and **Sadler's Wells** (*see p176*).

Theatre and musicals

For the 13th consecutive year, 2016 saw London's major theatres make more money than they had the year before. The secret of this success is pretty much the same as it's always been – big-production musicals. The most ancient of these (*Les Misérables* and *The Phantom of the Opera*) have been hoofing it on the London stage since the mid 1980s. Of late, homegrown musicals have been rather overtaken by Broadway imports: *The Book of Mormon*, *Aladdin* and *Kinky Boots* are packing them in, and even Andrew Lloyd Webber's latest smash *School of Rock* did Broadway first. It's a trend that's set to continue with Broadway mega-smash *Hamilton* ready to wipe out the dinosaurs when it hits the West End in November 2017. But drama is booming at the moment too, in large part thanks to the efforts of super-producer Sonia Friedman, responsible for a host of pioneering transfers from London's peerless subsidised sector, and for a little play by the name of *Harry Potter and the Cursed Child*.

The **Donmar Warehouse** (*see p150*) traditionally lures high-profile film stars to perform at its tiny Earlham Street home. And while Kevin Spacey may no longer be in charge at the **Old Vic** (*see p80*), heavyweight director Matthew Warchus has proved an inspired replacement, with an eclectic and busy programme that finds room for plenty of big names.

On a smaller scale, Off-West End houses such as the **Young Vic** (*see p80*) and the **Almeida** (*see p174*) continue to produce some of London's most exciting, best-value theatre – much of which moves on to the West End – while the **Barbican Centre** programmes visually exciting and physically expressive work from around the world.

Clubbing

When it comes to after-dark indulgence, London has all the variety you could possibly wish for. Yes, we have one of the world's largest and most influential nightclubs, **Fabric** (*see p161*), and high hopes for huge new venue the **Printworks** (Surrey Quays Road, Rotherhithe, SE16 7PJ, printworkslondon.co.uk), but spend a few moments hunting on Facebook and you'll unearth fabulous happenings in any number of shop basements and other informal spaces. Check out **The Hydra** (the-hydra.net) and **London Warehouse Events** (www.lwe.events) for a fix of big-name electronica.

Once the hub of the capital's nightlife, Shoreditch has become increasingly commercialised (witness the weekend trails of hen and office parties between Old Street and Spitalfelds), despite the groovy work still being done at live space and club **XOYO** (*see p186*). Nights at **Book Club** (100-106 Leonard Street, Shoreditch, EC2A 4RH), which range from disco to science drink-and-thinks, show a newer kind of Shoreditch nightlife. The city's cool kids now take the bus north up the Kingsland Road from Shoreditch into Dalston, where the **Dalston Superstore** (*see p185*) pulls huge crowds onto its intense pitch-black dancefloor.

There's more of interest to the south. Peckham has put itself at the heart of London nightlife with the superb **Bussey Building** (*see opposite* Eat, drink and party in... Peckham). Brixton has a multitude of venues, not least sleek **Phonox** (418 Brixton Road, SW9 7AY, phonox.co.uk).

Eat, drink and party in... Peckham

Londoners are flocking south of the river

The expansion of the Overground network of light rail links has opened south London up to the uninitiated, with some parts – notably Peckham – rivalling east London for hipster cred. What tipped many Londoners off to Peckham's credentials as the coolest part of town was a multistorey car park made over into an arty bar by Bold Tendencies back in 2009. An annual summer fixture since then, **Frank's Café** (95a Rye Lane, SE15 4ST, www.boldtendencies.com) is where to go to sip Campari and watch an urban sunset – it's always busy, so arrive early and expect to queue for food. London's finest club is also on focal Rye Lane. A four-storey warehouse overlooking a railway, the CLF Art Café, known by pretty much everyone as the **Bussey Building** (133 Copeland Road, SE15 3SN, 7635 0000, www.

clfartcafe.org) is a multi-discipline arts space to which top promoters consistently bring the best names on the underground and alternative dance scenes. Around these two complexes are a selection of avant-garde galleries, music venues, bars and restaurants, plus the excellent **PeckhamPlex** cinema (95A Rye Lane, SE15 4ST, 0844 567 2742, www.peckhamplex.london). Stand-out eateries include **Artusi** (161 Bellenden Road, SE15 4DH, 3302 8200, www.artusi.co.uk) for cutting-edge Italian and the **Begging Bowl** (168 Bellenden Road, SE15 4BW, 7635 2627, www.thebeggingbowl.co.uk) for Thai street food. There's a smattering of sights too: Will Allsop's striking, award-winning **Peckham Library** (122 Peckham Hill Street, E15 5JR) and Brit-art pioneer, the **South London Gallery** (65-67 Peckham Road, SE5 8UH, 7703 6120, www.southlondongallery.org).

Bussey Building

XOYO

And the gay village in Vauxhall is just as welcoming to open-minded, straightrolling types (*see p45*).

To the north, up in King's Cross, there are some good nights at **Egg** (200 York Way, N7 9AX), the **Big Chill House** (257-259 Pentonville Road, N1 9NL, 7427 2540, wearebigchill.com/house) and, with its late weekend licence and killer sound system, the **Star of Kings** pub-club (126 York Way, N1 0AX, 7458 4218, www.starofkings. co.uk). Further north, Camden has credible nights at indie student hangout **Proud** (Horse Hospital Stables Market, Chalk Farm Road, Camden, NW1 8AM), teeny pub-rave spot the **Lock Tavern** (35 Chalk Farm Road, Camden, NW1 8AJ) and bourbon-soaked gig haunt the **Blues Kitchen** (111-113 Camden High Street, Camden, NW1 7JN). **Koko** (*see p175*) runs some of the biggest student nights around.

Gigs

London's music scene is defined by rampant diversity. You might find yourself watching a US country star in a tiny basement, an African group under a railway arch or a torch singer in a church. While corporations have taken over some venues, there's still rough and ready individuality to be found in the likes of **XOYO** (*see p186*). The **O2 Arena** (*p187*) and **Wembley** (Wembley

LGBT London

The city's best events, shows, clubs and bars

Acceptance of gay lifestyles in London feels broader than ever. In fact, many clubs no longer bother much about sexual orientation, just as long as everyone gets to have a good time. The closure of key venues, however, has caused plenty of soul-searching. Has Grindr killed the gay bar? Is it rising rents? Noise complaints from intolerant neighbours? London's headline homo event remains **Pride** (see p59), while **BFI Flare** (www.bf.org.uk/flare) is a major LGBT film festival.

Roughly speaking, London's gay scene is split into three key zones: **Soho** is the most mainstream, **Vauxhall** is the most decadent, and **east London** the most outré. Centred on Old Compton Street, the Soho scene continues to attract the crowds. Notable venues here include **G-A-Y Bar** (30 Old Compton Street, 7494 2756, www.g-a-y.co.uk) and **Ku Bar & Club** (30 Lisle Street, Chinatown, 7437 4303, www.ku-bar.co.uk). A welcome addition is **SHE Soho** (see p143) – the city's only full-time drinking den for lesbians. The party continues down the road at the legendary **Heaven**, Under the Arches, Villiers Street, Covent Garden, WC2N 6NG (7930 2020, heavennightclub-london.com).

Down south, Vauxhall is the place to go if you want to stay up all night and the next day as well. Long-standing alt-cabaret venue **RVT** (Royal Vauxhall Tavern, 372 Kennington Lane, Vauxhall, SE11 5HY, 7820 1222) and club night **Horse Meat Disco** (Eagle London, 349 Kennington Lane, Vauxhall, SE11 5QY, 7793 0903, www.eaglelondon.com) are both utterly enjoyable. Popular nights at **Fire** (South Lambeth Road, SW8 1RT, www.freclub.co.uk) include Orange, a Sunday staple, or there's club night **Union** (no.66, www.clubunion.co.uk) on the Albert Embankment.

The most alternative, creative and vibrant of the capital's queer scenes is to be found in east London. In **Dalston Superstore** (see p185) and the **Glory** (281 Kingsland Road, Dalston, E2 8AS, 7684 0794), you'll rub shoulders with fashion and music movers and shakers (plus assorted straight folk), to soundtracks built by ferociously underground DJs.

Pride

Stadium, Empire Way, Wembley, HA9 0WS) remain London's most popular stadiums for classic rock and retro gigs. Several nightclubs multitask, staging regular gigs: **Corsica Studios** (*see p78*), **Proud Camden** (*see p44*) and **Nest** (36 Stoke Newington Road, Dalston, N16 7ZJ) are notable. **Borderline** (*see p141*) is known for country and folk gigs, but does hosts indie bands.

London has a lively home-grown jazz scene, inspired by freewheeling attractions at the **Vortex** (11 Gillett Square, Dalston, N16 8AZ) and the unhinged monthly **Boat-Ting Club** nights (www.boat-ting.co.uk). International names can be seen and heard at **Ronnie Scott's** (*see p143*) and there's more good quality mainstream fare at **Spice of Life** (6 Moor Street, Soho, W1D 5NA, 7437 7013, www.spiceoflifesoho.com). There's a lot of very good jazz at the excellent **Kings Place**; and both the **Barbican** and the **Southbank Centre** host dozens of big names. For something a little more down and dirty, try the **Borderline** (*see p141*).

Comedy and cabaret

While the big stadiums – especially the **O2 Arena** and **SSE Arena**, **Wembley** – host the massive shows, it's the circuit of pubs and smaller clubs that defines London's comedy scene. In addition to its stellar programme of plays and cabaret, the **Soho Theatre** (*see p144*) has become one of the best places to see new comics breaking into the scene. Another multi-tasking venue is the **Union Chapel** (*see p176*), whose monthly *Live at the Chapel* night provides line-ups of big guns (Noel Fielding and Stewart Lee, for example) supported by comics who are headliners in their own right. To see the best cabaret, head to the always interesting **Bethnal Green Working Men's Club** (42-44 Pollard Row, Bethnal Green, E2 6NB).

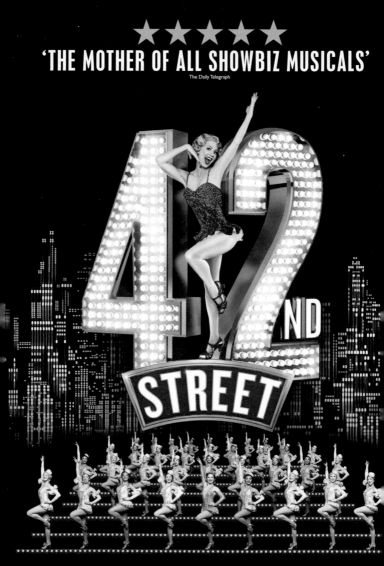

London Day by Day

Itineraries

Whether you visit for a weekend or longer, for hedonism or high culture, there's a whole world of things to see and do in the British capital - whatever your budget. While you can't expect to see all of London's sights in one trip, our tailored tours will help you to maximise your time in the city. Choose from Essential Weekend, Budget Break and Family Day Out, or cherry-pick elements from each to suit your own itinerary.

▶ *Budgets include transport, meals and admission prices, but not accommodation and shopping.*

ESSENTIAL WEEKEND

Budget £200-£250 per person
Getting around walking, tube and Overground trains

DAY 1

Morning

Today is a whistlestop walking tour of historic London. Get to Charing Cross or Leicester Square stations for 10am and start the day in **Trafalgar Square** (*see p89*). The centre of London is an impressive sight, especially when it isn't too full of tourists snapping pictures of themselves with the lions. Far beneath Nelson on his column, the Fourth Plinth bears contemporary art: check out David Shrigley's huge thumbs-up, *Really Good*, which will be replaced in 2018 by Michael Rakowitz's *The Invisible Enemy Should Not Exist*. The masterpieces of the **National Gallery** (*see p87*) – an encyclopaedia of Western art – are on the pedestrianised northern side of the square. But you've only got half an hour: at 10.45am you should head south down Whitehall, keeping an eye out for the red-coated cavalryman on sentry duty. At 11am, the Horse Guards in shiny helmets and with shiny swords perform the daily **Changing of the Guard** ceremony (*see p22*; it's an hour earlier on Sunday). After the ceremonials, head through the parade ground into **St James's Park** (*see p91*) to see the pelicans and admire **Buckingham Palace** (*see p84*) at the end of the lake. Just out of the park's south-eastern corner is **Parliament Square** (*see p86*). This is a UNESCO World Heritage Site: admire Westminster Abbey, Parliament and the Queen Elizabeth Tower ('Big Ben' to most people). Then cross Westminster Bridge to County Hall and the London Eye and take a stroll east along the **South Bank** (*see p66*). This walk is modern London's biggest tourist cliché, but it's also great fun.

Afternoon

Replenish your energy at one of the many restaurants around the **Southbank Centre** (*see p80*), before following the Thames past the **National Theatre** (*see p79*) to the newly expanded **Tate Modern** (*see p74*) and **Shakespeare's Globe** (*see p71*). Finish your afternoon by walking across the Millennium Bridge for the slow climb up to 17th-century architectural masterpiece **St Paul's Cathedral** (*see p162*). You'll need to arrive by about 3.30pm to give yourself time.

Evening

If you're cooked after all that walking, One New Change mall, next to St Paul's, has upmarket chain restaurants. But if you've still got a bit of puff, invest it in the 15-minute walk north into **Clerkenwell** (*see p153*) where there are infinitely superior eating options. Farringdon or Barbican tube stations are your best route back to your hotel.

British Museum

DAY 2

Morning

We're not quite done with culture: are you ready for one of the world's finest museums? You betcha – arrive as close to 10am as you can to miss most of the crowds. The **British Museum** (*see p126*) is so full of treasures, you may not know where to begin: try turning left out of the middle of the covered courtyard for the extraordinary monumental antiquities, including the Parthenon Marbles.

Afternoon

There are plenty of good eating options around Covent Garden (or queue at Barrafina, *p146*, for something really special). **Covent Garden Market** is catnip to tourists, but the fabulous **London Transport Museum** (*see p145*) is a better reason to linger. Shopaholics might want to explore the area around **Seven Dials**, which is crammed with boutiques.

Evening

For something a bit special, head south of the river to one of our favourite restaurants, **El Pastór** (*p76*), tucked away in one of the old railway arches near **Borough Market** (*p76*). You'll have to queue but it'll be worth the wait for the tasty tacos and Latin vibe that await. Alternatively, for excellent fine-dining views, book in advance at one of the Shard's (*p73*) four restaurants (we like **Hutong**, *see p76*) and finish off with a cocktail at **Gŏng**. If you've still got energy to burn, you can dance away until the sun comes up at one of Vauxhall's clubs.

BUDGET BREAK

For the pound-conscious visitor
Budget £50-£70 per person
Getting around tube, walking

Good news, pound-stretchers. London, although expensive in most terms, is incredibly cheap for culture. Almost all of the key museums are free, only charging for temporary exhibitions. The British Museum, both Tates and all three South Kensington museums are just the start, with many smaller collections (including the Soane, Wallace and Grant) also eschewing an admission price. To ensure your transport costs are as low as possible, get an Oyster card (*see p200*), or use the same contactless debit/credit card for all your journeys. Your fares for the day will be capped at the price of a one-day travelcard (*see p201*).

Morning

Start at South Kensington tube station, which is a short walk from three of London's – indeed, the world's – finest museums. Decide which appeals most and leave the others for another day. Our favourite, the **Victoria & Albert Museum** (*see p100*) combines a palatial Victorian setting with absorbing and awe-inspiring collections that are a fascinating history of art and design. The Arts and Crafts style tea room is a good spot for an early lunch, or take a picnic and head north to **Kensington Gardens** (*see p95*), the lovelier half of **Hyde Park**.

Afternoon

After lunch and a stroll in the park, it's worth popping in to see watever's on at the **Serpentine** and **Serpentine Sackler** (*see p98*) galleries. Afterwards, head to the north-east corner of the park, where you'll see **Marble Arch** (and pass the assorted soapbox crazies expounding their theories at Speakers' Corner, though they're mainly in attendance at weekends). You could sample the madness of **Oxford Street** by walking east along it, but we'd recommend saving your legs and getting the Central line one stop to Bond Street. Head north to the **Wallace Collection** (*see p115*), another free museum in another glorious setting, this time a grand 16th-century townhouse.

Evening

After a cheap but satisfying day, take the tube to Piccadilly Circus or Tottenham Court Road to **Soho** in the heart of the West End. Despite its reputation for naughtiness, Soho has become London's go-to place for cheap eats: almost everything in our selection of the city's best bargain eats is here. Rather than bust the budget boozing, why not finish the evening with a film at the **Prince Charles** (*see p143*)? There might be a triple-bill all-nighter – after which, the Night Tube runs through Piccadilly Circus station, and the fare is still part of your capped travel for the day, even after midnight...

FAMILY DAY OUT

Keeping the kids amused

Budget £300-£400 for a family of four

Getting around tube, walking, boat. Allow plenty of time in your schedule for last-minute wee stops, getting lost and other child-rearing distractions.

Morning

The trick with many of London's greatest attractions is getting out early – which can be a problem if you've multiple kids to corral, Get the tube to Tower Hill on the District and Circle lines and head down the steps to the **Tower of London** (*see p165*). There's lots to see and do here, with the experience enhanced by the presence of affable red-coated beefeaters. Hustle to the Crown Jewels first thing, though. Queues build up rapidly to glide on the travelator past Her Majesty's baubles.

Afternoon

For lunch on the go, grab a sandwich from the cluster of venues north-west of the Tower, and take them to the pier where you can eat during the 10-20 minute wait for the next **Thames Clipper** (*see p202*) to the South Bank. While the **Shard** (*see p73*) provides the more eye-popping views, the constantly changing vista from the pods of the **London Eye** (*see p72*) can be more fun with the kids. Book your timeslot in advance for the cheapest tickets. When you're disgorged, you'll be confronted by the **London Aquarium** (*see p74*) and the **London Dungeon** (*see p70*). They're all good, but you've already shelled out enough,

so be ready to chivvy the little pesterers on to the **Southbank Centre** (*see p80*), possibly buying them off along the way with a run around the playground or a ride on the vintage merry-go-round. If your luck's in, there'll be free child-focused entertainment in the foyer of the **Royal Festival Hall**; if there isn't, the combination of crowds and entertainers and ice-cream will keep the nippers happy.

Evening

The plan is to work your way steadily along the South Bank, with its fairy lights at night, as far as **Tate Modern** (*see p74*). Then you turn inland and head south to **Hixter Bankside** (16 Great Guildford Street, SE1 0HS, 7921 9508, www.hixrestaurants.co.uk/restaurant/hixter-bankside), where the open-plan layout feels relaxed, but the food is good enough to be a grown-up treat. Too ambitious? Not to worry: there are endless variations on pizza and burgers along the way. Head home from Waterloo (Northern, Bakerloo and Jubilee lines), if you don't get beyond the Southbank Centre, or Southwark (Jubilee line) from Hixter.

Tate Modern

Thames Clipper cruises past the Tower of London

THE NATIONAL GALLERY

The National Gallery houses one of the greatest collections of paintings in the world and admission to see them is free.

For details on our exhibitions, events and free talks, visit nationalgallery.org.uk

Opening hours
Daily 10am – 6pm, Fridays 10am – 9pm

Nearest tube
Charing Cross/ Leicester Square ⊖

Bonfire Night fireworks over Albert Bridge

Diary

Forget about British reserve. Festivals and events play increasingly elaborate variations on the age-old themes of parading and dancing, nowadays with ever-larger sprinklings of arts and culture. Some are traditional, some innovative, from the splendid ritual of the Changing the Guard to the outdoor spectacle of the Greenwich & Docklands International Festival. Weather plays a part in the timing, with a concentration of things to do in the warmer – and sometimes drier – months of summer, but the city's calendar is busy for most of the year.

Year round

London doesn't really have an off-season, with interesting things going on all through the year. The weather is never predictable, but nor is it particularly harsh – in winter you might even bless our polluted air, which keeps the temperature a degree or two higher than the surrounding countryside.

Ceremony of the Keys

www.hrp.org.uk/tower-of-london/ explore/ceremony-of-the-keys
Join the Yeoman Warders at the Tower of London as they lock the fortress's entrances in this 700-year-old ceremony. Apply two months ahead.

Gun Salutes

www.royal.uk/gun-salutes
Many important royal occasions are marked with gun salutes and dramatic cavalry charges.

Spring

Our favourite time of year. This is a surprisingly green city, with blossoming cherry trees and crocuses, primroses and daffodils in the Royal Parks that ring central London. Spring often brings better weather than summer – and, outside the school holidays, fewer crowds. The Old Smoke can feel lively, pretty and far more cheerful than our fellow Brits would ever believe.

Mar London Beer Week

drinkup.london/beerweek
A city-wide celebration of all things hop.

Mar WoW: Women of the World

www.southbankcentre.co.uk/ whats-on/festivals-series/women- of-the-world
Discussion, debate and performances about women.

Late Mar-May Kew at Springtime

www.kew.org
Five million flowers carpet the grounds in spring, *see p20*.

Mid Mar St Patrick's Day Parade & Festival

www.london.gov.uk/events
Sunday parade followed by toe-tapping tunes in Trafalgar Square.

Apr Oxford & Cambridge Boat Race

www.theboatrace.org
Elite rowers from Oxford and Cambridge universities battle it out on the Thames.

Mid Apr London Marathon

www.virginmoneylondonmarathon. com
Some 36,000 elite athletes and fundraisers run, jog and walk their way to the Mall.

Early May Breakin' Convention

www.breakinconvention.com/ events/festival
Jonzi D's street dance festival at Sadler's Wells Theatre provides spectacular entertainment.

May Museums at Night

museumsatnight.org.uk
Doors kept open after-hours at various cultural venues.

Mid May Covent Garden May Fayre & Puppet Festival

www.punchandjudy.com/ coventgarden.htm
All-day puppet mayhem devoted to Mr Punch at the scene of his first recorded sighting in England in 1662.

Mid May Chelsea Flower Show

www.rhs.org.uk/shows-events
Admire perfect blooms in entire laid-out gardens.

May/June State Opening of Parliament

www.parliament.uk
The Queen reopens Parliament after its recess, arriving and departing in the golden State Coach, accompanied by Household Cavalry troops.

Summer

Summers can be rainy, but at the slightest sniff of fine weather Londoners are boozing at pavement tables like some fantasy of the south of France. The Tube becomes a sweaty hellhole, but suck it up: this is the season of al fresco cinema, music festivals in the parks and sipping Camparis with the trendsters.

June Field Day

www.fielddayfestivals.com
Acts ranging from weird pop and indie rock to underground dance producers and folk musicians.

Aphex Twin plays Field Day

June London Festival of Architecture

www.londonfestivalofarchitecture.org
Talks, discussions, walks, screenings and other events.

June LIFT (London International Festival of Theatre)

www.liftfestival.com
Biennial festival featuring hundreds of artists. Next in 2018.

June Camden Rocks Festival

camdenrocksfestival.com
One-day festival of rock and metal bands.

June Bushstock

www.bushstock.co.uk
Run by independent record label Communion Presents focusing on new talent.

June-Aug Opera Holland Park

www.operahollandpark.com
A canopied outdoor theatre hosts a season of opera.

♥ Late June/early July Greenwich & Docklands International Festival

www.festival.org
This annual week of outdoor arts, theatre, dance and family entertainment is spectacular. Events take place at the Old Royal Naval College and other sites, including Canary Wharf and Mile End Park.

♥ Late June/early July Pride London

www.prideinlondon.org
This historic celebration of the LGBT community (taking place since 1972, initially in support of the Stonewall rioters) now welcomes some 800,000 revellers to a week of events, culminating in a celebratory parade held on Saturday.

Late June-mid July Wimbledon Tennis Championships
www.wimbledon.com
One of the world's most prestigious tournaments.

Early July Wireless Festival
www.wirelessfestival.co.uk
Three nights of rock and dance acts.

Every Sun in July Summer Streets
www.regentstreetonline.com/ campaigns/summerstreets
Regent Street's classy curve is pedestrianised for a street party.

Mid July Lovebox Weekender
www.loveboxfestival.com
Top-quality weekend music festival in Victoria Park, which has headlined everyone from Sly Stone and Blondie to MIA.

Mid July Somerset House Summer Series
www.somersethouse.org.uk/ whats-on/summer-series-somerset-house
A dozen big-name concerts in the fountain court.

July Citadel Festival
citadelfestival.com
Top musical line-up and arts-driven distractions in East London's Victoria Park.

2 weekends in July British Summer Time Festival
www.bst-hydepark.com
Hyde Park plays host to some of the planet's biggest musical stars.

♥ Mid July-mid Sept BBC Proms
www.bbc.co.uk/proms
The Proms overshadows all other classical music festivals in the city, with around 70 concerts, covering everything from early-music recitals to orchestral world premières, and from boundary-pushing debut performances to reverent career retrospectives. BBC Radio 3 plays recordings of the concerts.

Early Aug Carnaval del Pueblo
www.carnavaldelpueblo.com
Loud-and-proud day out for Latin American Londoners, attracting up to 60,000 people to Burgess Park in Southwark.

Carnaval del Pueblo

Aug Camden Fringe
www.camdenfringe.com
An eclectic bunch of new, experimental and short shows.

Aug Sunfall
www.sunfall.co.uk
Catch big names and cult heroes at Brixton's Brockwell Park day-and-night dance festival and its after-parties.

Mid Aug Meltdown
www.southbankcentre.co.uk
Music and cultural festival at the Southbank Centre, curated by a different musician every year.

❤ Aug bank holiday Notting Hill Carnival
www.thelondonnottinghillcarnival.com
Two million people stream into Notting Hill for Europe's largest street party. Massive mobile sound systems dominate the streets with whatever bass-heavy party music is currently hip, but there's plenty of tradition from the West Indies too: calypso music and a spectacular costumed parade.

Aug bank holiday South West Four
www.southwestfour.com
London's key dance-music festival, covering everything from trance to house on Clapham Common.

Autumn
Autumn has a good share of clear, crisp days, which often seem to fall kindly for Diwali and Bonfire Night fireworks. The kids are back at school after the summer holidays but it is rarely unpleasantly cold, so autumn is a great time of year for sightseeing.

Early Sept Tour of Britain
www.tourofbritain.co.uk
Join spectators on the streets of the capital for a stage of British cycling's biggest outdoor event.

Sept London African Music Festival
www.joyfulnoise.co.uk
A wonderfully eclectic affair, held over a fortnight in September in multiple venues.

❤ Sept Totally Thames Festival
www.totallythames.org
A giant party along the Thames, this month of events is London's largest free arts festival. It's a family-friendly mix of carnival, pyrotechnics, art installations and live music alongside craft and food stalls. Events include the Great River Race – a 22-mile marathon for all manner of traditional rowed and paddled boats. The festival is brought to an end with a lantern procession and fireworks.

Sun in Sept Horseman's Sunday
www.stjohns-hydepark.com
A cavalcade of over 100 horses in Hyde Park in celebration of riding in the capital.

Mid Sept Open-House London
www.open-city.org.uk
For one weekend only, there's access to some 500 amazing buildings that are normally closed to the public.

Mid Sept Kings Place Festival
www.kingsplace.co.uk/festival
More than 100 events over three days – classical, jazz and experimental music.

Mid Sept London Fashion Week

www.londonfashionweek.co.uk
The autumn edition of the biannual fashion jamboree in Somerset House.

Mid Sept OnBlackheath

www.onblackheath.com
Weekend music and food festival with past headliners including Massive Attack, Primal Scream, Hot Chip, Belle & Sebastian and James.

Mid Sept-mid Oct London Literature Festival

www.southbankcentre.co.uk/whats-on/festivals-series/london-literature-festival
Combining superstar writers with architects, comedians, sculptors and cultural theorists at the Southbank Centre.

Sept Pearly Kings & Queens Harvest Festival

www.visitlondon.com/things-to-do/event/26845942-pearly-kings-and-queens-harvest-festival
A proper Cockney knees-up as the Pearly Kings and Queens lead a parade to St Mary-le-Bow church. Expect maypole dancing, Morris dancers and a marching band.

Oct Museums at Night

museumsatnight.org.uk
Doors kept open after-hours at various cultural venues.

Oct Dance Umbrella

www.danceumbrella.co.uk
Innovative celebration of dance covering many styles and choreographers.

Mid Oct London Film Festival

www.bfi.org.uk/lff
The most significant of the capital's film festivals; expect red-carpet celebs at the BFI Southbank and Leicester Square's Vue West End.

❤ Mid Oct London Frieze Art Fair

friezelondon.com
The biggest contemporary carnival in London's art calendar occupies a purpose-built venue at the south end of Regent's Park, where some 1,000 artists are displayed over the four-day festival. Highlights include the daily-changing Projects; debates and discussions as part of the Talks strand; and Live, showing performance-based installations.

Oct/Nov Diwali

www.london.gov.uk
Hindu, Jain and Sikh Festival of Light in Trafalgar Square.

5 Nov & around Bonfire Night

Firework displays all over town, marking the arrest of Guy Fawkes, and the thwarting of the attempt to blow up Parliament on 5 November 1604.

❤ Early Nov Lord Mayor's Show

www.lordmayorsshow.org
This big show marks the traditional presentation of the new Lord Mayor for approval by the monarch's justices. The Lord Mayor leaves Mansion House in a fabulous gold coach at 11am, along with a colourful procession of floats and marchers. At 5.15pm, there's a fireworks display on the river.

▶ *The Lord Mayor is a City officer, elected each year by the livery companies and with no real power outside the City of London; don't confuse him with the Mayor of London, currently Sadiq Khan.*

Early Nov Remembrance Sunday Ceremony

Always held on the Sunday nearest to 11 November, this solemn commemoration honours those who died fighting in the World Wars and later conflicts. The

Queen, the prime minister and other dignitaries lay poppy wreaths at the Cenotaph. A two-minute silence at 11am is followed by a service of remembrance.

Mid Nov London Jazz Festival
efglondonjazzfestival.org.uk
London's biggest jazz festival features 10 days of music from trad to free improv.

Winter
There's plenty of fun to be had in the run-up to the big C, with roaring fires in trad pubs, the giant Christmas tree arriving in Trafalgar Square from Norway and the West End illuminations going up. Just don't count on seeing any snow. Christmas Day is pretty much the only time London closes down: there's no public transport and few attractions, shops or restaurants bother to open.

Dec Spitalfields Winter Music Festival
www.spitalfieldsmusic.org
Multi-genre music events, featuring world-class artists, in unusual venues across East London.

Early Dec Great Christmas Pudding Race
www.xmaspuddingrace.org.uk
Fancy-dress race in Covent Garden that involves balancing a Christmas pudding.

31 Dec New Year's Eve celebrations
www.london.gov.uk/events
A full-on fireworks display launched from the London Eye and rafts on the Thames.

1 Jan New Year's Day
www.lnydp.com
If your hangover isn't too bad you can join the costumed New Year's Day Parade in central London.

Jan/Feb London International Mime Festival
www.mimelondon.com/festival
Theatrical magic in many forms, from haunting visual theatre to puppetry for adults

Shrove Tuesday Great Spitalfields Pancake Race
www.alternativearts.co.uk
Fancy dress teams run through the cobbled streets of Spitalfelds flipping a pancake in the hope of winning a specially engraved frying pan.

Feb Chinese New Year Festival
www.lccauk.com
Celebrate the Year of the Dog (2018) and the Boar (2019) in style in Chinatown and Leicester Square.

Mid/late Feb London Fashion Week
www.londonfashionweek.co.uk
See p62 London Fashion Week.

London Fashion Week

RIGHT NEAR.
RIGHT NOW.

You're only seconds away
from a great bar, an amazing
new restaurant or the latest
things to do in New York.

DOWNLOAD
THE APP TODAY

DISCOVER | BOOK | SHARE

London by Area

South Bank

An estimated 14 million people come this way each year, and it's easy to see why. Between the London Eye and Tower Bridge, the south bank of the Thames offers a two-mile procession of diverting arts and entertainment venues and a host of London's must-see attractions.

Tourists have been visiting the area for centuries, but the entertainments have changed somewhat. **Shakespeare's Globe** remains as popular as ever, but the associated prostitutes, gamblers and bear-baiters have been replaced with art lovers, theatre-goers and culture vultures.

The area's modern-day life began in 1951 with the Festival of Britain, staged to boost morale in the wake of World War II. The **Royal Festival Hall** stands testament to the inclusive spirit of the project; it was later expanded into the **Southbank Centre** which, alongside the **BFI Southbank** (the UK's premier arthouse cinema) and the

Best for culture
Flagship thespian venue, the
National Theatre (*p79*). Step back
in time at Shakespeare's Globe
(*p71*). Major multi-arts hub, the
Southbank Centre (*p80*).

Best view
London's tallest building, The
Shard (*p73*). Taking it all in from
the London Eye (*p72*).

Best art gallery
Burgeoning artistic powerhouse,
the Tate Modern (*p74*).

Best restaurant
El Pastór at Borough Market (*p76*).

Best bar
Dandelyan (*p77*) for exhilarating
cocktails right by the Thames.

Best for nightlife
Corsica Studios (*p78*) for gigs, club
nights and freaky light shows.

Best museum
Conflict histories at the Imperial
War Museum (*p69*).

concrete ziggurat of the **National Theatre**, has developed
into a thriving cultural hub.

The riverside really took off in the new millennium,
when money was ploughed in to revitalise the area.
The conversion of the old Bankside Power Station into
the world-class **Tate Modern** was so spectacularly
popular that a 60 per cent extension of exhibition
space was added in 2016.

Skyline landmarks such as the ever-popular
London Eye and the ever-visible **Shard** offer some of
the best views in the city, while closer to the ground,
the 13th-century **Borough Market** is a superb
foraging place for both street-food enthusiasts and
fine-dining aficionados.

Meanwhile in Lambeth, the impressive – and
steadily revamped – **Imperial War Museum** provides
a compelling, frequently hard-hitting history of armed
conflict since World War I.

➜ **Getting around**
The area is best accessed by tube/rail and, once there, most of the sights
can be reached on foot. The riverside walkway from Westminster Bridge to
Tower Bridge can take anything from 40 minutes to three hours.

Sights & museums

Currently undergoing substantial refurbishment, the **Hayward Gallery** (Southbank Centre, Belvedere Road, SE1 8XX, 7960 4200, www.southbankcentre. co.uk) is set to reopen in January 2018. This versatile gallery has no permanent collection, but has always run a good programme of temporary exhibitions, among them Antony Gormley's fog-filled chamber for 'Blind Light' and Carsten Höller's roller-coaster slides.

Garden Museum

Lambeth Palace Road, SE1 7LB (7401 8865, www.gardenmuseum. org.uk). Lambeth North tube or Waterloo tube/rail. **Open** *10.30am-5pm Mon-Fri, Sun; 10.30am-4pm Sat; check website for occasional closures.* **Admission** *Museum £10; £5-£8.50 reductions; free under-6s. Tower £3, free under-18s.* **Map** *p68 M11.*
Saved from demolition in the 1970s, the deconsecrated church of St Mary's is a fitting site for the world's first horticulture museum: it was the last resting place of intrepid plant hunter and gardener to Charles I, John Tradescant (c1570-1638). Recently reopened after a £7.5 million redevelopment, the museum's interior features seven galleries containing gardening memorabilia from 1600 to the modern day, including Britain's oldest watering can and Harold Gilman's intriguing *Portrait of a Black Gardener*. The new courtyard extension contains a garden of rare plants, designed by Dan Pearson, and a café. You can climb the 14th-century tower and explore the Ark Gallery – based on the Tradescants' 17th-century cabinet of curiosities – as well as visiting temporary exhibitions. It's a quiet place for reflection, too.

HMS Belfast

The Queen's Walk, SE1 2JH (7940 6300, www.iwm.org.uk). London Bridge tube/rail. **Open** *Mar-Oct 10am-6pm daily. Nov-Feb 10am-5pm daily.* **Admission** *£14.50; £8-£12.80 reductions; free under-5s.* **Map** *p68 S9.*
This 11,500-ton 'Edinburgh' class large light cruiser is the last surviving big-gun World War II warship in Europe. It's also a floating branch of the Imperial War Museum, and is a popular if unlikely playground for children, who tear around its complex of gun turrets, bridge, decks and engine room. The *Belfast* was built in 1936, ran convoys to Russia, supported the Normandy Landings and helped UN forces in Korea before being decommissioned in 1963.

❤ Imperial War Museum

Lambeth Road, SE1 6HZ (7416 5000, www.iwm.org.uk). Lambeth North tube or Elephant & Castle tube/rail. **Open** *10am-6pm daily.* **Admission** *free. Special exhibitions vary.* **Map** *p68 O11.*
One of London's great museums – but probably the least famous of them – IWM London focuses on the military action of British and Commonwealth troops during the 20th century. One of the highlights, built to commemorate the 2014 centenary, are the state-of-the-art

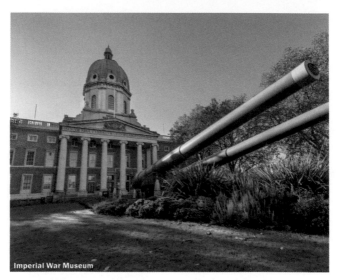

Imperial War Museum

First World War galleries that take a more considered, contemporary look at the conflict, examining the Home Front as much as the Western Front. Alongside huge set pieces like a walk-through trench is a heart-stopping collection of small, personal items and medical objects, including a magnet used to pull shrapnel from wounds. The Central Hall is an attention-grabbing repository of major artefacts: guns, tanks and aircraft hang from the ceiling (not least a Harrier GR9 that saw action in Afghanistan).

The museum's tone darkens as you ascend. On the third floor, the Holocaust Exhibition (not recommended for under-14s) traces the history of European anti-Semitism and its nadir in the concentration camps. Upstairs, Crimes Against Humanity (unsuitable for under-16s) is a minimalist space in which a film exploring contemporary genocide and ethnic violence rolls relentlessly.

London Dungeon

*County Hall, Westminster Bridge Road, SE1 7PB (www.thedungeons. com/london). Westminster tube or Waterloo tube/rail. **Open** 10am-4pm Mon-Wed, Fri; 11am-5pm Thur; 10am-6pm Sat, Sun. School holidays varies. **Admission** £30; £24 reductions; free under-3s. Book online for 30% reductions. **Map** p68 N9.*

Visitors to this jokey celebration of torture, death and disease journey back in time to London's plague-ridden streets (rotting corpses, rats, vile boils, projectile vomiting) and meet some of the city's least savoury characters, from Guy Fawkes to Sweeney Todd. A cast of blood-splattered actors are joined by 'virtual' guests, such as Brian Blessed as Henry VIII, as well as 18 different shows and 'surprises' – which could see you on the run from Jack the Ripper or getting lost in London's Victorian sewers. There are two thrill rides too: a turbulent boat trip down the Thames for execution, and a dark

💙 Shakespeare's Globe

*21 New Globe Walk, Bankside, SE1 9DT (information 7902 1400, tickets 7401 9919, www. shakespearesglobe.com). Southwark tube or London Bridge tube/rail. **Tours** 9.30am-5pm daily (except during performances). **Admission** £16; £12.50-£14.50 reductions; £43 family; free under-5s. **Map** p68 P8.*

Back in the 1990s, Sam Wanamaker – an American actor and director – dreamt a big dream: why not recreate the theatre where Shakespeare first staged many of his plays, using the original methods and materials? The amazing thing is that in 1997 this flight of fancy became, with a great deal of hard work and determination, a fabulously entertaining reality. Concessions were made along the way – the theatre is some 750 feet from the site of the original – but Wanamaker's conception resulted in an extraordinarily historically accurate facsimile, perched on the bank of the Thames, where Shakespeare is still performed in a theatre as close to the original Globe as could be imagined. After successful tenures as artistic director by Mark Rylance and Dominic Dromgoole, the Globe has had a weird time of late: Emma Rice's time in the post was marked by popular success but clashes with a tradition-loving board who hated her extensive use of electric light and sound. She duly departs in 2018 after just two years at the top to be replaced by actress Michelle Terry, who plans to perform in rather than

direct future productions. As well as being one of the greatest theatres in the country, the Globe can also be the most affordable, with the open-air, standing-room pit sensational value at £5 a pop. Open April to October, the open-air main space is stunning, but the Globe's indoor Jacobean theatre, the **Sam Wanamaker Playhouse** (completed in 2014), is arguably even more atmospheric. The 340-seat space is made entirely out of wood, exquisitely decorated and lit by candles, just as the Blackfriars theatre that Shakespeare and his King's Men troupe moved to in 1609 would have been. If you can't see a play here, visit the Globe Exhibition and take a theatre tour.

The Tempest

drop ride that plunges three storeys in the pitch black.

❤ London Eye

Jubilee Gardens, SE1 7PB (www. londoneye.com). Westminster tube or Waterloo tube/rail. **Open** *varies.* **Admission** *£24.95; £19.95 reductions; free under-3s. Ticket office in County Hall, next to London Eye. Book online for reductions.* **Map** *p68 N9.*
Here only since 2000, the Eye is nonetheless up there with Tower Bridge and 'Big Ben' among the capital's most postcard-friendly tourist assets. Assuming you choose a clear day, a 30-minute circuit on the Eye affords predictably great views of the city, with touchscreens in each of the 32 pods providing a guide to what you can see. Take a few snaps from the comfort of your pod and, there, your sightseeing's just about done. The Eye was the vision of husband-and-wife architect team Julia Barfield and David Marks, who entered a 1992 competition to design a structure for the millennium. Their giant wheel idea came second, but the winning entry is conspicuous by its absence. The Eye was planned as a temporary structure but its removal now seems unthinkable.

Newport Street Gallery

Newport Street, SE11 6AJ (3141 9320, www.newportstreetgallery. com/about). Vauxhall tube/rail or Lambeth North tube. **Open** *10am-6pm Tue-Sun.* **Admission** *free.* **Map** *p68 N11.*
Damien Hirst, the Young British Artist par excellence, isn't a man to do things by halves – unless, that is, taking half a street of listed warehouses and converting them into a huge gallery. Across two levels, six exhibition spaces and some 37,000sq ft of floor, his private collection of 3,000 works is displayed in temporary exhibitions: with holdings that include Picasso, Francis Bacon and Jeff Koons alongside YBA chums like Sarah Lucas and Gavin Turk, he's got plenty of art to choose from, but there's also taxidermy, indigenous art from the Pacific Northwest and anatomical models. The space was brilliantly reworked by Caruso St John (the architects won the 2017

❤ The Shard

32 London Bridge Street, SE1 9SG (0844 499 7111, www. theviewfromtheshard.com). London Bridge tube/rail. **Open** *10am-8.30pm daily.* **Admission** *£30.95; £21.95-£26.95 reductions; free under-4s. Book online for reductions.* **Map** *p68 R9.*

You can't miss the Shard – which is, after all, the point of the structure. Looking oddly similar to Saruman's tower in *The Lord of the Rings*, it shoots into the sky 'like a shard of glass' – to use the words of its architect, Renzo Piano, who doodled the idea for this vast edifice for its developer, Irving Sellar, on the back of a menu. In 2011, the Shard became the tallest building in the EU, but wasn't to reach its full height until 2012, when it topped out at 1,016ft.

But height isn't everything: it's the shape of this slim, slightly irregular pyramid that makes it noteworthy, an instantly recognisable centrepiece of views from pretty much everywhere in London – except, ironically, from the Victorian alleys at its foot, where the monstrous building plays peek-a-boo with visitors as they scurry around looking for a good snapshot.

Once you're inside, high-speed lifts whisk passengers up 72 floors to enjoy stunning 360°, 40-mile views, but the real joy of a visit is looking down: even seasoned London-watchers find peering down on the likes of the Tower of London from this extreme height oddly revelatory, like Google Earth in real-time.

If you've got a few quid in your pocket, a stay at the Shangri-La

(see p194) gives you plenty of time to take it all in without the hoi polloi – and with the opportunity to swim in a rather narrow infinity pool on the 52nd floor. But you don't have to be resident to enjoy cocktails at Gŏng *(see p77)* or eat at one of the four restaurants; Hutong is our favourite *(see p76)*.

▶ *If you're planning to take your time up there, note there are no toilets or refreshments on the viewing platforms.*

Stirling Prize for their efforts) and has a fine restaurant run by the estimable Mark Hix.

Old Operating Theatre, Museum & Herb Garret

9A St Thomas' Street, SE1 9RY (7188 2679, oldoperatingtheatre.com). London Bridge tube/rail. **Open** *10.30am-5pm daily.* **Admission** *£6.50; £3.50-£5 reductions; £14 family.* **Map** *p68 R9.*

The tower that houses this reminder of the surgical practices of the past used to be part of the chapel of St Thomas' Hospital. Before moving there, operations took place in the wards. Visitors enter via a vertiginous spiral staircase to inspect a pre-anaesthetic operating theatre dating from 1822, with tiered viewing seats for students. The operating tools look more like torture implements.

Sea Life London Aquarium

County Hall, Westminster Bridge Road, SE1 7PB (www2.visitsealife. com/london). Westminster tube or Waterloo tube/rail. **Open** *10am-6pm Mon-Fri; 9.30am-7pm Sat, Sun. School holidays varies.* **Admission** *£25; £17.55 reductions; free under-3s. Book online for reductions.* **Map** *p68 N10.*

This is one of Europe's largest aquariums, and a huge hit with kids – perhaps too huge: it does get awfully crowded in the school holidays and at weekends. The inhabitants are grouped by geographical origin, beginning with the Atlantic, where blacktail bream swim alongside the Thames Embankment. The 'Rainforests of the World' exhibit has introduced poison arrow frogs, crocodiles and piranhas. The Ray Lagoon is still popular, though touching the friendly flatfish is no longer allowed (it's bad for their health). Starfish, crabs and anemones can be handled in special open

rock pools instead, and the clown fish still draw crowds. There's a mesmerising Seahorse Temple, a tank full of turtles and enchanting Gentoo penguins. The centrepieces, though, are the massive Pacific and Indian Ocean tanks, with menacing sharks quietly circling fallen Easter Island statues.

❤ Tate Modern

Bankside, SE1 9TG (7887 8888, www.tate.org.uk). Blackfriars tube/rail or Southwark tube. **Open** *10am-6pm Mon-Thur, Sun; 10am-10pm Fri, Sat.* **Admission** *free. Temporary exhibitions vary.* **Map** *p68 P8.*

Thanks to its industrial architecture, this powerhouse of modern art is awe-inspiring even before you enter. Built after World War II as Bankside Power Station, it was designed by Sir Giles Gilbert Scott, architect of Battersea Power Station. The power station shut in 1981; nearly 20 years later, it opened as an art museum, and has enjoyed spectacular popularity ever since. The gallery attracts five million visitors a year – twice as many as the original building was intended for, hence the ten-storey extension that rose from the power station's former fuel tanks to completion in 2016. This vast, partly folded tower has increased exhibition space by 60 per cent and features a top-floor viewing level, restaurant, and three new floors of galleries. It has allowed for a 'progressive rehang' of Tate Modern's permanent collection, with more room for lesser-known international art. The cavernous Turbine Hall, used to jaw-dropping effect for the massive Hyundai Commission installation each year, has become what the Tate is calling 'the street' that connects both buildings.

Beyond, the permanent collection draws from the Tate's many post-1900 international works, featuring heavy-hitters

Tate Modern

such as Matisse, Rothko and Beuys. The polka-dotted **Tate-to-Tate boat** zooms to Tate Britain every 40 minutes, via the London Eye (tickets £8, £2.65-£5.35 reductions, free under-5s).

Restaurants

Anchor & Hope ££

36 The Cut, SE1 8LP (7928 9898, www.anchorandhopepub.co.uk). Southwark tube or Waterloo tube/rail. **Open** *5-11pm Mon; 11am-11pm Tue-Sat; 12.30-3.15pm Sun. Food served 6-10.30pm Mon; noon-2.30pm, 6-10.30pm Tue-Sat; 12.30-3.15pm Sun.* **Map** *p68 O9* ① *Gastropub*

Open for more than a decade, the Anchor & Hope is still a leading exponent of using 'head-to-tail' ingredients (offal and unusual cuts of meat) in simple but artful combinations, served in a relaxed setting. Bookings aren't taken, so most evenings you'll join the waiting list for a table (45mins midweek is typical) and have to hover at the crammed bar. But

the food is terrific: beautifully textured venison kofte, say, served on perkily dressed gem lettuce leaves; or rabbit served savagely red, with salty jus, fat chips and béarnaise sauce.

Casse-Croûte £££

109 Bermondsey Street, SE1 3XB (7407 2140, cassecroute.co.uk). London Bridge tube/rail. **Open** *noon-10pm Mon-Sat; noon-4pm Sun.* **Map** *p68 R10* ② *French*

Romantically lit, with checked tablecloths and a tiny bar lined with digestifs, Casse-Croûte is a shot of warm, villagey France in Bermondsey. On the site of a former sandwich shop, Hervé Durochat's intimate bistro has space for just over 20 covers and feels genuinely familial. Best of all, the sensibly priced blackboard menu of boldly chosen French classics really delivers. From delicate shavings of calf's head in a tangy sauce *ravigote* to creamy mackerel fillets pepped up with a scoop of mustard ice-cream, dishes are fresh, simple and smartly executed.

❤ El Pastór ££

*7a Stoney Street, SE1 9AA (www.
tacoselpastor.co.uk). London
Bridge tube/rail.* **Open** *noon-3pm,
5-11pm Mon-Fri; noon-4pm, 6-11pm
Sat.* **Map** *p68 Q9* ❸ *Mexican*

El Pastór is a little bit special.
This high-class taco joint, in a
railway arch next to foodie magnet
Borough Market, is the most recent
offering from the Hart Brothers
(of Barrafina fame, *see p146*).
Drawing on their experience of
running a nightclub in Mexico, it's
is a fun space with a Latin party
vibe. And the food is delicious:
carefully sourced ingredients,
served in simple, flavour-punch
combinations. To kick off, you
might try a tuna tostada, a bowl
of fresh guac and a prawn taco on
a nicely firm corn tortilla. Or the
strip of stonebass and some juicy
chunks of chargrilled chicken.
Larger plates include the signature
24-hour marinated 'al pastór' pork
and 'DIY' beef short rib. The no
bookings policy means you could
be in for a two-hour wait, but they'll
text you when your table is ready so
you can go and find a nearby bar.
Highly recommended.

Hutong ££££

*The Shard, Level 33, 31 St Thomas
Street, SE1 9RY (3011 3234, hutong.
co.uk). London Bridge tube/rail.*
Open *noon-2.30pm, 6-10.30pm
Mon-Fri; 11.30am-3.30pm,
6-10.30pm Sat, Sun.* **Map** *p68
R9* ❹ *Chinese*

Like the original Hutong in Hong
Kong, the Shard version is a glitzy
place with amazing views, ersatz
Old Beijing decor, and a Sichuan/
northern Chinese menu. The
traditionally fiery cuisine, big
on chilli and sichuan pepper,
has been toned down a little for
the *gweilo* (foreigner) palate, but
there's plenty to set the tastebuds
alight. Delicate starters of chilled
sliced scallops served with pomelo
segments or octopus salad with

hot and sour sauce, are followed by
mouthwatering mains such as prawn
wontons with *ma-la* ('numbing, spicy
hot' sauce), a 'red lantern' of softshell
crabs or Mongolian-style barbecue
rack of lamb. It's not cheap but then
this is the Shard, not Chinatown.

M Manze £

*87 Tower Bridge Road, SE1 4TW
(7407 2985, www.manze.co.uk).
Bus 1, 42, 188.* **Open** *11am-2pm
Mon; 10.30am-2pm Tue-Thur;
10am-2.30pm Fri; 10am-2.45pm
Sat.* **Map** *p68 R11* ❺ *Pie & mash*

One of the few remaining purveyors
of the dirt-cheap traditional
foodstuff of London's working
classes. It's the oldest pie shop in
town, established in 1902, with tiles,
marble-topped tables and wooden
benches – and is almost as beautiful
as L Manze's on Walthamstow High
Street, now Grade II-listed. Orders
are simple: minced beef pies or,
for braver souls, stewed eels with
mashed potato and liquor (a thin
parsley sauce).

Padella ££

*6 Southwark Street, SE1 1TQ (www.
padella.co). London Bridge tube/
rail.* **Open** *noon-4pm, 5-10pm
Mon-Sat; noon-5pm Sun.* **Map** *p68
Q9* ❻ *Italian*

This sleek pasta bar, from the duo
behind Islington's Trullo (*see p172*),
is ideal for a classy express lunch.
There's a changing mix of classics
and lesser-spotted varieties, such as
tagliarini (skinny tagliatelle) or *pici
cacio* (a kind of hand-rolled no-egg
noodle from Siena), smothered
in a simple yet moreish sauce of
parmesan, butter and cracked black
pepper. The eight-hour beef shin ragu
served over pappardelle is a perennial
favourite, while the smoked eel
and cream tagliatelle – with just a
hint of Sicilian lemon – is sublime.
Dishes are small enough (and, at
around £5-£9, cheap enough) to let
you to order three between two.

Pubs & bars

♥ Dandelyan

Mondrian London, 20 Upper Ground, SE1 9PD (3747 1000, www.morganshotelgroup. com/mondrian). Blackfriars or Southwark tube. **Open** *4pm-1am Mon-Wed; noon-2am Thur-Sat; noon-12.30am Sun.* **Map** *p68 O8* ❶

The second bar opened by Ryan Chetiyawardana (aka bartender Mr Lyan) couldn't be more different from his first. Rather than occupying a converted Hoxton pub, Dandelyan has a prime spot off the lobby of the multimillion-pound Mondrian (*see p194*). The bar might be glamorous, luxurious and a bit formal, but the drinks show Chetiyawardana's invention and attention to detail are intact: the botanically themed drinks list includes ingredients such as 'chalk bitters', 'crystal peach nectar' and the archaic-sounding 'dandelion capillaire'. Everything is surprising without being show-off, and, importantly, it's all very drinkable.

Doodle Bar

60 Druid Street, SE1 2EZ (7403 3222, www.thedoodlebar.com). Bermondsey tube. **Open** *noon-11pm Thur; noon-midnight Fri, Sat; noon-6pm Sun.* **Map** *p68 S10* ❷

One of London's more original pop-up bars, Doodle now resides in an atmospheric Bermondsey railway arch. The concrete floor is high gloss, there's table football by the bar, and a street food van parks outside on weekends. But the real action is at the back: a narrow arch of a room with ping pong tables, where drinkers are encouraged to draw all over the walls. A well-curated wine list is accompanied by a handful of cocktails and the bar's own-brewed pale ale.

Gŏng

Level 52, The Shard, 31 St Thomas Street, SE1 9QU (7234 8208, www. gong-shangri-la.com). London Bridge tube/rail. **Open** *noon-1am Mon-Sat; noon-midnight Sun.* **Map** *p68 R9* ❸

Take the express lift up the Shard to the 52nd floor to find London's highest bar. At this altitude, it's actually not so easy to pick out landmarks, but the views of the City are simply spectacular, especially if you book a two-hour slot across sunset. Be warned: you'll pay a premium for drinking in such an elevated location. Bermondsey Bubbles, for example, made with Jensen's gin, rose liqueur and champagne – is perfectly pleasant, but it doesn't leave much change from a £20 note.

There's usually a minimum £30 spend per person, but on Sunday, Monday or Tuesday (except bank holidays) you can enjoy the view for just the price of a bottle of beer or a glass of wine.

Waterloo Tap

Corner of Sutton Walk & Concert Hall Approach, SE1 8RL (3455 7436, www.waterlootap.com). Waterloo tube. **Open** *noon-11pm Mon-Wed; noon-11.30pm Thur, Fri; 11am-11.30pm Sat; 11am-10pm Sun.* **Map** *p68 N9* ❹

Tucked away in a railway arch a short dash from Waterloo station, the Tap has bucked the trend towards the new breed of high-alcohol brews and stuck to its roots as a more traditional alehouse. You'll find no filament bulbs or scruffily chalked-up beer lists here. The 20-strong keg collection is British-focused, with the north especially well represented (no surprise, given the original Tap is in Sheffield). If they're on, try something from Manchester's Cloudwater Brew Co, whose one-off, seasonal brews are never around for long.

(including hops), as well as hosting workshops, tastings and foodie demonstrations. You can also nip in with your snack if the weather's poor.

Shops & services

Borough Market

8 Southwark Street, SE1 1TL (7407 1002, www.boroughmarket.org. uk). London Bridge tube/rail. **Open** *10am-5pm Mon-Thur; 10am-6pm Fri; 8am-5pm Sat.* **No cards.** **Map** *p68 Q9* ❶ *Market*

The food hound's favourite market is also London's oldest, dating back to the 13th century. It's the busiest, too, occupying a sprawling site near London Bridge. Gourmet goodies run the gamut, from fresh loaves and rare-breed meats, via fish, game, fruit and veg, to cakes and all manner of preserves, oils and teas; head out hungry to take advantage of the numerous free samples. A rail viaduct, vigorously campaigned against, is now in place, which means restored historic features have been returned and works disruption should be at an end. As if to celebrate, a Market Hall, facing on to Borough High Street, was opened: it acts as a kind of greenhouse for growing plants

Entertainment

BFI IMAX

1 Charlie Chaplin Walk, South Bank, SE1 8XR (0330 333 7878, www.bfi.org.uk/imax). Waterloo tube/rail. Tickets £16.60-£20.80; £11.20-£16.40 reductions. Screens 1. **Map** *p68 N9* ❶ *Cinema*

London's – indeed, the UK's – biggest cinema screen at 5800sq ft, the BFI IMAX is in the centre of a busy roundabout next to Waterloo station. As well as the massive screen, you get superlative sound quality and seats arranged at such a vertiginous angle there's no chance of a head blocking your view. It's not cheap – just over £20 for a premium seat – but if you like your blockbusters vast and noisy, there's really nothing else like it in town. Film aficionados will likely prefer **BFI Southbank** (7928 3232, www.bfi.org.uk), under Waterloo bridge, which screens significant British and foreign films.

❤ Corsica Studios

4-5 Elephant Road, Elephant & Castle, SE17 1LB (7703 4760, www. corsicastudios.com). Elephant & Castle tube/rail. **Open** *8pm-6am Fri, Sat; 8pm-3am Sun-Thur.* **Admission** *free-£15.* **Map** *p68 P11* ❷ *Music club and arts venue*

An independent, not-for-profit arts complex, Corsica Studios seeks to breed a culture of creativity. The flexible warehouse space is one of London's most adventurous, supplementing the DJs that play here with bands, poets, painters and lunatic projectionists. Sure, it's rough around the edges, with makeshift bars and toilets, but the events are second to none. The

 National Theatre

South Bank, SE1 9PX (7452 3000, www.nationaltheatre.org.uk). Embankment or Southwark tube, or Waterloo tube/rail. **Box office** *9.30am-8pm Mon-Sat.* **Tickets** *£15-£52.* **Map** *p68 N9* ❸ *Theatre*

A still-startling jewel of brutalist design, the National is surely the world's greatest theatre. Nobody would say it gets everything right, but it is worthy of a pilgrimage for anybody remotely interested in the arts. Having passed its 50th anniversary in 2013, the National first completed a major programme of expansion and upgrades, then waved goodbye to its hugely appreciated artistic director, Nicholas Hytner, who had been in the post since 2003: Hytner rescued the NT from the doldrums, launching endless hit transfers to the West End, got Travelex to sponsor tickets to bring down the prices, and adroitly balanced the programme to mix big, crowd-pleasing stuff by Shakespeare with startling new work and some properly obscure rediscoveries. His landmark successes – Alan Bennett's *The History Boys* and *War Horse* – showed that the state-subsidised home of British theatre could turn out quality drama at a profit.

Successor Rufus Norris has had a slightly more difficult time of it. Big West End money-spinner *War Horse* finally closed, and *The Curious Incident of the Dog in the Night-Time* followed suit, with no obvious sign of replacements. Meanwhile, the theatre's Arts Council subsidy is on the wane as the government's austerity programme continues. The press has been occasionally unkind, criticising Norris for everything from staging work that's too weird to putting on too much new writing. If a new West End hit remains elusive, that's not for want of popular, agenda-setting productions, with a starry revival of Tony Kushner's epic *Angels in America* and van Hove's take on the classic '70s film *Network*, starring *Breaking Bad*'s Bryan Cranston, keeping the returns queue busy throughout 2017. The Travelex seasons continue, widening audiences by offering tickets for £15, as does the free outdoor performing arts River Stage, held outside the NT during the summer.

War Horse

live-music roster has included gigs from Silver Apples, Acoustic Ladyland and Lydia Lunch.

Old Vic

The Cut, Waterloo, SE1 8NB (0844 871 7628, www.oldvictheatre. com). Southwark tube or Waterloo tube/rail. **Box office** *In person 10am-6pm Mon-Sat. By phone 9am-7.30pm Mon-Fri; 9am-4pm Sat; 9.30am-4pm Sun. Tickets £10-£90.* **Map** *p68 O10* ④ *Theatre*

London's most famous artistic director, Kevin Spacey, moved out in 2015, but don't be fooled into thinking his less famous successor Matthew Warchus is some sort of step down. A seriously heavyweight director (he has been pencilled in to direct the Broadway adaptation of *Frozen*), Warchus has all of Spacey's celebrity pulling power, topped with a bolder, more eclectic approach to programming. His USP is heavyweight new musical work: his brilliant *Groundhog Day* had its tryout run at the Vic in 2016 before heading off to conquer Broadway, and an adaptation of Warchus' hit film *Pride* (2014) is said to be in the works.

❤ Southbank Centre

Belvedere Road, South Bank, SE1 8XX (7960 4200, www. southbankcentre.co.uk). Embankment tube or Waterloo tube/rail. **Box office** *In person 10am-8pm daily. By phone 9am-8pm daily. Tickets £7-£75.* **Map** *p68 N9* ⑤ *Concert venue*

The centrepiece of the cluster of cultural venues collectively known as the Southbank Centre is the 2,500-seat **Royal Festival Hall**; the neighbouring 900-seat **Queen Elizabeth Hall** and attached 365-seat **Purcell Room** will reopen after refurbishment in early 2018. All three programme a wide variety of events – spoken word, jazz, rock and pop gigs – but classical is very

well represented. The RFH has four resident orchestras and hosts music from medieval motets to Messiaen via Beethoven and Elgar. Beneath this main hall, facing the foyer bar, a stage puts on hundreds of free concerts each year.

Young Vic

66 The Cut, Waterloo, SE1 8LZ (7922 2922, www.youngvic.org). Waterloo tube/rail. **Box office** *10am-6pm Mon-Sat. Tickets £10-£57.* **Map** *p68 O9* ⑥ *Theatre*

As the name suggests, this Vic has more youthful bravura than its older sister up the road, and draws a younger crowd, who pack out the open-air balcony and its restaurant and bar on the weekends. They come to see European classics with a modern edge, new writing with an international flavour and collaborations with leading companies. Recent winners have included *Yerma*, an update of Lorca's play from Aussie director Simon Stone that included a paintstripper-intense turn from Billie Piper, while summer 2017 saw Sienna Miller star in Benedict Andrews' take on *Cat On a Hot Tin Roof*, which is going straight into the West End.

Riverside at Southbank Centre

Westminster & St James's

The whole of the United Kingdom is ruled from this small portion of London on the north bank of the Thames. The monarchy has been in residence in **Westminster** since the 11th century, when Edward the Confessor moved west out of the walled City, and as the role of British kings and queens became increasingly ceremonial, Parliament was already here to take on the real business of government. Many visitors find the imposing buildings of Westminster more formal than inviting, but it's a key destination with the most significant area designated a UNESCO World Heritage Site back in 1987.

Parliament Square has some of the capital's most impressive architecture: the Gothic masterpiece of

♥ Shortlist

Best sights
The historic Houses of Parliment (*p86*) and Westminster Abbey (*p85*).

Best decadent dining
Brunch at the Wolseley (*p90*).

Best café
Art deco greasy spoon, Regency Café (*p89*).

Best pub
London's finest brews at Cask (*p90*).

Best shops
Upmarket department store, Fortnum & Mason (*p92*). Achingly cool brands at Dover Street Market (*p90*).

Best park
St James's Park (*p91*) for a peaceful stroll.

Best art galleries
Famous paintings at the National Gallery (*p87*). Tate Britain (*p88*) for fine British art.

Westminster Abbey has been the site of almost every British coronation, while the **Houses of Parliament** and its '**Big Ben**' clock tower have starred in many holiday snaps. Heading north along **Whitehall** – one of London's most majestic streets – is **Trafalgar Square** where visitors flock in their thousands to pose for photographs in front of **Nelson's Column**.

Westminster is also packed with culture. The **National Portrait Gallery** and **Tate Britain** – often overlooked in favour of its modern cousin on the other side of the river – offer a walk through British history. The perennially popular **National Gallery** continues to draw visitors with one of the greatest collections of paintings in the world.

And for such an important part of London, the area is surprisingly spacious. **The Mall** offers a regally broad approach route to **Buckingham Palace**, which presides over lovely **St James's Park**. Traditional, quiet and exclusive, the residential area of **St James's** is dignified and unhurried, whether you're shopping at **Fortnum's** or entertaining at the **Wolseley**.

→ Getting around
This central area is very well served by tube and bus, but you'll see more if you walk. Most sights are within half a mile of each other.

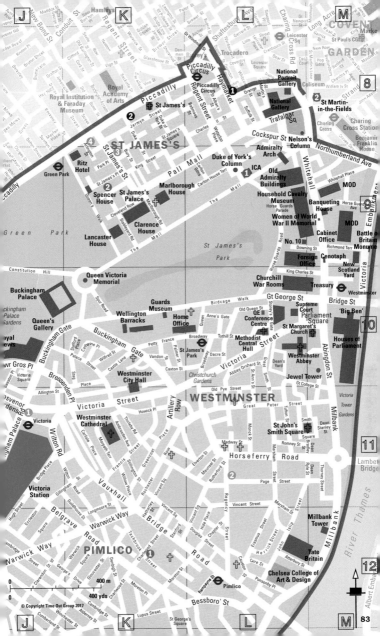

Sights & museums

Banqueting House

Whitehall, SW1A 2ER (3166 6000, www.hrp.org.uk/banqueting-house). Westminster tube. **Open** *10am-5pm daily; phone to check.* **Admission** *£6; £5 reductions; free under-16s.* **Map** *p83 M9.*

This handsome Italianate mansion, which was designed by Inigo Jones and constructed in 1620, was the first true Renaissance building in London. The sole surviving part of the Tudor and Stuart kings' Whitehall Palace, the Banqueting House features a lavish painted ceiling by Rubens, glorifying James I, 'the wisest fool in Christendom'. Regrettably, James's successor, Charles I, did not rule so wisely. After losing the English Civil War to Cromwell's Roundheads, he was executed in front of Banqueting House in 1649 – the subject of a set of displays here.

Buckingham Palace & Royal Mews

The Mall, SW1A 1AA (Palace 0303 123 7300, Royal Mews 0303 123 7302, Queen's Gallery 0303 123 7301, www.royalcollection.org.uk). Green Park tube or Victoria tube/rail. **Open** *admission times & prices vary.* **Map** *p83 J10.*

Constructed as a private house for the Duke of Buckingham in 1703 and converted into a palace by John Nash in 1820, Buckingham Palace has been used as the primary home of every British monarch since Queen Victoria. The palace is open to the public each year while the family are away on their summer hols; you'll be able to see the State Apartments, which are still used to entertain guests of state. At other times of year, visit the Queen's Gallery to see the Queen's personal collection of treasures, including paintings by Rembrant, Sèvres porcelain and the Diamond Diadem crown.

Further along Buckingham Palace Road, the **Royal Mews** is a grand garage for the royal fleet of Rolls-Royces and home to the splendid royal carriages and the horses, individually named by the Queen, that pull them.

Churchill War Rooms

Clive Steps, King Charles Street, SW1A 2AQ (7930 6961, www.iwm.org.uk). St James's Park or Westminster tube. **Open** *9.30am-6pm daily.* **Admission** *£17.25; £8.60-£13.80 reductions; free under-5s.* **Map** *p83 L10.*

Out of harm's way beneath Whitehall, this cramped and spartan bunker was where Winston Churchill planned the Allied victory in World War II, and the rooms powerfully bring to life the reality of a nation at war. The cabinet rooms were sealed on 16 August 1945, keeping the complex in a state of suspended animation: every pin stuck into the vast charts was placed there in the final days of the conflict. The humble quarters occupied by Churchill and his deputies give a tangible sense of wartime hardship, an effect reinforced by the wailing sirens and wartime speeches on the audio guide (free with admission).

Guards Museum

Wellington Barracks, Birdcage Walk, SW1E 6HQ (7414 3428, www.theguardsmuseum.com). St James's Park tube. **Open** *10am-4pm daily.* **Admission** *£6; £2-£3 reductions; free under-16s.* **Map** *p83 K10.*

Just down the road from Horse Guards, this small museum tells the 350-year story of the Foot Guards, using flamboyant uniforms, period paintings, medals and intriguing memorabilia, such as the stuffed body of Jacob the Goose, the Guards' Victorian mascot, who was regrettably run over by a van in barracks. Appropriately, the shop is well stocked with toy soldiers of the British regiments. *See also p22.*

❤ Westminster Abbey

20 Dean's Yard, SW1P 3PA (information 7222 5152, tours 7654 4834, www.westminster-abbey.org). St James's Park or Westminster tube. **Open** *May-Aug 9.30am-3.30pm Mon, Tue, Thur-Sat; 9.30am-3.30pm, 4.30-6pm Wed. Sept-Apr 9.30am-3.30pm Mon, Thur, Fri; 2-3.30pm Tue; 9.30am-3.30pm, 4.30-6pm Wed; 9.30am-1.30pm Sat. Abbey Museum, Chapter House, College Gardens & Tours times vary; check website for details.* **Admission** *£20; £9-£17 reductions; £45 family; free under-5s. Tours £5.* **Map** *p83 L10.*

The cultural, historic and religious significance of Westminster Abbey is impossible to overstate, but also hard to remember as you're shepherded around, forced to elbow fellow tourists out of the way to read a plaque or see a tomb. The best plan is to get here as early in the day as you can – although it also quietens down towards closing time.

Edward the Confessor commissioned a church to St Peter on the site of a seventh-century version, but it was only consecrated on 28 December 1065, eight days before he died. William the Conqueror subsequently had himself crowned here on Christmas Day 1066 and, with just two exceptions, every English coronation since has taken place in the abbey.

Many royal, military and cultural notables are interred here. The most haunting memorial is the Grave of the Unknown Warrior, in the nave. Elaborate resting places in side chapels are taken up by the tombs of Elizabeth I and Mary Queen of Scots. In Innocents Corner lie the remains of two lads believed to be Edward V and his brother Richard (their bodies were found at the Tower of London). Poets' Corner is the final resting place of Chaucer, who was the first writer to be buried here. The remains of Dryden, Johnson, Browning and Tennyson are also present.

Set to open in 2018, the new Queen's Diamond Jubilee Galleries will present treasures and historic oddities that tell the long and complex history of this glorious place.

▶ *Even when the abbey is at its most crowded, the 900-year-old College Garden – one of the oldest cultivated spaces in Britain, with some lovely mulberry trees – remains tranquil.*

North door

❤ Houses of Parliament

Parliament Square, SW1A 0AA (Commons information 7219 4272; Lords information 7219 3107; tickets 7219 4114, www.parliament. uk). Westminster tube. **Open** *(when in session) House of Commons Visitors' Gallery 2.30-10.30pm Mon; 11.30am-7.30pm Tue, Wed; 9.30am-5.30pm Thur; 9.30am-3pm Fri. House of Lords Visitors' Gallery 2.30-10pm Mon, Tue; 3-10pm Wed; 11am-7.30pm Thur; from 10am Fri. Tours 9.15am-4.30pm Sat & summer recess; check website for details.* **Admission** *Visitors' galleries free. Tours £25.50; £11-£21 reductions; free under-5s.* **Map** *p83 M10.*

The British parliament has an extremely long history, with the first parliamentary session held in St Stephen's Chapel in 1275. The Palace of Westminster, however, only became the permanent seat of Parliament in 1532, when Henry VIII moved to a new des-res in Whitehall.

The current palace is a wonderful mish-mash of styles, dominated by Gothic buttresses, towers and arches. It looks much older than it is: the Parliament buildings were designed in 1860 by Charles Barry (ably assisted by Augustus Pugin) to replace the original building, which had been destroyed by fire in 1834. Of the original palace, only the Jewel Tower and, within the Parliament buildings, Westminster Hall, remain.

Visitors are welcome (subject to stringent security checks) to observe the political debates in the House of Lords and House of Commons, but tickets must be arranged in advance through your embassy or MP, who can also arrange tours – even free trips up the 334 spiral steps of the Elizabeth Tower to hear 'Big Ben'. The experience of listening in on the Houses of Parliament in session is often soporific, but Prime Minister's Question Time at noon on Wednesday is often sparky.

Alternatively, book one of the revealing 90-minute guided tours (7219 4114, www.parliament.uk/ visiting) on Saturday or during summer recess. Tours take in both Houses, Westminster Hall, the Queen's Robing Room and the Royal Gallery.

Houses of Parliament and Westminster Bridge

Household Cavalry Museum

Horse Guards, Whitehall, SW1A 2AX (7930 3070, www. householdcavalrymuseum.co.uk). Westminster tube or Charing Cross tube/rail. **Open** *Apr-Oct 10am-6pm daily. Nov-Mar 10am-5pm daily.* **Admission** *£7; £5 reductions; £18 family; free under-5s.* **Map** *p83 L9.*
Household Cavalry is a fairly workaday name for the military peacocks who make up the Queen's official guard. They tell their stories through video diaries at this small but entertaining museum, which also offers the chance to see medals, uniforms and shiny cuirasses (breastplates) up close. You also get a peek – and sniff – of the magnificent horses that parade just outside every day: the stables are separated from the main museum by no more than a screen of glass. *See also p22.*

♥ National Gallery

Trafalgar Square, WC2N 5DN (7747 2885, www.nationalgallery. org.uk). Charing Cross tube/rail. **Open** *10am-6pm Mon-Thur, Sat, Sun; 10am-9pm Fri. Tours 11.30am, 2.30pm Mon-Thur; 11.30am, 2.30pm, 7pm Fri; 11.30am, 2.30pm Sat, Sun.* **Admission** *free. Special exhibitions vary.* **Map** *p83 L8.*
Founded in 1824, the National Gallery is one of the world's great repositories for art. There are masterpieces from virtually every European school of art, from austere 13th-century religious paintings to the sensual delights of Titian, Caravaggio and Van Gogh.

The gallery itself is huge; don't try to see everything in one visit. The modern Sainsbury Wing extension contains the gallery's earliest works: Italian paintings by masters such as Giotto and Piero della Francesca, as well as the medieval *Wilton Diptych*, showing Richard II with the Virgin and Child.

In the West Wing are Italian Renaissance masterpieces by Correggio, Titian and Raphael. The North Wing, displays 17th-century Dutch, Flemish, Italian and Spanish Old Masters, including Rembrandt's *A Woman Bathing in a Stream* and Caravaggio's *Supper at Emmaus*.

In the East Wing, you'll find works by the French Impressionists and Post-Impressionists, including Monet's *Water-Lilies*, one of Van Gogh's *Sunflowers* and Seurat's *Bathers at Asnières*. Don't miss Renoir's astonishingly lovely *The Skiff* (*La Yole*).

Downstairs, the opening of Gallery B has transformed the ground floor. 'Rubens and Rembrandt', kicked off the programme of free temporary exhibitions here in 2017.

National Portrait Gallery

St Martin's Place, WC2H 0HE (7306 0055, www.npg.org.uk). Leicester Square tube or Charing Cross tube/rail. **Open** *10am-6pm Mon-Wed, Sat, Sun; 10am-9pm Thur, Fri.* **Admission** *free. Special exhibitions vary.* **Map** *p83 L8.*
Portraits don't have to be stuffy. The NPG has everything from oil paintings of stiff-backed royals to photographs of soccer stars and gloriously unflattering political caricatures. Portraits are arranged in chronological order from the top of the gallery to the bottom. On the second floor are the earliest works, portraits of Tudor and Stuart royals and notables, including Holbein's 'cartoon' of Henry VIII and the 'Ditchley Portrait' of his daughter, Elizabeth I, her pearly slippers placed firmly on a colourful map of England. On the same floor, the 18th-century collection features Georgian writers and artists (including Congreve, Dryden, Wren and Swift), as well as Regency greats, military men such as

💙 Tate Britain

Millbank, SW1P 4RG (7887 8888, www.tate.org.uk). Pimlico tube. **Open** *10am-6pm daily. Tours 11am, noon, 2pm, 3pm daily.* **Admission** *free. Special exhibitions vary.* **Map** *p83 L12.*

Especially since the opening of its dramatic extension in 2016, **Tate Modern** (*see p74*) has been getting all the attention. But (whisper it) we prefer the original Tate Gallery – or Tate Britain, as it's now known. This isn't nostalgia. Tate Britain was handsomely refurbished a few years ago, has a better organised collection than its illustrious counterpart and is much less busy – the lack of visitors (relative lack, of course) wasn't much fun for outgoing director Penelope Curtis, but it sure makes viewing art more enjoyable.

Unlike the themed galleries at Tate Modern which can be disorientating, the main floor of the Tate Britain is a logical journey through the history of British Art from Holbein in the 1540s. Key artists are given more substantial treatment: Blake and Henry Moore have their own rooms, while JMW Turner occupies his own extensive Clore Gallery.

Founded by sugar magnate Sir Henry Tate, Tate Britain opened in a stately riverside building in 1897 – built on the site of the pentagonal Millbank Prison, which held criminals destined for transportation to Botany Bay – with a display of 245 British paintings. Now, the collection is rather more extensive. Constable, Millais, Whistler, Hogarth and Bacon are all represented; the blockbuster exhibitions – not

least a stunning Hockney retrospective in 2017 – are increasingly excellent.

Tate Britain has also been surreptitiously stealing a bit of the limelight back from its starrier sibling with a long-term redevelopment plan called the Millbank Project; this has upgraded the galleries while conserving original features, opening new spaces to the public and adding a new café. Also, sturdier floors meant that more sculpture could be displayed, and the amount of natural light was increased. The Millbank entrance is lovely these days, with its stained glass and striking spiral staircase; downstairs in the restaurant, a new Alan Johnston ceiling mural complements the restored 1926-27 Rex Whistler wall mural *Pursuit of Rare Meats*.

Wellington and Nelson, plus Byron, Wordsworth and other Romantics. The first floor is devoted to the Victorians (Dickens, Brunel, Darwin) and to 20th-century luminaries, such as TS Eliot and Ian McKellen.

Trafalgar Square

Leicester Square tube or Charing Cross tube/rail. **Map** *p83 L8.*
Trafalgar Square was conceived in the 1820s as a homage to Britain's naval power. Always a natural gathering point, the square now regularly hosts celebrations and festivals, and even some protests. The focus is **Nelson's Column**, a Corinthian pillar topped by a statue of the naval hero, supported by four lions, but the changing contemporary sculpture on the **Fourth Plinth** bring fresh colour – David Shrigley's huge thumbs-up, *Really Good*, will be followed in 2018 by Michael Rakowitz's *The Invisible Enemy Should Not Exist.*

Westminster Cathedral

42 Francis Street, SW1P 1QW (7798 9055, www.westminstercathedral. org.uk). Victoria tube/rail. **Open** *6.30am-7pm Mon-Fri; 7.30am-7.30pm Sat; 7.30am-8pm Sun.* **Admission** *free; donations appreciated.* **Map** *p83 K11.*
With its domes, arches and soaring tower, the most important Catholic church in England looks surprisingly Byzantine. There's a reason: architect John Francis Bentley, who built it between 1895 and 1903, was heavily influenced by Hagia Sophia in Istanbul. Compared to the candy-cane exterior, the interior is surprisingly restrained (in fact, it's unfinished), but there are still some impressive marble columns and mosaics. Eric Gill's sculptures of the Stations of the Cross (1914-18) were dismissed as 'Babylonian' when they were first installed, but worshippers have come to love them. An upper gallery holds the 'Treasures of the Cathedral' exhibition, where you can see an impressive Arts and Crafts coronet, a Tudor chalice, holy relics and Bentley's amazing architectural model of his cathedral, complete with tiny hawks.

Restaurants

Bleecker ££

205 Victoria Street, SW1E 5NE (www.bleeckerburger. co.uk). Victoria tube/rail. **Open** *11.30am-11pm Mon-Sat; 11.30am-10pm Sun.* **Map** *p83 J11* ❶
Burgers
The first bricks-and-mortar shop from this popular street-food burger outfit is pure filth… in the best possible way. Made with rare-breed, dry-aged beef, the burgers don't compromise on quality but there's nothing pretentious about them – they're just bun, cheese and killer pucks of meat. Serious carnivores will adore the award-winning 'Bleecker black': two pink patties sandwiching a slice of black pudding. But given the inevitable, crippling post-scoff food coma, be sure to come hungry and eat fast.

❤ Regency Café £

17-19 Regency Street, SW1P 4BY (7821 6596, regencycafe.co.uk). St James's Park tube or Victoria tube/ rail. **Open** *7am-2.30pm, 4-7.15pm Mon-Fri; 7am-noon Sat.* **Map** *p83 L11* ❷ *Café*
Behind its black-tiled art deco exterior, this classic caff has been here since 1946. Customers sit on brown plastic chairs at Formica-topped tables, watched over by muscular boxers and Spurs stars of yore, whose photos hang on the tiled walls. Lasagne, omelettes, salads, every conceivable cooked breakfast and mugs of tannin-rich tea are meat and drink to the Regency. Still hungry? The

improbably gigantic cinnamon-flavoured bread and butter pud will see you right for the rest of the week.

Sake no Hana ££££

23 St James's Street, SW1A 1HA (7925 8988, sakenohana.com/london). Green Park tube. **Open** noon-3pm, 6-11pm Mon-Thur; noon-3pm, 6-11.30pm Fri; noon-3.30pm, 6-11.30pm Sat. **Map** p83 K9 ❸ *Japanese*

As you'd expect from the Hakkasan restaurant group, Sake No Hana is beautifully designed. That and the fine range of contemporary Japanese dishes and slick service make it popular place for business lunches and well-heeled families. For a filling meal, the 'Taste of Sake No Hana' (£29) consists of miso soup, a choice of sukiyaki, tempura or grilled dish, a handful of sushi and a dessert. There's also plenty for wine and saké buffs to get stuck into. Don't forget to glance upwards while you're dining: the sculptural wood slating above your head definitely deserves a look.

♥ Wolseley £££

160 Piccadilly, W1J 9EB (7499 6996, www.thewolseley.com). Green Park tube. **Open** 7am-midnight Mon-Fri; 8am-midnight Sat; 8am-11pm Sun. **Map** p83 K8 ❹ *Brasserie*

A self-proclaimed 'café-restaurant in the grand European tradition', the Wolseley combines London heritage and Viennese grandeur. The kitchen is much celebrated for its breakfasts, and the scope of the main menu is admirable. From oysters, steak tartare or soufflé suisse, via wiener schnitzel or grilled halibut with wilted spinach and béarnaise, to Portuguese custard tart or apple strudel, there's something for everyone. On Sunday afternoons, three-tiered afternoon tea stands are in abundance.

Pubs & bars

♥ Cask

6 Charlwood Street, Pimlico, SW1V 6EE (7630 7225, www.caskpubandkitchen.com). Pimlico tube. **Open** noon-11pm Mon-Sat; noon-10.30pm Sun. Food served noon-3pm, 5-10pm Mon-Fri; 12.30-9.30pm Sat, Sun. **Map** p83 K12 ❶

It's not much to look at – an awkward shape at the bottom of a new-build block – but Cask has been blazing the trail for better beer for years. Its fridges and cellar are filled with an absurdly generous range of the finest brews from London, Britain and beyond, with something to satisfy the most ardent hophead or convert the most timid quaffer of fizzy yellow lager. Staff really know their stuff too – ask for a recommendation and you won't be disappointed.

Dukes Bar

Dukes Hotel, 35 St James's Place, SW1A 1NY (7491 4840, www.dukeshotel.com/dukes-bar). Green Park tube. **Open** 2-11pm Mon-Sat; 4-10.30pm Sun. **Map** p83 K9 ❷

If you want to go out for a single cocktail, strong and expensive and very well made, go to Dukes. It's in a luxury hotel, but everyone gets the warmest of welcomes. There are three small rooms, all decorated in discreetly opulent style; you feel cocooned. The bar is famous for the theatre of its Martini-making – at the table, from a trolley, using vermouth made exclusively for them at the Sacred distillery in Highgate – but other drinks are just as good.

Shops & services

♥ Dover Street Market

18-22 Haymarket, SW1Y 4DG (7518 0680, www.doverstreetmarket.com). Green Park tube. **Open** 11am-7pm Mon-Sat; noon-6pm Sun. **Map** p83 L8 ❶ *Fashion*

💙 St James's Park

*St James's Park tube. **Open** 5am–midnight daily. **Map** p83 L9.*

There's only one London park where you might spot a pelican swallow a pigeon. St James's Park, a 90-acre wedge of green between Westminster, Trafalgar Square and Buckingham Palace, is the oldest of eight royal parks – those parks that are Crown rather than municipal property. It is also one of London's finest, with narrow lanes meandering around a lake and gorgeous sculpted flower beds, a lakeside café, copious wildfowl and one of the most romantic views in the city. This comes from a bridge across the graceful central lake, which was created from a more formal canal by John Nash in the 1820s. Look east and, above the trees in the near distance, hover the spires, pinnacles and domes of Whitehall – with no square modern towers in sight, it looks like something from Prague or Disneyland; look west and, if the leaves are off the trees, you'll see **Buckingham Palace** (*see p84*). It's a peaceful place – except when

it's used for ceremonial events like **Trooping the Colour** (*see p22*).

It's quite a transformation for a park, formed from a marshy field attached to a leper hospital, that later became a haunt of prostitutes. Henry VIII was the first to use the land for leisure, creating a bowling alley and ground for hunting. James I had more formal gardens laid out and imported a menagerie that included two crocodiles. In the 17th century, Charles II had it redesigned again, by the French landscape gardener from Versailles, adding a pair of pelicans that had been a gift from the Russian ambassador – pelicans have been resident ever since. In fact, wildlife has been a constant theme. Early occupants included deer, leopards and an elk, but by the 18th century the park was being used to graze cows – fresh milk could be bought here until 1905. Now, wildfowl are the draw, with 17 different species splashing about in the central lake. Those bag-jawed pelicans are fed between 2.30pm and 3pm daily.

Combining the energy of London's indoor markets with rarefied labels, Rei Kawakubo's ground-breaking multistorey store is a mecca for the fashion obsessed. Housing some of London's brightest stars – Grace Wales Bonner's wonderfully elegant menswear and Molly Goddard's dream dresses woven out of tulle – it's a real champion of the capital's pioneering fashion designers. All 14 of the Comme des Garçons collections are here, alongside exclusive lines from such designers as Lanvin and Azzedine Alaïa.

❤ Fortnum & Mason

*181 Piccadilly, W1A 1ER (7734 8040, www.fortnumandmason. co.uk). Green Park or Piccadilly Circus tube. **Open** 10am-8pm Mon-Sat; noon-6pm Sun (11.30am for browsing). **Map** p83 K8 ❷ Department store*

In business for over 300 years, Fortnum & Mason is as historic as it is inspiring. A sweeping spiral staircase soars through the four-storey building, while light floods down from a central glass dome. The iconic eau de nil blue and gold colour scheme with flashes of rose pink abounds on both the store design and the packaging of the fabulous ground-floor treats, such as chocolates, biscuits, teas and preserves. A food hall in the basement has a good range of fresh produce; Fortnum's Bees honey comes from beehives on top of the building. There are various eateries, including an ice-cream parlour. The famous hampers start from £55 – though they rise to a whopping £1,000 for the most luxurious.

Entertainment

Institute of Contemporary Arts

*The Mall, SW1Y 5AH (7930 0493 information, 7930 3647 tickets, www.ica.org.uk). Piccadilly Circus tube or Charing Cross tube/ rail. **Open** 11am-11pm Tue-Sun. Galleries (during exhibitions) 11am-6pm Tue, Wed, Fri-Sun; 11am-9pm Thur. **Admission** free. **Map** p83 L9 ❶ Arts venue*

Founded in 1947 by a collective of poets, artists and critics, the ICA offers exhibitions, arthouse cinema, performance art, philosophical debates, art-themed club nights and anything else that might challenge convention – but 'convention' is so much harder to challenge now that everyone's doing it. Perhaps new director Stefan Kalmár – whose CV includes stints at New York's Artists Space and Munich's Bonner Kunstverein – will make it a must-visit for the culturati once more.

St Martin-in-the-Fields

*Trafalgar Square, WC2N 4JH (7766 1100, www.smitf.org). Leicester Square tube or Charing Cross tube/ rail. **Open** 8.30am-1pm, 2-6pm Mon, Tue, Fri; 8.30am-1.15pm, 2-5pm Wed; 8.30am-1pm, 2-6pm Thur; 9.30am-6pm Sat; 3.30-5pm Sun. Brass Rubbing Centre 10am-6pm Mon-Wed; 10am-8pm Thur-Sat; 11.30am-5pm Sun. **Admission** free. Brass rubbing £4.50. **Map** p83 M8 ❷ Concert venue*

There's been a church 'in the fields' between Westminster and the City since the 13th century. The current one was built in 1726 by James Gibbs, using a fusion of neoclassical and Baroque styles. The parish church for Buckingham Palace (the royal box is to the left of the gallery), St Martin's interior was restored a few years back, with Victorian furbelows removed and the addition of a brilliant altar window that shows the Cross, stylised as if rippling on water. The lunchtime and evening concerts in the church are often delightful, especially when candlelit.

Kensington & Chelsea

It was Prince Albert who oversaw the inception of **South Kensington's** world-class museums, colleges and concert hall, using the profits of the 1851 Great Exhibition. The area was nicknamed 'Albertopolis' in his honour. Here you'll find the **Natural History Museum**, the **Science Museum** and the **Victoria & Albert Museum** (V&A), **Imperial College**, the **Royal College of Art** and the **Royal College of Music**. The last forms a unity with the **Royal Albert Hall**, variously used for boxing, motor shows, marathons, table-tennis tournaments, fascist rallies and rock concerts.

Neighbouring **Knightsbridge**, on the other hand, has no cultural pretensions: a certain type of Londoner comes here to spend, spend, spend, in the designer shops

❤ Shortlist

Must-see museum
The then and now of great design at the V&A (*p100*) and the Design Museum (*p108*).

Best outdoor attraction
Botanical delights at Chelsea Physic Garden (*p103*).

Best for kids
Life on earth at the Natural History Museum (*p96*). How the world works at the Science Museum (*p98*).

Best restaurant
French-inspired bistro, Bar Boulud (*p102*). Rabbit (*p105*) for tasty small plates.

Best shop
Luxury department store, Harrods (*p103*).

Best cultural venue
BBC Proms at the Royal Albert Hall (*p101*). Classical music at the art deco Cadogan Hall (*p106*).

and world-famous department stores. Expensive brands – Gucci, Prada, Chanel – dominate, but for many tourists Knightsbridge means one thing: **Harrods**.

Bordering the area to the north, **Hyde Park** and **Kensington Gardens** form one of London's largest Royal Parks and are of great historic interest. The land was appropriated in 1536 from the monks of Westminster Abbey by Henry VIII for hunting deer and has long been a hotspot for mass demonstrations. London's oldest boating lake, the **Serpentine**, is here, along with art at the **Serpentine** and **Serpentine Sackler** galleries.

Heading south down Exhibition Road, **Chelsea** has a couple of worthwhile attractions in the mercilessly modern art of the **Saatchi Gallery** and the botanical marvel that is the **Chelsea Physic Garden**. West of Kensington Gardens, meanwhile, is the ambitious new **Design Museum** and delightful **Holland Park**, with **Portobello Road Market** and **Notting Hill** to the north.

→ Getting around
This is a large district, served by a similarly large number of tube stations. For the Natural History Museum, Science Museum and V&A, take the District, Circle or Piccadilly lines to South Kensington. Buses also run along the main routes.

South Kensington

Sights & museums

Albert Memorial

Kensington Gardens (0300 061 2000, www.royalparks.org.uk). South Kensington tube. Tours Mar-Dec 2pm, 3pm 1st Sun of mth. **Admission** *£8; £7 reductions.* **Map** *p96 E9.*

'I would rather not be made the prominent feature of such a monument,' was Prince Albert's reported response when the subject of his commemoration arose. Hard, then, to imagine what he would have made of this extraordinary thing, unveiled 15 years after his death. Created by Sir George Gilbert Scott, it centres on a giant, gilded Albert holding a catalogue of the 1851 Great Exhibition, guarded on four corners by the continents of Africa, America, Asia and Europe. The pillars are crowned with bronze statues of the sciences, and the frieze at the base depicts major artists, architects and musicians.

It's one of London's most dramatic monuments.

Kensington Palace & Kensington Gardens

Kensington Gardens, W8 4PX (0844 482 7777, 0844 482 7799 reservations, www.hrp.org. uk). High Street Kensington or Queensway tube. **Open** *Palace Mar-Oct 10am-6pm daily. Nov-Feb 10am-5pm daily.* **Admission** *£16.50; free-£13.75 reductions.* **Map** *p96 D9.*

It was in 1689 that William III – averse to the dank air of Whitehall – relocated here, sectioning off a corner of Hyde Park for his residence, and the Palace is still occupied by royalty today - William and Kate have a flat here. Kensington Gardens is delineated from Hyde Park (*p102*) only by the line of the Serpentine and the Long Water. It's lovelier than its easterly neighbour, with gorgeous trees, a bronze Peter Pan statue, the paddling-friendly Diana, Princess of Wales Memorial Fountain

Natural History Museum *Stegosaurus*

(near the Serpentine Gallery, *p98*) and the Diana, Princess of Wales Memorial Playground, with its massive wooden pirate ship in a vast sandpit.

The Palace itself was radically altered first by Wren and again under George I, when intricate trompe l'oeil ceilings and staircases were added. Visitors follow a whimsical trail focused on four 'stories' of former residents – Diana; William and Mary, and Mary's sister Queen Anne; Georges I and II; Queen Victoria – unearthing the facts through handily placed 'newspapers'. Artefacts include paintings by the likes of Tintoretto, contemporary art and fashion installations, and even Victoria's (tiny) wedding dress.

❤ Natural History Museum
Cromwell Road, SW7 5BD (7942 5000, www.nhm.ac.uk). South Kensington tube. **Open** *10am-5.50pm daily.* **Admission** *free. Special exhibitions vary. Tours free.* **Map** *p96 E11.*

Both a research institution and a fabulous museum, the NHM opened in Alfred Waterhouse's purpose-built, Romanesque palazzo on the Cromwell Road in 1881. Now joined by the splendid Darwin Centre extension, the original building still looks quite magnificent. The pale blue and terracotta façade just about prepares you for the natural wonders within.

The vast entrance hall – previously home to the iconic *Diplodocus* skeleton – has undergone a transformation. While 'Dippy' is on tour, he has been replaced by another huge beast: a blue whale. Suspended dramatically from the ceiling, the 25m-long, 4.5-tonne skeleton takes centre-stage in a new exhibition telling the tale of evolution

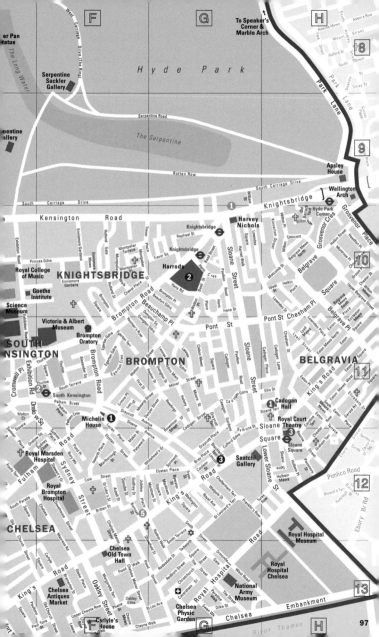

and of human impact on the natural world.

From the entrance hall, a left turn leads into the west wing, or Blue Zone, where queues form to see animatronic dinosaurs – especially the endlessly popular *T rex*. Here too, is the Mammals Hall, where you can stare out all manner of stuffed animals from a polar bear to a pygmy shrew.

A right turn from the central hall leads past the Creepy Crawlies exhibition to the Green Zone. Stars include a cross-section through a giant sequoia tree and an amazing array of stuffed birds.

Beyond is the Red Zone, where a *Stegosaurus* skeleton takes pride of place. Earth's Treasury is a mine of information on a variety of precious metals, gems and crystals; From the Beginning is a brave attempt to give the expanse of geological time a human perspective; Volcanoes and Earthquakes explores the immense energy and power of the natural world through dramatic film footage, interactive games and an earthquake simulator.

Many of the museum's 22 million insect and plant specimens are housed in the Darwin Centre, where they take up nearly 17 miles of shelving. With its eight-storey

Cocoon, this is also home to the museum's research scientists, who can be watched at work.

Serpentine & Serpentine Sackler galleries

*Kensington Gardens, near Albert Memorial, W2 3XA (7402 6075, www.serpentinegalleries. org). Lancaster Gate or South Kensington tube. **Open** 10am-6pm Tue-Sun. **Admission** free; donations appreciated. **Map** p96 E9 & F8.*

The Serpentine Gallery – much-loved for its sometimes challenging exhibitions of contemporary art – was originally squeezed into one small 1930s tea house. Here, the rolling two-monthly programme of exhibitions features a mix of up-to-the-minute artists and edgy career retrospectives, but – perhaps symbolic of the gallery's limitations of space – every spring it also commissions a renowned architect, who's never before built in the UK, to build a temporary pavilion outside. The pavilion then hosts a packed programme of cultural events (June to September).

A permanent solution to the issue of space was found in 2013, when the gallery opened a second location, the Serpentine Sackler, just across the bridge from the original. Devoted to emerging art in all forms, the Sackler is a Grade II-listed, Palladian former gunpowder store, with a clean-lined restaurant over which the late architect Zaha Hadid cast a billowing white cape of a roof.

❤ Science Museum

*Exhibition Road, SW7 2DD (7942 4000, www.sciencemuseum.org. uk). South Kensington tube. **Open** 10am-6pm daily. **Admission** free. Wonderlab £8; £6 reductions; £22.50 family. Special exhibitions vary. **Map** p96 E10.*

The Science Museum is a celebration of the wonders of

In the know
Clues to the queues

Especially in school holidays, there are often long queues at the main entrance of the Natural History Museum on Cromwell Road. Try the side entrance on Exhibition Road, instead: it is usually less busy and provides an impressive introduction to the collections as you ascend the escalator up into the Earth Galleries. Tickets to the dinosaur room can be booked online for free and allow you to enter at a specific time slot rather than queue.

Science Museum

technology in the service of our daily lives. In the ground floor Energy Hall, Making the Modern World is introduced by *Puffing Billy*, the world's oldest steam locomotive, and contains Stephenson's Rocket, the Apollo 10 command module and an absorbing collection of technological marvels dating back to 1750. Also here, is Exploring Space where rocket science and the lunar landings are illustrated by dramatically lit mock-ups and full-size models.

On the second floor, Information Age is dedicated to the history of communications technology, from the 19th-century international telegraph network all the way up to the worldwide web. The stunning new Winton Gallery – designed by Zaha Hadid Architects as a wind tunnel for the gallery's centrepiece, a 1929 Handley Page aircraft – reveals how mathematics has shaped the modern world, from foetal monitoring and artificial intelligence to World War II code-breaking and astronomy.

The third floor is dedicated to flight, including the hands-on Launchpad Gallery, which has levers, pulleys, explosions and all manner of experiments. It is also home to Wonderlab: The Statoil Gallery (entry costs from £6), where visitors are encouraged to learn about the physical world through play. Fun mirrors help to explain geometry, plasma globes are effectively bottled lightning, and the chemistry bar is home to live experiments that let you get messy and spectacular with crystals, dry ice, bubble volcanoes and non-Newtonian fluids.

Bathed in an eerie blue light, are the three floors of the Wellcome Wing, where the museum makes sure it stays on the cutting edge of science. Antenna is a web-savvy look at breaking science stories, while the enjoyable and troubling Who Am I? gallery features engaging interactive displays – from a cartoon of ethical dilemmas that introduces you to your dorsolateral prefrontal cortex to a chance to find out what gender your brain is. Compelling

❤ Victoria & Albert Museum

*Cromwell Road, SW7 2RL (7942 2000, www.vam.ac.uk). South Kensington tube. **Open** 10am-5.45pm Mon-Thur, Sat, Sun; 10am-10pm Fri. Tours 10.30am, 12.30am, 1.30pm, 3.30pm daily. **Admission** free. Special exhibitions vary. **Map** p96 F11.*

It comes to something when a museum can lay claim to having been opened as Queen Victoria's last public engagement. In 1899, the current premises of the V&A enjoyed that privilege. It has gone on to become one of the world's – let alone London's – most magnificent museums.

The details? There are some 150 grand galleries over seven floors. They contain countless pieces of furniture, ceramics, sculpture, paintings, posters, jewellery, metalwork, glass, textiles and dress, spanning several centuries. You could run through the highlights for the rest of this guide, but key artefacts include the seven Raphael Cartoons, painted in 1515 as tapestry designs for the Sistine Chapel; the finest collection of Italian Renaissance sculpture outside Italy; the Ardabil carpet, the world's oldest and arguably most splendid floor covering, in the Jameel Gallery of Islamic Art; and the Luck of Edenhall, a 13th-century glass beaker from Syria. The fashion galleries run from 18th-century court dress right up to contemporary chiffon numbers, while the architecture gallery has videos, models, plans and descriptions of various styles.

The ongoing FuturePlan project has seen more than 85 per cent of the V&A's public spaces transformed, from the stunning Medieval & Renaissance Galleries to the ambitious galleries of 'European 1600-1815'. The Toshiba Gallery of Japanese Art includes 550 works running from the sixth century AD to the first Sony Walkman and an origami outfit by Issey Miyake. New additions include the museum's 'Rapid Response Collection', which features contemporary design and architecture reflecting important news events, while major temporary exhibitions – Alexander McQueen, David Bowie – are frequently blockbuster sell-outs.

Summer 2017 saw the opening of a new entrance through the porcelain-tiled Sackler Courtyard to the purpose-built Sainsbury Gallery. It's a fitting introduction to a fabulous museum.

▶ *The V&A also runs the Museum of Childhood in Bethnal Green (see p179).*

objects include a jellyfish that's 'technically immortal', the statistically average British man (he's called Jose), a pound of human fat, displayed alongside a gastric band, and half of Charles Babbage's brain (the other half is in the Hunterian Museum).

Restaurants

Daquise ££

20 Thurloe Street, SW7 2LT (7589 6117, www.daquise.co.uk). South Kensington tube. **Open** *noon-11pm daily.* **Map** *p96 F11* ❷ *Polish*

This much-loved grande dame of London Polish restaurants (established 1947) offers a home-from-home ambience with a stylish twist. In the shabby-chic, light and airy interior, enlivened with fresh flowers, robust, flavourful, no-nonsense traditional dishes are served with great charm. Classic cold starters of meltingly tender herring with cream, apple, onion and flax oil, or beetroot with subtly warming horseradish, are ladled directly from capacious earthenware bowls, while mains are assembled directly at the table from well-worn saucepans, borne by the chefs who lovingly prepared the dishes.

Shops & services

Conran Shop

Michelin House, 81 Fulham Road, SW3 6RD (7589 7401, www.conranshop.co.uk). South Kensington tube. **Open** *10am-6pm Mon, Tue, Fri; 10am-7pm Wed, Thur; 10am-6.30pm Sat; noon-6pm Sun.* **Map** *p96 F11* ❶ *Homewares*

Sir Terence Conran's flagship store in the Fulham Road's beautiful 1909 Michelin Building showcases furniture and design for every room in the house as well as the garden. In addition to design classics, such as the Eames DAR chair, there are plenty of portable accessories, gadgets, books, stationery and toiletries that make great gifts or souvenirs. There's another branch at 55 Marylebone High Street, W1U 5HS (7723 2223).

Entertainment

❤ Royal Albert Hall

Kensington Gore, South Kensington, SW7 2AP (7589 8212, www.royalalberthall.com). South Kensington tube or bus 9, 10, 52, 360, 452. **Box office** *9am-9pm daily. Tickets £15-£275.* **Map** *p96 E10* ❷ *Concert hall*

In constant use since opening in 1871, with boxing matches, motor shows and Allen Ginsberg's 1965 International Poetry Incarnation among the headline events, the Royal Albert Hall continues to host a very broad programme. The classical side is dominated by the superb BBC Proms (*see p60*), which runs every night for two months in summer and sees a huge array of orchestras and other ensembles battling the difficult acoustics. It's well worth catching a concert that features the thunderous Grand Organ.

Knightsbridge

Sights & museums

Apsley House

149 Piccadilly, W1J 7NT (7499 5676, www.english-heritage.org.uk). Hyde Park Corner tube. **Open** *Nov-Mar 10am-4pm Sat, Sun. Apr-Oct 11am-5pm Wed-Sun. Tours by arrangement.* **Admission** *£9.30; £5.60-£8.40 reductions; £24.20 family; free under-5s. Joint ticket with Wellington Arch £11.20; £6.70-£10.10 reductions; £29.10 family.* **Map** *p96 H9.*

Called No.1 London because it was the first London building encountered on the road to the city from the village of Kensington, Apsley House was built by Robert Adam in the 1770s. The Duke of Wellington kept it as his London home for 35 years. Although his descendants still live here, several rooms are open to the public, providing a superb feel for the man and his era. Admire the extravagant porcelain dinnerware and plates or ask for a demonstration of the crafty mirrors in the scarlet and gilt picture gallery, where a fine Velázquez and a Correggio hang near Goya's portrait of the Iron Duke after he defeated the French in 1812. This was a last-minute edit: X-rays have revealed that Wellington's head was painted over that of Joseph Bonaparte, Napoleon's brother. In winter, the twilight tours at Apsley House are very atmospheric.

Hyde Park

7298 2000, www.royalparks.gov.uk. Hyde Park Corner, Lancaster Gate or Marble Arch tube. Map p96 FG8
One of the largest Royal Parks, Hyde Park is 1.5 miles long and a mile wide. It was a hotspot for demonstrations in the 19th century and remains so – a 2003 march against the Iraq War that ended in the park was the largest in British history. The legalisation of public assembly here led to the creation of Speakers' Corner in 1872 (near Marble Arch tube), where political and religious ranters still have the floor on Sunday afternoons, and Marx, Orwell and the Pankhursts once spoke. Rowing boats can be hired on the Serpentine – but adjoining Kensington Gardens (*p95*) is really much prettier.

Wellington Arch

Hyde Park Corner, W1J 7JZ (7930 2726, www. english-heritage.org. uk). Hyde Park Corner tube. Open Apr-Oct 10am-6pm daily. Nov-Mar 10am-4pm daily. Admission £5; £3-£4.50 reductions; £13
family; free under-5s. Joint ticket with Apsley House £11.20; £6.70-£10.10 reductions; £29.10 family. Map p96 H9.
Built in the late 1820s to mark Britain's triumph over Napoleonic France, Decimus Burton's Wellington Arch was initially topped by an out-of-proportion equestrian statue of Wellington. However, Captain Adrian Jones's 38-ton bronze *Peace Descending on the Quadriga of War* has finished it with a flourish since 1912. The Arch has three floors, with an English Heritage bookshop and various displays, covering the history of the arch and the Blue Plaques scheme, and in the Quadriga Gallery providing space for excellent temporary exhibitions. There are great views from the balcony in winter (leafy trees obscure the sightlines in spring and summer).

Restaurants

❤ Bar Boulud £££

Mandarin Oriental Hyde Park, 66 Knightsbridge, SW1X 7LA (7201 3899, www.barboulud.com). Knightsbridge tube. Open noon-midnight Mon-Sat; noon-11pm Sun. Map p96 G10 ❶ *French*
Overseen by renowned chef Daniel Boulud, the restaurant has an eye-catching view of the open-plan kitchen, where chefs work in meditative calm. Charcuterie from Gilles Verot is a big draw, as are the elegant French brasserie options and finger-licking American staples. We've had burgers here and loved every bite – try a beef patty topped with pulled pork and green chilli mayonnaise – but other culinary gems might include a robust French onion soup, resplendent with caramelised onions and topped with molten gruyère.

Harrods

Shops & services

The other landmark department store here is **Harvey Nichols** (109-125 Knightsbridge, SW1X 7RJ, 7235 5000, www.harveynichols.com).

💙 Harrods

87-135 Brompton Road, SW1X 7XL (7730 1234, www.harrods. com). Knightsbridge tube. **Open** *10am-9pm Mon-Sat; noon-6pm Sun (browsing from 11.30am).* **Map** *p96 G10* **2** *Department store*
It might be unashamedly ostentatious, stuffed with tourists and in possession of the world's most vulgar statue (Dodi and Diana in bronze by the Egyptian escalators), but Harrods – London's most famous department store – is still spectacular. Serious shoppers browse the elegantly tiled and fragrant food halls on the ground floor or the wealth of exclusives in the beauty halls. But indulge the excesses too: Harrods has an art gallery, a stunning new interiors department and a kitchenware floor that hosts live cooking lessons from household names. Got kids? Head straight to Toy Kingdom on the third floor, with its enchanted forest, intergalactic science lab and bespoke sweets-maker. Elsewhere,

Harrods excels at shoes – with a gargantuan footwear department stocking labels such as Ferragamo, Charlotte Olympia and Giuseppe Zanotti – and the Fashion Lab, on the fourth floor, is dedicated to young designer labels such as Zadig & Voltaire, Wildfox and the Kooples.

Chelsea

Sights & museums

💙 Chelsea Physic Garden

66 Royal Hospital Road, SW3 4HS (7352 5646, www. chelseaphysicgarden.co.uk). Sloane Square tube or bus 11, 19, 22. **Open** *Apr-June, Sept, Oct 11am-5pm Mon, 11am-6pm Tue-Fri, Sun. July, Aug 11am-5pm Mon, 11am-6pm Tue, Thur, Fri, Sun; 11am-10pm Wed. Nov-Mar 11am-3pm Mon-Fri. Tours times vary; phone to check.* **Admission** *£9.50; £6.25 reductions; free under-5s. Tours free.* **Map** *p96 G13.*
Passing through these modest red-brick walls is like stepping into a secret garden: a place by the Thames but with its own microclimate, where rare plants from Britain and across the globe

have been collected – and now thrive. Set up by apothecaries in 1673, Chelsea Physic Garden contains the world's oldest rock garden, created in 1773 from black Icelandic basalt imported by Joseph Banks (the most-famous plant hunter of all) and decorated with masonry from the Tower of London. Today the garden is also home to Britain's first garden of ethnobotany (the study of the botany of different ethnic groups and indigenous peoples), and a Garden of Medicinal Plants, tracing the chronology of plant remedies over almost an acre, from ancient Greek herbs to plants that are likely to be used in future medicine. There's also a shop where visitors can buy unusual plants, and a café serving very good homemade cakes.

Chelsea Physic Garden

National Army Museum
Royal Hospital Road, SW3 4HT (7730 0717, www.nam.ac.uk). Sloane Square tube or bus 170. **Open** *10am-5.30pm daily; until 8pm 1st Wed of the mth.* **Admission** *free.* **Map** *p96 G13.*
The National Army Museum reopened in 2017 after a three-year, £24m redesign – and a major rethink. A huge atrium has been carved out of the middle of the building, and the whole place is much lighter and less gloomy, but the structural redevelopment isn't the biggest change. The museum now reflects evolving perceptions of the history of the British Army. As one graph on display reveals, there are fewer people serving in the regular army today than at any time in the last 200 years, yet its public profile has never been higher. To reflect this, the museum has five new galleries representing different aspects of the armed forces, with a much keener focus on social history and diversity. Some old-fashioned models of

battles (notably Waterloo) and uniforms remain, of course, along with favourite exhibits such as Major Michael 'Bronco' Lane's frost-bitten fingertips and the skeleton of Napoleon's horse Marengo. In Play Base, under-eights can take on an assault course, climb aboard a command liaison vehicle or develop their fieldcraft skills.

Saatchi Gallery
Duke of York's HQ, King's Road, SW3 4RY (7811 3070, www. saatchigallery.com). Sloane Square tube. **Admission** *free.* **Map** *p96 G12.*
Charles Saatchi's gallery offers 50,000sq ft of space for temporary exhibitions. Given his fame as a promoter in the 1990s of what became known as the Young British Artists – Damien Hirst, Tracey Emin, Gavin Turk, Sarah Lucas et al – it will surprise many that the focus of exhibitions here has been internationalist in outlook,

with China, Africa and India all featuring. Still, Richard Wilson's superb oil-sump installation *20:50* has survived from the Saatchi Gallery's previous incarnations and remains here as the only permanently displayed artwork.

Restaurants

Harwood Arms £££
*Corner of Walham Grove & Farm Lane, SW6 1QP (7386 1847, www. harwoodarms.com). Fulham Broadway tube. **Open** Snacks served 5.30-11pm Mon; noon-11pm Tue-Thur; noon-midnight Fri, Sat. Lunch served noon-3pm Tue-Sun. Dinner served 6.15-9.30pm Mon-Sat; 6.15-9pm Sun. **Map** p96 off map ❸ British*

It might look an upmarket pub, but the Harwood Arms is a serious restaurant with wine list to match. It showcases prime British produce through skilled, imaginative modern cooking. The mounted deer's head is a reminder that game and wild food are a speciality, with mains such as grilled haunch of Berkshire roe deer accompanied by beetroot, slivers of roast onion and pickled mushrooms. Expect fine dining, rather than pub portions, and you'll be more than happy. Be sure to book ahead.

Medlar £££
*438 King's Road, SW10 0LJ (7349 1900, www.medlarrestaurant. co.uk). Fulham Broadway tube or bus 11, 22. **Open** noon-3pm, 6.30-10.30pm Mon-Fri; noon-3pm, 6-10.30pm Sat; noon-3pm, 6-9.30pm Sun. **Map** p96 E13 ❹ Modern European*

The decor here is understated: a soothing grey-green colour scheme and unobtrusive artwork. The real artistry arrives on the plates, dishes of astounding excellence. Assemblies are complex and have lengthy names: crisp calf's brain with smoked duck breast, aïoli, pink fir potatoes and *tardivo* (raddichio), for example. But every ingredient justifies its place in entirely natural-seeming juxtapositions of flavour, texture and colour. And the execution is nearly flawless. Save room for wonderful (and relatively simple) puddings, such as cardamom custard with saffron oranges, pomegranate and langues de chat.

♥ Rabbit £££
*172 King's Road, SW3 4UP (3750 0172, www.rabbit-restaurant.com). Sloane Square tube. **Open** 6-11pm Mon; noon-midnight Tue-Sat; noon-6pm Sun. **Map** p96 F12 ❺ British*

More than a restaurant, Rabbit feels a bit like a theme bar that does food, right down to a 'stable door' entrance, outside which smokers linger. But to see it as a party venue does the cooking a disservice: the Gladwins dish up inventive mouthfuls of joy that warm you up for heavy, slow-cooked mains (perhaps pigs' cheeks with malt, stout, garlic and pennywort) and lighter, faster-cooked dishes (such as tempura duck liver). However, the 'British with a twist' ethos is best summed up by the desserts: try a Viennetta parfait made of Magnum ice-cream lollies, or an intriguing cep and white-chocolate bourbon.

Shops & services

John Sandoe
*10 Blacklands Terrace, SW3 2SR (7589 9473, www.johnsandoe. com). Sloane Square tube. **Open** 9.30am-6.30pm Mon-Sat; 11am-5pm Sun. **Map** p96 G12 ❸ Books & music*

Tucked away on a side street, this 50-year-old independent has always looked just as a bookshop should, with stock literally packed to the rafters. The enthusiasm and knowledge of the staff can be taken as, forgive us, read – several have worked here for decades, their passion for books undimmed.

The Shop at Bluebird
*350 King's Road, SW3 5UU (7351 3873, www.theshopatbluebird.com). Sloane Square tube. **Open** 10am-7pm Mon-Sat; noon-6pm Sun. **Map** p96 E13* ❹ *Fashion/homewares*

Browsing the Shop at Bluebird is an unusually tranquil experience. The 10,000sq ft space, which began life as a garage back in the 1930s, has a white tiled floor and lots of natural light, tempting shoppers to roam calmly through its delightfully curated mix of fashion, beauty, homewares, books and music. The Shop was opened by John and Belle Robinson in 2005; it now has a reputation for tempting luxury brands and for discovering up-and-coming designers. There's an in-store spa, too.

Entertainment

❤ Cadogan Hall
*5 Sloane Terrace, off Sloane Street, Chelsea, SW1X 9DQ (7730 4500, www.cadoganhall.com). Sloane Square tube. **Box office** Non-performance days 10am-6pm Mon-Sat. Performance days 10am-8pm Mon-Sat; noon-6pm Sun. Tickets £15-£50. **Map** p96 H11* ❶ *Concert hall*

Jazz groups and rock bands have been attracted by the acoustics in this renovated former Christian Science church, but the programming at the austere yet comfortable 950-seat hall is dominated by classical. The Royal Philharmonic is resident; other orchestras also perform, and there's regular chamber music.

Royal Court Theatre
*Sloane Square, Chelsea, SW1W 8AS (7565 5000, www.royalcourttheatre.com). Sloane Square tube. **Box office** 10am-6pm Mon-Sat. Tickets £12-£40. **Map** p96 H12* ❸ *Theatre*

From John Osborne's *Look Back in Anger*, staged in the theatre's opening year of 1956, to the more recent likes of Jez Butterworth, Simon Stephens and debbie tucker green, the emphasis at the Royal Court has always been on new voices in British and international theatre. Since Vicky Featherstone took over as artistic director (the first woman in the role) in 2013, the shows have got artier, though there's still room for established names, including the legendary Caryl Churchill. Expect to find punchy, socially engaged new work by

Kyoto Gardens, Holland Park.

Leighton House

first-time and international playwrights upstairs, and bigger, state-of-the-nation works by household names downstairs.

Holland Park & Notting Hill

Sights & museums

18 Stafford Terrace

18 Stafford Terrace, W8 7BH (tours 7602 3316 Mon-Fri, 7938 1295 Sat, Sun, www.rbkc.gov.uk). High Street Kensington tube. **Open** *2-5.30pm Wed, Sat, Sun. Tours (pre-booked only) 11am Wed, Sat, Sun. Closed end June-Sep.* **Admission** *£7; £5 reductions; free under-5s. Tours £10; £8 reductions.*
The home of cartoonist Edward Linley Sambourne was built in the 1870s and has almost all of its original fittings and furniture. On Saturdays, tours are led by an actor in period costume.

Holland Park

Ilchester Place, W8 6LU (7361 3003, www.rbkc.gov.uk/leisure-and-culture/parks/holland-park). Holland Park/Kensington High Street tube. **Open** *7.30am-30mins before dusk daily.*
Holland Park, whose 55 acres add up to one of London's finest green spaces, was formerly the grounds of Jacobean mansion Holland House, named after its second owner, the Earl of Holland, whose wife was the first person in England to successfully grow dahlias. In the 19th century, Holland House was a hub of political and literary activity, visited by Disraeli and Lord Byron among others, but it was largely destroyed by the Blitz during World War II – enough of it remains to have been Grade I-listed and for a fancy-pants youth hostel, Safestay Holland Park (7870 9629, www.safestay.com/ss-london-holland-park.html), to move in. These days, dahlias are still grown, but there are also the Japanese-style Kyoto Gardens with their koi carp and bridge at the foot of a waterfall. Holland Walk, along the park's eastern edge, is one of the most pleasant paths in central London, and there's a fine café. In summer, open-air theatre and opera are staged.

Leighton House

12 Holland Park Road, W14 8LZ (7602 3316, www.rbkc.gov.uk). High Street Kensington tube. **Open** *10am-5.30pm Mon, Wed-Sun. Tours 3pm Wed, Sat.* **Admission** *£12; £5-£10 reductions. Tours free.*
In the 1860s, artist Frederic Leighton commissioned a showpiece house. He ensured that, behind the sternly Victorian red-brick façade, it was full of treasures from all over the world, as well as his own works and those of his contemporaries. The house is decorated in high style: magnificent downstairs

❤ Design Museum

KENSINGTON & CHELSEA

*224-238 Kensington High Street, W8 6AG (3862 5900, designmuseum.org). High Street Kensington tube. **Open** 10am-6pm (last admission 5pm) daily. **Admission** free; temporary exhibitions vary.*

It's a fitting destination for a rather itinerant museum. Terence Conran's seed notion of a collection that would introduce the public to the wonders of contemporary design started life as the Boilerhouse Project series of exhibitions at the V&A (*see p100*) in the early 1980s, before setting up as a museum in a converted Thameside banana warehouse in 1989. Nearly three decades later, it finally has the grand space its ambition deserves.

Dating to 1962, the Grade II*-listed former Commonwealth Institute building on Kensington High Street is itself a classic piece of modern architecture, with a pioneering hyperboloid roof made of copper-clad concrete. The vast space allows plenty of room for temporary exhibitions, the archive, a library, two shops, a café, mezzanine restaurant and, for the first time in its history, a permanent collection.

So how does it work? Brilliantly, as it happens. The main collection is small but crammed with 1,000 interesting things. Called 'Designer Maker User', the exhibition traces the development of 20th- and 21st-century design, starting with a detailed timeline at the entrance. Thereafter there are plenty of artefacts to satisfy those looking for some fuzzy

hey-wow tech nostalgia – Sony Walkmans, Xbox controllers and early iPhones – but the tale of design is told, from major urban infrastructure and industrial design to crowdfunding and 3D printing.

All this – and the designers-in-residence gallery – is free, but the ticketed temporary exhibitions that were the lifeblood of the museum's previous incarnation remain, and they remain excellent. Some take a look at particular designers, including Cartier and Camper; some explore broader themes, such as cycling or recycling; and some do a bit of both, as at the necessarily loose but always compelling annual Designs of the Year awards exhibition.

reception rooms designed for lavish entertaining; a dramatic staircase leading to a light-filled studio that takes up most of the first floor; and, above all, the Arab Hall, which showcases Leighton's huge collection of 16th-century Middle Eastern tiles. The only private space in the whole house is a tiny single bedroom – there are even theatrically Moorish-style screens allowing you to observe the downstairs without being seen.

Museum of Brands, Packaging & Advertising
111-117 Lancaster Road, W11 1QT (7243 9611, www.museumofbrands. com). Notting Hill Gate tube. **Open** *10am-6pm Tue-Sat; 11am-5pm Sun.* **Admission** *£9; £5-£7 reductions; £24 family; free under-7s.*
In 2015, the Museum of Brands found itself a glam new home: it's still in Notting Hill, but now has extra space for its seemingly endless collection of wrappers, posters, toys, boxes and general collectibles. The main part of the display is the 'time tunnel', a winding corridor of dark cabinets stuffed with colourful curios arranged chronologically. With the arrival of each new decade an information panel helps to put the changing designs and new fashions into context. A separate gallery functions as a sort of shrine to a few favourite brands: one cabinet holds every iteration of can and bottle produced by Guinness, another is packed with Kellogg's cereal boxes. We'd prefer a bit more analysis of the social trends that created all these designs – but as a nostalgia-stuffed tribute to the many, many things we buy, the museum is unparalleled.

Restaurants

Ledbury £££
127 Ledbury Road, W11 2AQ (7792 9090, www.theledbury.com). Westbourne Park tube. **Open** *6.30-9.45pm Mon, Tue; noon-2pm, 6.30-9.45pm Wed-Sun. French*
Few haute establishments have the hospitable hum of the Ledbury, and even fewer boast two Michelin stars. But this former pub remains top-tier for gustatory good times. British ingredients – smoked eel, Cumbrian lamb – line up alongside delicacies such as Tokyo turnips, Bresse chicken and black truffle, but it's chef Brett Graham's clever contemporary treatment of them that sets the place apart. Ledbury signatures are consistently thrilling – particularly the flame-grilled mackerel with pickled cucumber, celtic mustard and shiso; and, well, all the desserts.

Nama ££
110 Talbot Road, W11 1JR (7313 4638, namafoods.com). Westbourne Park tube. **Open** *noon-10pm Tue, Wed; noon-11pm Thur; 9am-11pm Fri, Sat; 9am-6pm Sun. Vegan*
Against an austerely stylish backdrop (stark white walls, high ceilings, throbbing beats) that's more art gallery than restaurant, Nama isn't the cuddliest vegan eaterie – the staff and diners are far too cool for hugging trees. But what it lacks in warmth, it makes up for in frighteningly good cooking. 'Rice' is fashioned from tiny grated *kohlrabi* (a sweet cabbage). In the must-order 'sushi', this is combined with tiny pieces of cashew (for richness) as well as cucumber, avocado and sesame (for authentic flavours); in the Thai coconut curry, it's sprinkled with black sesame seeds and served with a creamy yellow-curry sauce and folds of mandolin-thin pickled fennel.

Snaps & Rye £

93 Golborne Road, W10 5NL (8964 3004, www.snapsandrye.com). Westbourne Park tube. **Open** *8am-6pm Tue, Wed; 8am-11pm Thur-Sat; 10am-5pm Sun. Food served 8am-3pm Tue, Wed; 8am-3pm, 6.30-9.30pm Thur-Sat; 10am-3pm, 6.30-9pm Sun.* Danish
Snaps (alcohol infusions) & Rye (the accompanying food) embodies all that's best about Scandinavian design: simple and functional, but every detail designed or chosen with aesthetic pleasure in mind. The owners have also taken great pains to make their food, prepared by British chef Tania Steytler, as good as it can possibly be. While Denmark's famous open-faced sandwiches (smørrebrød) are simple in concept, Steytler raises them to great heights through the use of superb ingredients, masterly cooking skills and attention to detail. Other options are meatballs, herring, cured salmon and apple cake. Feeling the cold but don't fancy snaps? Try cocio, a Nordic hot chocolate.

Shops and services

Portobello Road Market

Portobello Road, W10 (www. portobelloroad.co.uk). Ladbroke Grove or Notting Hill Gate tube. **Open** *General 9am-6pm Mon-Wed; 9am-1pm Thur; 9am-7pm Fri, Sat.* **No cards.** *Market*
Best known for antiques and collectibles, this is actually several markets rolled into one: antiques start at the Notting Hill end; further up are food stalls; under the Westway and along the walkway to Ladbroke Grove are emerging designer and vintage clothes on Fridays (usually marginally less busy) and Saturdays (invariably manic).

There are more than 2,000 specialist antiques dealers squeezed tightly into any available space along Portobello Road, with bargain-hunters jostling with camera-laden tourists to the soundtrack of live jazz. Pickings around Elgin Crescent are meagre, so push on to explore the fashion market under the Westway flyover. Best visited on a less-frantic Friday morning, it's here you'll find fashionistas and trendy teens delving through troves of prized vintage, boutique fashion and retro memorabilia. And don't stop there: continue up to Golborne Road for bargains away from the masses, helped by the presence of eccentric second-hand interiors stalls.

Snaps & Rye

West End

Oxford Street is working hard to stay top of London's shopping destinations, with wider pavements, a revamped roundabout at Marble Arch and the shiny new Tottenham Court Road superstation. The neighbourhoods north of Oxford Street are bookish and bohemian. The luxury cafés and boutiques of **Marylebone** lead to graceful Regent's Park, while in **Fitzrovia** the days of post-war drunken poets have given way to an era of new-media offices. South of London's busiest commercial artery, **Mayfair** oozes wealth, while neon-lit **Piccadilly Circus** is a bit of town every Londoner does their best to avoid.

The academic heart of London, **Bloomsbury**, is best known as the home of the superb **British Museum**, To the north, the legendarily seedy **King's Cross** has been transformed by the **British Library**, the rebirth of

♥ Shortlist

Best restaurants
Fabulous fish dishes at J Sheekey (*p147*). Jason Atherton's excellent Social Eating House (*p136*). Treat yourself at glamorous Roka (*p116*) Culinary fireworks at Chiltern Firehouse (*p115*).

Best bars
Connaught Bar (*p121*) for pure Mayfair class. Pub roof terrace at Scottish Stores (*p130*). Swift (*p137*) for wonderful cocktails. A mixed crowd at the Friendly Society (*p142*).

Best gigs and giggles
Borderline (*p141*) for intimate indie gigs. Alt comedy and improv at the Comedy Store (*p141*). Ronnie Scott's (*p143*), a jazz institution.

Best for kids
Interactive fun at the London Transport Museum (*p145*). Running around the fountains at Granary Square (*p128*).

Must-see museums
A treasure trove of history at the British Museum (*p126*). Science made scintillating at the Wellcome Collection (*p129*).

Best shop
Tradition and fashion combined at Liberty (*p122*).

Best cultural venue
Blockbuster shows at the Royal Academy of Arts (*p120*). Classical music and late-night gigs at Wigmore Hall (*p119*).

St Pancras Station as an international rail hub and the emergence of the buzzing King's Cross Central district.

Soho – once notorious as the West End's sleazy late-night party zone – may not be as debauched as it once was, but it's still a lively bohemian area with an almost inconceivable number of bars, restaurants and shops. Even the most crowd-averse Londoner can't help but find some aspects of **Covent Garden** appealing: grudgingly the buskers; eagerly the **London Transport Museum**.

➜ Getting around

London's West End is a large area so you'll need to use public transport to get around. The main tube stations include Oxford Circus, Covent Garden, Piccadilly Circus and Leicester Square. It's worth noting that it only takes 10 minutes to walk from Piccadilly Circus to Covent Garden or Oxford Circus, and a similar time from Tottenham Court Road to Leicester Square.

► For a map of Bloomsbury and King Cross, see p125; for Soho and Covent Garden, see p133.

Oxford Street & North

There is relentless trade on Oxford Street, home to hip **Selfridges** (*see p119*), doughty **John Lewis** and chain flagships for **Uniqlo** and **Topshop**, but few locals esteem the historic thoroughfare: clogged pavements make for unpleasant shopping. Escape the crowds among the pretty boutiques on **Marylebone High Street** to the north. Highlights of the area include the overlooked **Wallace Collection** and **Regent's Park** (open 5am-dusk daily), one of London's most delightful open spaces. Originally a hunting ground for Henry III, it was formally designed by John Nash in 1811, but only opened to the public in 1845. For **ZSL London Zoo**, *see p171*.

Heading east, **Fitzrovia** – once home to radicals, writers and boozers, mostly in reverse order – retains sufficient traces of bohemianism to appeal to the media types that now frequent it. Fine hotels and restaurants cluster at Charlotte Street.

Sights & museums

Madame Tussauds

Marylebone Road, NW1 5LR (www. madametussauds.com/london). Baker Street tube. **Open** *varies.* **Admission** *£29; £24 reductions; free under-4s. Cheaper tickets available online in advance. Timed tickets available to avoid queueing.* **Map** *p113 H5.*

Madame Tussaud brought her show to London in 1802, 32 years after it was founded in Paris, and it's been expanding ever since on these very premises since 1884. There are now some 300 waxen figures in the collection: current movie A-listers who require no more than a first name (Angelina, Brad), a bevy of Royals (not least Wills and Kate), and sundry sports stars including Nadal, Bobby Moore and Mo Farah. Rihanna and One Direction can be found hanging out among the Music Megastars, while Dickens, Einstein and Madame Tussauds herself kick back in the Culture section. Proving they remain right on top of trends and current affairs, there's a section dedicated to YouTube stars Zoe and Alfie, as well as a Donald Trump alongside political luminaries such as Nelson Mandela, Martin Luther King and Barack Obama. What must they be thinking. If you're not already overheating, your palms will be sweating by the time you descend to the Chamber of Horrors in 'Scream', where only teens claim to enjoy the floor drops and scary special effects.

Tussauds also hosts Marvel Super Heroes 4D where waxworks of Iron Man, Spider-man and an 18-ft Hulk provide further photo ops, but the highlight is the nine-minute film in 4D with 'real' effects such as a shaking floor and smoke. There's a truly impressive Star Wars area where visitors can explore Yoda's swamp and the lava fields of Mustafar, as well as the new Sherlock Holmes Experience (an extra £5) and King Kong-themed Skull Island Experience, complete with 18ft-tall animatronic gorilla head.

Pollock's Toy Museum

1 Scala Street, W1T 2HL (7636 3452, www.pollockstoys.com). Goodge Street tube. **Open** *10am-5pm Mon-Sat.* **Admission** *£6; £3-£5 reductions; free under-3s.* **Map** *p113 K6.*

Named after Victorian toy theatre printer Benjamin Pollock, this place is in turns beguiling and creepy, a nostalgia-fest of old board games, tin trains, porcelain dolls and gollies. It is fascinating for adults but less so for children: describing a pile of painted

Wallace Collection

woodblocks in a cardboard box as a 'Build a skyscraper' kit may make them feel lucky to be going home to *Minecraft*. Having said that, the Pollock's Toy Museum shop is good for wind-up toys and other funny little gifts for children.

Wallace Collection

Hertford House, Manchester Square, W1U 3BN (7563 9500, www.wallacecollection.org). Bond Street tube. **Open** *10am-5pm daily.* **Admission** *free.* **Map** *p113 H6.*
Built in 1776 and tucked away on a quiet square, the Wallace is looking particularly lovely after extensive refurbishment. This handsome house contains an exceptional collection of 18th-century French furniture, paintings and objets d'art, as well as an amazing array of medieval armour and weaponry taking up much of the ground floor. It all belonged to Sir Richard Wallace, who, as the illegitimate offspring of the fourth Marquess of Hertford, inherited in 1870 the treasures his father had amassed in the last 30 years of his life. Room after grand room contains Louis XIV and XV furnishings and Sèvres porcelain; the galleries are hung with paintings by by heavyweights including Titian, Gainsborough, Canaletto, Rembrandt, Velázquez and Rubens.

Restaurants

♥ Chiltern Firehouse £££££
1 Chiltern Street, W1U 7PA (7073 7676, www.chilternfirehouse. com). Baker Street tube. **Open** *7-10.30am, noon-2.30pm, 5-10.30pm Mon-Wed; 7-10.30am, noon-3pm, 6-10.30pm Thur, Fri; 8-10am, 11am-3pm, 6-10.30pm Sat, Sun.* **Map** *p113 H6* ⑧ *Modern European*
This lovely 1889 Grade II-listed Victorian Gothic fire brigade building has been rebuilt from the inside out to create London's buzziest hotel, but the discreetly gated garden is also the entrance to one of London's finest restaurants. The kitchen can do fiddly and pretty, exemplified by appetisers such as the tiny, slider-like 'doughnuts' filled with crab meat, but pretty is only part of the story. The restaurant's success is built on its reputation as a celeb-magnet but when that fades, the flavour combinations and exemplary modern cooking techniques, as 'curated' by Portuguese superchef Nuno Mendes, will remain. The best seats are at the kitchen counter, from which you can watch the chefs work their magic.

Honey & Co £

25A Warren Street, W1T 5LZ (7388 6175, www.honeyandco.co.uk). Warren Street tube.
Open *8am-10.30pm Mon-Fri; 9.30am-10.30pm Sat.* **Map** *p113 K5* ⓭ *Middle Eastern*

A bijou delight, with small tables and chairs packed closely together. The kitchen is run by an accomplished Israeli husband-and-wife team. This pedigree shines in a daily-changing menu that draws influences from across the Middle East. The meze selection includes fabulously spongy, oily bread, sumac-spiked tahini, smoky taramasalata, crisp courgette croquettes with *labneh*, pan-fried feta and a bright salad with lemon and radishes. A main might be a whole baby chicken with lemon and a chilli and walnut *muhamara* paste. It's imaginative home-style cooking, and service is charming.

Providores & Tapa Room £££

109 Marylebone High Street, W1U 4RX (7935 6175, www. theprovidores.co.uk). Baker Street or Bond Street tube. **Open** *Providores noon-3pm, 6-10.30pm Mon-Fri; 10am-3pm, 6-10.30pm Sat; 10am-3pm, 6-10pm Sun. Tapa Room 8-11.30am, noon-10.30pm Mon-Fri; 9am-3pm, 4-10.30pm Sat; 9am-3pm, 4-10pm Sun.* **Map** *p113 H6* ㉑ *Fusion*

Fusion cuisine is common in London these days, but Peter Gordon was one of the pioneers – and his flagship restaurant continues to shine. On the ground floor is the Tapa Room, a casual, buzzy space heaving with well-dressed locals knocking back top-quality coffee, New Zealand wines and an all-day menu of small plates. Upstairs is the more formal but still intimate Providores restaurant, where everything is ratcheted up a notch. The menu of small plates – roughly a sonnet in

length and style – might include scallops with a bright salad and beurre noisette hollandaise or coconut laksa with a fish dumpling and quail's eggs.

Portland £££

113 Great Portland Street, W1W 6QQ (7436 3261, portlandrestaurant.co.uk). Oxford Circus tube. **Open** *noon-2.30pm, 6-10pm Mon-Sat.* **Map** *p113 J6* ⓴ *Contemporary European*

It is rare to go to a restaurant and be astonished, but nothing prepared us for this bold, powerful, surprising food: chef Merlin Labron-Johnson was cooking like a wizard. For this level of cooking, the menu is great value, offering small plates at £5-£7. Favourite dishes include pig's head croquettes, aged mimolet cheese and granola, or pickled shiitake mushrooms. Desserts – such as 'chocolate bar, peanut butter praline, peanut ice-cream' – are skilfully executed and the wine list is short but imaginative. It's a small, bare-wood, no-frills kind of place, but it's very attractive and the flavours are sensational.

♥ Roka ££££

37 Charlotte Street, W1T 1RR (7580 6464, www.rokarestaurant.com). Goodge Street or Tottenham Court Road tube. **Open** *noon-3.30pm, 5.30-11.30pm Mon-Fri; 12.30-4pm, 5.30-11.30pm Sat; 12.30-4pm, 5.30-10.30pm Sun.* **Map** *p113 K6* ㉒ *Japanese*

Roka gets top marks for glitz and glamour. Much of the action takes place at the central robata grill, where a repertoire of contemporary *izakaya*-inspired food is created in full view. The 13-course tasting menu is popular with first-time diners, taking them on a spin of the best Roka has to offer: elegant dishes such as hand-made *kimchi*, sashimi and sticky skewers of *tebasaki* (chicken wings) are finished off with a trio of desserts, featuring delights such as Pocky-style chocolate and sesame biscuit sticks. It isn't cheap, but each dish is impeccable.

Roti Chai ££

3 Portman Mews South, W1H 6AY (7408 0101, www.rotichai.com). Marble Arch tube. **Open** *Dining room noon-10.30pm Mon-Sat; 12.30-9pm Sun. Street kitchen noon-10.30pm Mon-Sat; 12.30-9pm Sun.* **Map** *p113 H7* ㉓ *Pan-Indian*
The ground-floor 'street kitchen', with its utilitarian furniture and canteen vibe, is ideal for a swift midday feed – and the alert young staff keep things pacy. The menu is modelled on those of urban India's snack shacks, so you'll find food such as bhel pooris, chilli paneer and pani puri. Larger dishes include 'railway lamb curry' (tender meat and potato in a rich gravy spiced with star anise and cinnamon bark). In the basement, the evening-only 'dining room' is a darker, sexier (and pricier) space.

Zoilo ££

9 Duke Street, W1U 3EG (7486 9699, zoilo.co.uk). Bond Street tube. **Open** *noon-2.30pm, 5.30-10.30pm Mon-Sat.* **Map** *p113 H7* ㉖ *Argentinian*
If the idea of deconstructed, small-plates Argentinian cooking seems a contradiction in terms, pull up a counter seat and prepare to be amazed. With few actual tables, most of the seating is around the ground-floor bar or the downstairs kitchen – it shouts 'watch us work, look how good we are!'. Diners can witness the creation of dazzling offerings like octopus cooked sous vide, fried *queso de chancho* ('head cheese'), or miniature steak, each rustled up with flair and a feel for authenticity. Desserts run from a traditional, ultra-sweet 'tres leches' milk cake to a tart passionfruit sorbet, and most of the all-Argentinian wine list is available by the glass or small carafe. Plates might be small, but when flavours are as compelling as these, you want as many different dishes as you can get.

Shops & services

Browns

24-27 South Molton Street, W1K 5RD (7514 0016, www. brownsfashion.com). Bond Street tube. **Open** *10am-7pm Mon-Wed, Sat; 10am-8pm Thur, Fri; noon-6pm Sun.* **Map** *p113 J7* ❹ *Fashion*
The buying team at Browns are magicians, with an uncanny ability to pull in the most interesting, talking-point pieces of a designer's collection. Having been owned by Joan Burnstein and her family for the past four decades, Browns was acquired by fashion website Farfetch in 2015, with the aim of bringing technological innovation to its offerings. Among the 100-odd designers jostling for attention across five interconnecting shops are fashion heavyweights Chloé, Dries Van Noten and Balenciaga. You'll also find designs from rising stars, and shop exclusives are common. No.24 now houses Browns Focus, a younger and more casual look; while Labels for Less is loaded with last season's leftovers.

Collaborative Store

58 Blandford Street, W1U 7JB (7935 8123, www.instagram.com/the_ collaborative_store). Baker Street tube. **Open** *11am-7pm Mon-Sat; noon-6pm Sun.* **Map** *p113 H6* ❻ *Fashion*
Following a couple of great pop-ups, this concept store found a permanent place to call home. Only stocking independent designers and makers, it features plenty of under-the-radar brands. In the same space, you can pick up delicate, geometric jewellery from Clerkenwell's Miya Bonner,

Selfridges

colourful furniture from Jennifer Newman and brilliant shoes from Ganor Dominic – all of them London-based. Every month the store also hosts workshops and pop-up events.

Daunt Books
83-84 Marylebone High Street, W1U 4QW (7224 2295, www. dauntbooks.co.uk). Baker Street tube. **Open** *9am-7.30pm Mon-Sat; 11am-6pm Sun.* **Map** *p113 H6* **❼** *Books & music*
This beautiful Edwardian shop's elegant three-level back room – complete with oak balconies, viridian-green walls and stained glass window – houses a much praised travel section (guidebooks, maps, travelogues) and is a first-rate stop for literary fiction, biography, gardening and more. There's a good range of author readings to boot.

Gallery of Everything
4 Chiltern Street, W1U 7PS (7486 8908, shop.musevery.com). Baker Street tube. **Open** *11am-6.30pm Tue-Sat; 2-6pm Sun.* **Map** *p113 H6* **❾** *Art & merchandise*
It all started in a former dairy in Camden – or perhaps with Duchamp's urinal. The former

was, in 2009, the site of the hugely popular Museum of Everything exhibition of outsider or non-academic or naïve or private or... well, of art you don't usually see in galleries. Further exhibitions followed, here and in other cities, all delivered with a winning pop sensibility and a shrewd eye for artistry and interest. This gallery-shop continues the good work – even if you're not in the hunt for original art, the excellent merchandise makes winningly idiosyncratic souvenirs.

Postcard Teas
9 Dering Street, W1S 1AG (7629 3654, www.postcardteas.com). Bond Street or Oxford Circus tube. **Open** *10.30am-6.30pm Mon-Fri; 11am-6.30pm Sat. Tastings £20; £15 reductions.* **Map** *p113 J7* **㉑** *Food & drink*
The range in this exquisite little shop is not huge, but it is selected with great care, and all teas are sourced from small cooperatives. There's a central table for those who want to try a pot; or book in for one of the tasting sessions held on Saturdays between 10am and 11am. Stunning tea-ware and accessories are also sold.

Selfridges

400 Oxford Street, W1A 1AB (0800 123400, www.selfridges.com). Bond Street or Marble Arch tube. **Open** *9.30am-9pm Mon-Sat; noon-6pm Sun (browsing from 11.30am).* **Map** *p113 H7* ❷ *Department store*
With its plethora of concession boutiques, store-wide themed events and collections from all the hottest brands, Selfridges is as dynamic as a department store could be. While the basement is chock-full of hip home accessories and stylish kitchen equipment, it's Selfridges' fashion floors that really get hearts racing. With a winning combination of new talent, hip and edgy labels, high-street brands and luxury high-end designers, the store stays ahead of the pack. Highlights include the huge denim section, the extensive Shoe Galleries and, on the fifth floor, the 37,000sq ft Body Studio, a temple of top-notch activewear that aims to kit out people of all shapes and sizes. Level 4 hosts the predictably excellent Toy Shop. There are always new excitements in the food hall, ranging from great deli and bakery produce to classy packaged goods, while regularly changing pop-ups and special events keep customers on their toes.

Entertainment

❤ Wigmore Hall

36 Wigmore Street, Marylebone, W1U 2BP (information 7258 8200; tickets 7935 2141, www.wigmore-hall.org.uk). Bond Street tube. **Box office** *Non-performance days 10am-7pm Mon-Sat; 10am-2pm Sun. Performance days 10am-7pm daily. Tickets free-£35.* **Map** *p113 J6* ㉖ *Concert hall*
Built in 1901 as the display hall for Bechstein pianos, this world-renowned, 550-seat concert venue has perfect acoustics for the 460 concerts that take

place each year. Music from the classical and romantic periods are mainstays, usually performed by major classical stars to an intense audience, but under artistic director John Gilhooly there has been a broadening in the remit: more baroque and jazz (with heavyweights like Brad Mehldau), including late-night gigs. Monday lunchtime recitals are broadcast live on BBC Radio 3.

Mayfair

Mayfair has long meant money, but these days not necessarily stuffy exclusivity, with even the tailors of **Savile Row** loosening their ties.

Despite a £14m revamp, there's no reason to stop at **Piccadilly Circus**, other than to see the famous illuminating advertising panels, technically here since the late 19th century but these days fired by LEDs rather than neon.

Sights & museums

Handel & Hendrix in London

25 Brook Street, W1K 4HB (7495 1685, handelhendrix.org). Bond Street tube. **Open** *11am-6pm Mon-Sat (last entry 5pm).* **Admission** *£10; £5 reductions; free under-5s.* **Map** *p113 J7.*
Separated by just a brick wall are the former homes of two of history's most innovative and influential musicians – George Frideric Handel (1685-1759) and Jimi Hendrix (1942-1970). George Frideric Handel moved to Britain from his native Germany aged 25 and settled in this house 12 years later, remaining here until his death in 1759. The house – where he composed his *Messiah*, *Music for the Royal Fireworks* and several operas – has been faithfully restored, with original and recreated furnishings, paintings and some of the composer's scores. The programme of events includes

Royal Academy of Arts

Thursday recitals on the museum's several period instruments, which – along with engaging staff – enliven what is otherwise a bit of a worthy experience. The Hendrix section of the museum couldn't be more different. The upstairs flat at no.23 where, in 1968, Jimi lived with one of his girlfriends has also been painstakingly restored, with his bedroom detailed down to the discarded fag butts. But here the life of the former occupant really comes through: in addition to the period bedroom, there's a timeline room with a few artefacts and plenty of audio and film, and a brilliant, revealing annex where Jimi's record collection is itemised and explored.

❤ Royal Academy of Arts

Burlington House, W1J 0BD (7300 8000, www.royalacademy.org. uk). Green Park or Piccadilly Circus tube. **Open** *10am-6pm daily (last admission 5.30pm.* **Admission** *free. Exhibitions vary.* **Map** *p113 K8.*
Britain's first art school was founded in 1768 and moved to the extravagantly Palladian Burlington House a century later, but it's now best known not for education but for exhibitions. Ticketed blockbusters are generally

held in the Sackler Wing or the main galleries; shows in the John Madejski Fine Rooms are drawn from the RA's holdings, which range from Constable to Hockney, and are free. The biggest event here is the annual Summer Exhibition, which for more than two centuries has drawn from works entered by the public.

The RA expanded into a 19th-century building at 6 Burlington Gardens, which has been exhibiting unabashedly contemporary art, from Tracey Emin and David Hockney to lightworks by Mariko Mori.

As part of its 250th anniversary celebrations in 2018, the Royal Academy is undergoing major works to connect Burlington House and Burlington Gardens for the first time.

Restaurants

Kitty Fisher's £££££
10 Shepherd Market, W1J 7QF (3302 1661, www.kittyfishers.com). Green Park tube. **Open** *noon-2.30pm, 6.15-9.30pm Mon-Sat.* **Map** *p113 J9* ⑱ *Contemporary European*
Named after an 18th-century courtesan, known for her wit and

extravagance, Kitty Fisher's will leave you with a big smile on your face – if you don't mind paying for the privilege. The signature dish is beef cut from a ten- to 12-year-old Galician milking cow, chargrilled and served with cheese-stuffed salad potatoes and blackened onion (£80, serves two). To cut your bill in half, stick to small plates (£6-£12.50) such as melted taleggio with London honey, wholegrain mustard and loads of shaved truffle, or whipped cod's roe on dainty soldiers. The basement dining room is intimate and hugely atmospheric, but tables do get booked up well in advance.

Pubs & bars

♥ The Connaught Bar

The Connaught, Carlos Place, W1K 2AL (7499 7070, www.the-connaught.co.uk). Bond Street or Green Park tube. Open 11am-1am Mon-Sat; 11am-midnight Sun. Map p113 J8 **5**

Inside one of the more discreet of London's mega-expensive hotels, the Connaught Bar is all about old-school style and glamour. Designed by David Collins, its mirrors, low lighting, silver leaf and tasteful palette will put you in mind of a deco steamship. Even if you can only stretch to a single drink, it's worth it, especially if you order a Martini – the trolley is wheeled up beside you and the drink mixed on top.

Mr Fogg's

15 Bruton Lane, W1J 6JD (7036 0608, mr-foggs.com/residence). Green Park tube. Open 5.01pm-1.01am Mon-Wed; 4.01pm-2.01am; 2.01pm-2.01am Sat; 3.01pm-12.01am Sun. Map p113 J8 **8**

For sheer spectacle, Mr Fogg's is hard to beat. The place is stuffed with the detritus left by the titular Victorian explorer: every wall is covered with hunting rifles, stuffed animals, weathered flags and maps – all imaginary souvenirs of course, but that doesn't make the profusion of clutter any less fun. With an interior like this, it would be easy for cocktails to take second place, but seriously knowledgeable bar staff make sure the drinks are punchy and altogether sensational.

Shops & services

Despite the arrival of US import Abercrombie & Fitch a few years ago, bespoke tailoring is managing to hold out on Savile Row – but there isn't much to see if you're not getting a suit made.

Burlington Arcade

51 Piccadilly, W1J 0QJ (7493 1764, www.burlington-arcade.co.uk). Green Park tube. Open 9am-7.30pm Mon-Sat; 11am-6pm Sun. Map p113 K8 **5** *Mall*

In 1819, Lord Cavendish commissioned Britain's very first shopping arcade. Nearly two centuries later, the Burlington is still one of London's most prestigious shopping 'streets', patrolled by 'beadles' decked out in top hats and tailcoats. Highlights include collections of classic watches at David Duggan, established British fragrance house Penhaligon's, and Sermoneta, selling Italian leather gloves in a range of bright colours. High-end food shops come in the form of Luponde Tea and Ladurée; head to the latter for exquisite Parisian macaroons. Burlington also houses a proper shoe-shine boy working with waxes and creams for just £6. This may not offer the best shopping in London, but it's certainly one of the best shopping experiences.

❤ Liberty

Regent Street, W1B 5AH (7734 1224, www.liberty.co.uk). Oxford Circus tube. **Open** *10am-8pm Mon-Sat; noon-6pm Sun.* **Map** *p113 K7* ⓲ *Department store*

Founded in 1875, Liberty's present site was built in 1925 – its distinctive half-timbered frontage constructed from the remains of a couple of decommissioned warships, HMS *Hindustan* and HMS *Impregnable*. Which goes a good way to summarising the place: it's a superbly loveable mix of tradition and fashion. The store's interconnecting jumble of rooms, with the odd fireplace and cushioned window seat, have an intimate feel – as if you've strayed into a private room in a stately home. At the main entrance is Wild at Heart's exuberant floral concession and a room devoted to the store's own label. Fashion brands focus on high-end British designers, such as Vivienne Westwood and Christopher Kane. The Paper Room is the place to find Liberty's micro-floral print stationery and gifts, while the Dining Room offers quirky cookware and gadgetry. In the Literary Lounge, opened by French publishing powerhouse Assouline, you can flick through fashion, art and photography coffee-table books. The Beauty Hall stocks cult brands such as Aesop, Le Labo, Byredo and celebrated skin products from Egyptian Magic. Despite being up with the latest fashions, Liberty respects its dressmaking heritage in its third-floor haberdashery

department and extensive men's tailoring chamber. For all its pomp and fizz, Liberty doesn't take itself too seriously – there's a genuine sense of whimsy in its approach to retail. Collaborations with brands such as Puma and Nike produce floral sneakers (that instantly sell out) and, via its Art Fabrics project, Liberty has worked with babydoll-dress fancier Grayson Perry and even Hello Kitty to create exclusive fabrics. Visitors can also have their moustache expertly trimmed and waxed at Murdock barbers or their barnacles plucked off by expert chiropodists in the Margaret Dabbs Sole Spa.

Hamleys

Hamleys

*188-196 Regent Street, W1B 5BT
(0371 704 1977, www.hamleys.
com). Oxford Circus tube.* **Open**
*10am-8pm Mon-Wed; 10am-9pm
Thur, Fri; 9.30am-9pm Sat; noon-
6pm Sun.* **Map** *p113 K7* ⑪ *Toys*
Visiting Hamleys is certainly an
experience – whether a good one or
not will depend on your tolerance
for noisy, over-excited children,
especially during school holidays
and the run-up to Christmas,
when the store runs special kids'
events. As you doubtless know,
Hamleys is a ginormous toy shop,
perhaps the most ginormous toy
shop, with attractive displays of
all this season's must-have toys
across five crazed floors, and perky
demonstrators ramping up the
temptation levels.

Bloomsbury

In bookish circles, Bloomsbury is a
name to conjure with: it is the HQ
of London University and home to
the superb **British Museum**. The
name was famously attached to a
group of early 20th-century artists
and intellectuals (Virginia Woolf
and John Maynard Keynes among
them), and more recently to the
(Soho-based) publishing company

that gave us Harry Potter. Its
green squares are perfect for an
afternoon stroll.

Sights & museums

Cartoon Museum

*35 Little Russell Street, WC1A 2HH
(7580 8155, www.cartoonmuseum.
org). Tottenham Court Road tube.*
Open *10.30am-5.30pm Tue-Sun.*
Admission *£7; £3-5 reductions;
free under-18s.* **Map** *p125 M6.*
The best of British cartoon
art is displayed on the ground
floor of this former dairy. The
displays start in the early 18th
century, when high-society
types back from the Grand Tour
introduced the Italian practice
of caricatura to polite company.
From Hogarth, it moves through
Britain's cartooning 'golden
age' (1770-1830) to examples of
wartime cartoons, ending up with
modern satirists such as Gerald
Scarfe and the wonderfully loopy
Ralph Steadman. Upstairs is a
celebration of UK comic art, with
original 1921 Rupert Bear artwork
by Mary Tourtel, Frank Hampson's
Dan Dare, Leo Baxendale's Bash
Street Kids and a painted Asterix
cover by that well-known Briton,
Albert Uderzo.

Foundling Museum

*40 Brunswick Square,
WC1N 1AZ (7841 3600, www.
foundlingmuseum.org.uk). Russell
Square tube.* **Open** *10am-5pm Tue-
Sat; 11am-5pm Sun.* **Admission**
*£8.25; £5.50 reductions; free
under-16s.* **Map** *p125 M5.*

This museum recalls the social
history of the Foundling Hospital,
set up in 1739 by shipwright and
sailor Thomas Coram. Returning
to England from America in
1720, Coram was appalled by the
number of abandoned children he
saw. Securing royal patronage, he
persuaded Hogarth and Handel to
become governors; it was Hogarth
who made the building Britain's
first public art gallery; works by
artists as notable as Gainsborough
and Reynolds are on display. The
most heart-rending display is a tiny
case of mementoes that were all
mothers could leave the children
they abandoned here.

Grant Museum of Zoology

*University College London,
Rockefeller Building, 21 University
Street, WC1E 6DE (3108 2052, www.
ucl.ac.uk/culture/grant-museum).
Goodge Street tube.* **Open** *1-5pm
Mon-Sat.* **Admission** *free.*
Map *p125 L5.*

Now rehoused in a former
Edwardian library belonging to
University College, The Grant
Museum retains the air of an avid
Victorian collector's house, but
visitors are engaged in dialogue
about the distant evolutionary
past via the most modern means
available, including iPads and
smartphones. The museum's
67,000 specimens include the
remains of many rare and extinct
creatures, including skeletons of
the dodo and the zebra-like quagga
(which lived in South Africa and
was hunted out of existence in the
1880s), as well as pure oddities,
not least the jar of moles. Don't
miss the Micrarium – a kind of

booth walled with little illuminated
microscope slides.

Pubs & bars

All Star Lanes

*Victoria House, Bloomsbury Place,
WC1B 4DA (7025 2676, www.
allstarlanes.co.uk). Holborn tube.*
Open *Bar 3-11.30pm Mon-Wed;
3pm-midnight Thur; noon-2am
Fri; 11am-2am Sat; 1am-10.30pm
Sun. Kitchen closes 1hr earlier.*
Map *p125 M6* ❶

Of Bloomsbury's two subterranean
bowling dens, this is the one with
aspirations. Walk past the lanes
and smart, diner-style seating,
and you'll find yourself in a
comfortable, subdued side bar
with chilled glasses, classy red
furnishings, an unusual mix of
bottled lagers and some impressive
cocktails. There's an American
menu and, at weekends, DJs.
Bloomsbury Bowling Lanes
(basement of Tavistock Hotel,
Bedford Way, WC1H 9EU, 7183 1979,
www.bloomsburybowling.com)
offers a pints-and-worn-carpets
take on the same game – as well as
gigs and private karaoke booths.

Shops & services

Tucked among the residential
backstreets, **Lamb's Conduit
Street** is worth a browse for
its independent shops, two
Victorian pubs – **The Lamb**
and **The Perseverence** – and an
innovative food cooperative, **The
People's Supermarket**.

Blade Rubber Stamps

*12 Bury Place, WC1A 2JL (7831 4123,
www.bladerubberstamps.co.uk).
Holborn or Tottenham Court Road
tube.* **Open** *10.30am-6pm Mon-
Sat; 11.30am-4.30pm Sun.* **Map**
p125 M6 ❸

Blade Rubber Stamps is a shrine to
wooden-handled rubber stamps.

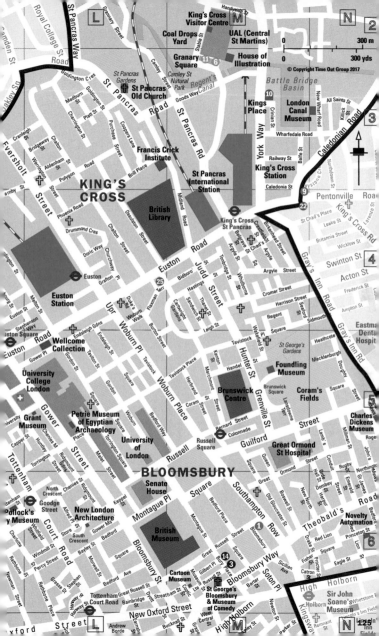

💜 British Museum

Great Russell Street, WC1B 3DG (7323 8299, www.britishmuseum. org). Russell Square or Tottenham Court Road tube. **Galleries** *10am-5.30pm Mon-Thur, Sat, Sun; 10am-8.30pm Fri.* **Great Court** *9am-6pm Mon-Thur, Sat, Sun; 9am-8.30pm Fri.* **Multimedia guides** *10am-4.30pm Thur, Sat, Sun; 10am-7.30pm Fri.* **Tours** *Eye Opener tours throughout the day. Highlights tours (Fri-Sun, 90mins).* **Admission** *free; donations appreciated. Temporary exhibitions vary. Multimedia guides £6; £5.50 reductions. Eye Opener tours free. Highlights tours £12.* **Map** *p125 L6.*

With more than six million visitors a year, the British Museum is officially the country's most popular tourist attraction. When it opened in 1759 it was the first national public museum anywhere in the world. The current building is a neoclassical marvel built in 1847 by Robert Smirke, one of the pioneers of the Greek Revival style. In 2000, Lord Foster added a glass roof to the Great Court, now claimed to be 'the largest covered public square in Europe' and a popular public space ever since. This £100m landmark surrounds the domed Reading Room, where Marx, Lenin, Dickens, Darwin, Hardy and Yeats once worked. The Sainsbury Exhibitions Gallery, new in 2014, is dedicated to blockbuster shows including *Vikings: Life and Legend*. Previous exhibitions included a rare visit from China's Terracotta Army and an eye-opening tour of Ice Age art.

In the museum proper, star exhibits include ancient Egyptian artefacts – the Rosetta Stone on the ground floor, mummies upstairs – and Greek antiquities, including the marble friezes from the Parthenon known as the Elgin Marbles. Room 41 displays Anglo-Saxon artefacts, including the famous Sutton Hoo treasure. Also upstairs, the Celts gallery has Lindow Man, killed in 300 BC and so well preserved in peat you can see his beard, while the ground-floor Wellcome Gallery of Ethnography holds an Easter Island statue and regalia collected during Captain Cook's travels. The King's Library is home to a permanent exhibition entitled 'Enlightenment: Discovering the World in the 18th Century', which covers archaeology, science and the natural world.

Time won't permit you to see everything in one day, so concentrate on a particular area or plan on making several visits.

Assyrian lion hunt reliefs

Neatly stacked shelves display arty stamps depicting chandeliers, cityscapes, images of Henry VIII, London buses, *Alice in Wonderland* characters, cutesy puppies and telephone boxes. Handy potential purchases include homework stamps ('check spelling', 'keep trying') and adorable love-letter writing kits. Unmounted sheets of rubber stamps, ink pads in every shade, glitters, glues, stencils, stickers, sticks of sealing wax, and a range of magazines and books complete the stock.

London Review Bookshop
14 Bury Place, WC1A 2JL (7269 9030, www.lrbshop.co.uk). Holborn or Tottenham Court Road tube. **Open** *10am-6.30pm Mon-Sat; noon-6pm Sun.* **Map** *p125 M6* ⓮ *Books & music*
From the inviting and stimulating presentation to the quality of the books selected, this is an inspiring bookshop. Politics, current affairs and history are well represented on the ground floor; downstairs, audio books lead on to exciting poetry and philosophy sections, everything you'd expect from a shop owned by the purveyor of long-form critical writing that is the *London Review of Books*. Browse through your purchases in the adjoining London Review Cakeshop.

Entertainment
The Place
17 Duke's Road, Bloomsbury, WC1H 9PY (7121 1100, www.theplace.org. uk). Euston tube/Overground/ rail. **Box office** *10.30am-5.30pm Mon-Sat. Performance days 10.30am-7pm. Tickets £11-£14.* **Map** *p125 L4* ㉕ *Dance*
For genuinely emerging dance, look to the Place, which is home to the London Contemporary Dance School and the Richard

Alston Dance Company. The theatre is behind the biennial Place Prize for choreography (next in 2018), which rewards the best in British contemporary dance, as well as regular seasons showcasing new work, among them Resolution! (Jan/Feb) and Spring Loaded (Apr/May).

King's Cross

North-east of Bloomsbury, the once-insalubrious area of King's Cross has undergone massive redevelopment around the grand **St Pancras International** station, with its dramatic Victorian glass-and-iron train shed roof, and the vast **British Library**. **King's Cross** station (location of Harry Potter's **Platform 9¾**) has also been restored and expanded, while, to the north of the station, derelict land has been extensively and imaginatively redeveloped as **King's Cross Central**.

Sights & museums
British Library
96 Euston Road, NW1 2DB (01937 546060, www.bl.uk). Euston or King's Cross St Pancras tube/rail. **Open** *9.30am-8pm Mon-Thur; 9.30am-6pm Fri; 9.30am-5pm Sat; 11am-5pm Sun.* **Admission** *free; donations appreciated.* **Map** *p125 L4.*
'One of the ugliest buildings in the world,' opined a Parliamentary committee on the opening of the new British Library in 1997. But don't judge a book by its cover: the interior is a model of cool, spacious functionality and the collection is unmatched (150 million items and counting). The focal point of the building is the King's Library, a six-storey glass-walled tower housing George III's collection, but the library's main treasures are on permanent display in the John

Statue of Newton at the British Library

Ritblat Gallery: the Lindisfarne Gospels, a Diamond Sutra from AD 868, original Beatles lyrics. Upstairs are engaging blockbuster shows covering meaty themes such as sci-fi, Gothic literature, the 800th anniversary of Magna Carta and the English language itself.

♥ Granary Square

www.kingscross.co.uk/granary-square. King's Cross St Pancras tube/rail. **Map** *p125 M3.*
Granary Square lies at the heart of the King's Cross redevelopment. Filled with choreographed fountains (1,080 water spouts, operating 8am-8pm daily, and lit in many colours at night), the square's terracing down to the canal is already populated most sunny days. No wonder: there's a ready supply of students from UAL Central Saint Martins college of art, which in 2011 moved into the building behind – a sensitively and impressively converted, Grade II-listed 1850s industrial building. Fronting on to the square are two restaurants and a café.

House of Illustration

2 Granary Square, N1C 4BH (3696 2020, www.houseofillustration. org.uk). King's Cross St Pancras tube/rail. **Open** *10am-6pm Tue-Sun.* **Admission** *£7.50; £4-£5 reductions; family £18; free under-5s.* **Map** *p125 M3.*
The world's first gallery dedicated to the art of illustration has demonstrations, talks, debates and hands-on workshops covering all aspects of illustration, from children's books and scabrous cartoons to advertising and animation, as well as a regular programme of temporary exhibitions, usually dedicated to a single illustrator: Quentin Blake, for instance, or EH Shepard, who drew the captivating pictures for *Winnie-the-Pooh*.

London Canal Museum

12-13 New Wharf Road, off Wharfdale Road, N1 9RT (7713 0836, www.canalmuseum.org. uk). King's Cross St Pancras tube/rail. **Open** *10am-4.30pm Tue-Sun (until 7.30pm 1st Thur of mth).* **Admission** *£5; £2.50-£4 reductions; family £12; free under-4s.* **Map** *p125 N3.*

Housed on two floors of a former 19th-century ice warehouse, the London Canal Museum has a barge cabin to sit in and models of boats, but the displays on the history of the ice trade (photos and videos about ice-importer Carlo Gatti) are perhaps the most interesting. The canalside walk (download a free MP3 audio tour from the museum website) from Camden Town to the museum is lovely, and in summer don't miss the tours – organised by the museum – that explore dank Islington Tunnel, an otherwise inaccessible Victorian canal feature.

♥ Wellcome Collection

183 Euston Road, NW1 2BE (7611 2222, www.wellcomecollection. org). Euston Square tube or Euston tube/Overground. **Open** *Galleries 10am-6pm Tue, Wed, Fri, Sat; 10am-10pm Thur; 11am-6pm Sun. Library 10am-6pm Mon-Wed, Fri; 10am-8pm Thur; 10am-4pm Sat.* **Admission** *free.* **Map** *p125 L5.*

Wellcome Collection is a free museum and library for the 'incurably curious'. Celebrating its tenth birthday in 2017, this gathering of international and medical oddities (Napoleon's toothbrush, Victorian amulets, Polynesian medical aids) is complemented by brilliant temporary exhibitions ('Bedlam' explored mental health and asylums; 'The Institute of Sexology' was all about bumping uglies) that explore art, health and what it means to be human. Over its first decade, the museum has attracted far more visitors than the original premises could cope with so the historic collection (Medicine Man) downstairs and science-themed temporary art gallery (Medicine Now) upstairs have been enhanced with a showpiece spiral staircase and two new exhibition spaces. The handsome Reading Room is manned by explainers and librarians who can introduce you to historic artwork (some of it in boxes that must be opened with protective white gloves) and extraordinary artefacts (a dentist's workstation, a Smoky Sue Smokes for Two pregnancy doll). Fascinating interactives include the 'Virtual Autopsy' table – effectively a giant tablet where you can swipe cuts through 3D cadavers – and a replica of Freud's couch.

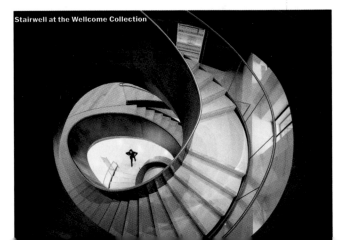

Stairwell at the Wellcome Collection

Restaurants

Caravan King's Cross ££

Granary Building, 1 Granary Square, N1C 4AA (7101 7661, www.caravankingscross.co.uk). King's Cross St Pancras tube/rail. Open 8am-10.30pm Mon-Fri; 10am-10.30pm Sat; 10am-4pm Sun. Map p125 M3 **6** *Global*

This is an altogether bigger, more urbane operation than the original Caravan on Exmouth Market. The ethos is the same, however: welcoming staff and a menu of what they call 'well-travelled food'. Most are small plates – deep-fried duck egg with baba ganoush, chorizo oil and crispy shallots, say, or grits, collard greens and brown shrimp butter – plus a few large plates and (at King's Cross only) a handful of first-class pizzas. Recent favourites include a naughty-but-nice crispy fried chicken with jerk mayo and pawpaw salsa. The setting, overlooking the fountains of Granary Square, is another plus, and there's a good range of drinks, including cocktails.

Grain Store £££

Granary Square, 1-3 Stable Street, N1C 4AB (7324 4466, www. grainstore.com). King's Cross St Pancras tube/rail. Open noon-2.30pm, 5.45-10.30pm Mon-Fri; 10am-10.30pm, 6-10.30pm Sat; 10.30am-3.30pm Sun. Map p125 M3 **11** *Modern European*

Grain Store, right next to Caravan, is a rather different proposition. The restaurant is run by Bruno Loubet, whose cooking is grounded in the classical traditions of south-west France, but not bound by them. The menu is a pick 'n' mix of fine ingredients and cuisines – a dish such as sticky pork belly with a corn and quinoa tamale is typical – but throughout there are consistency of style and imaginative, successful flavour pairings that are recognisably

Loubet. There's a bar, too, with excellent cocktails conceived by barmeister Tony Conigliaro – try the bellini, made not with peach purée but with celeriac purée.

Pubs & bars

❤ Scottish Stores

2-4 Caledonian Road, N1 9DT (3384 6497, www.thescottishstores. co.uk). King's Cross St Pancras tube/rail. Open 8am-11pm Mon-Wed; 8am-midnight Thur-Sat. Map p125 M4 **9**

Transformed from a seedy strip club into a handsome wood-panelled pub, the Scottish Stores is a reflection of the area's transformation from grotty to gleaming over the last decade or so. Run by a good old-fashioned gentleman, it specialises in interesting beers, such as the Basqueland Brewing Project IPA, as well as some more traditional draught options, all of which can be enjoyed out on the roof terrace – quite a find in this area.

Entertainment

Kings Place

90 York Way, King's Cross, N1 9AG (7520 1490, www.kingsplace.co.uk). King's Cross-St Pancras tube/rail. Box office noon-8pm Mon, Wed-Sat; noon-5pm Tue; noon-7pm Sun. Tickets free-£50. Map p125 M3 **10** *Concert hall*

Once a lone pioneer in the revival of King's Cross, Kings Place suddenly finds itself part of the King's Cross Central cultural hub. Beneath seven floors and a ground-floor restaurant-bar (with prized seats on the canal basin outside), the 415-seat main hall is a beauty, dominated by wood carved from a single, 500-year-old oak tree and ringed by invisible rubber pads that kill unwanted noise that might interfere with the immaculate acoustics. There's also a versatile second hall and a number of smaller rooms for workshops and lectures. The programming is tremendous and includes curated weeks featuring composers as wide-ranging as atonalist Arnold Schoenberg and jazzer Kit Downes. Other strands include chamber music and experimental classical, and there are spoken-word events too.

Scala

275 Pentonville Road, King's Cross, N1 9NL (information 7833 2022, tickets 0844 477 1000, scala.co.uk). King's Cross tube/rail. **Box office** *10am-6pm Mon-Fri. Tickets free-£25.* **Map** *p125 M4* ㉒ *Live music*
Although the venue has vacillated between use as a picturehouse and concert hall, the Scala's one consistent trait has been its lack of respect for authority: its stint as a cinema was ended after Stanley Kubrick sued it into bankruptcy for showing *A Clockwork Orange*. Nowadays, it's one of the most rewarding venues at which to push your way to the front for those cusp-of-greatness shows by big names in waiting – names as varied as the Chemical Brothers and Joss Stone.

Soho

Through the 1950s and '60s, Soho was London at its most game – now the prostitutes and mackintosh-wearing perverts have largely shipped out to leave PRs, shoppers and tourists to mingle with sundry party-people. Still, if you want to drink or eat, you could hardly find a better part of town in which to do so. And a wander among the skinny streets off **Old Compton Street**, Soho's main artery, should show you a bit of mischief.

Sights & museums

Leicester Square

Leicester Square tube. **Map** *p133 L8.*
One of London's most exclusive addresses in the 17th and 18th centuries, Leicester Square more recently became known for antisocial behaviour, pickpocketing and over-priced cinema tickets. But the arrival of a couple of high-class hotels and the reopening of the castle-like red-brick Hippodrome as a high-rolling casino, have given the area a bit of pull. Not all memories of the square's cheerfully tacky phase have gone, however: the Swiss Glockenspiel has returned, with its 27 bells and

Soho Square

mechanical mountain farmers chiming out the time on behalf of Switzerland Tourism.

Photographers' Gallery

16-18 Ramillies Street, W1F 7LW (7087 9300, www. thephotographersgallery.org. uk). Oxford Circus tube. Open 10am-6pm Mon-Wed, Fri, Sat; 10am-8pm Thur during exhibitions; 11am-6pm Sun. Admission £4; £2.50 reductions; free before noon. Temporary exhibitions vary. Map p133 K7.

Given a handsome refit by Irish architects O'Donnell+ Tuomey, this old, brick corner building is home to London's only gallery dedicated solely to the photographic arts. The upper floors have two airy exhibition spaces, while a bookshop, print sales room and café (open from 9.30am Mon-Fri) are tucked into the ground floor and basement. The exhibitions are varied, and enhanced by quirky details such as the camera obscura in the third-floor Eranda Studio and a projection wall in the café.

Ripley's Believe It or Not!

The London Pavilion, 1 Piccadilly Circus, W1J 0DA (3238 0022, ripleyslondon.com). Piccadilly Circus tube. Open 10am-midnight daily (last entry 10.30pm). Admission £27.95; £20.95 reductions; free under-4s. Book online 14 days in advance for 50% reductions. Map p133 L8.

This 'odditorium' follows a formula more or less unchanged since Robert Ripley opened his first display at the Chicago World Fair in 1933: an assortment of 800 curiosities is displayed, ranging from the world's smallest road-safe car to da Vinci's *Last Supper* painted on a grain of rice – via the company's signature shrunken heads. There are strange works of art created from everyday objects (a portrait of Michelle

Obama depicted in bottletops; Michael Jackson made out of sweets), exhibits that tell you about the curious traditions of obscure cultures, and a showcase of incredible human feats – the man who had his body reshaped so he looked like a lizard, the tallest man on earth, and so on. It's all brilliantly silly, offbeat fun.

Soho Square

Tottenham Court Road tube. Map p133 L7.

This tree-lined quadrangle, with a weather-beaten Charles II at the centre, beside the Mock Tudor gardeners' hut, fills with smoochy couples and snacking workers on sunny days.

Restaurants

10 Greek Street ££

10 Greek Street, W1D 4DH (7734 4677, www.10greekstreet.com). Tottenham Court Road tube. Open noon-2.30pm, 5.30-10.30pm Mon-Fri; noon-2.30pm, 5.30-10.45pm Wed-Sat. Lunch bookings taken; dinner walk-in only. Map p133 L7 ❶ *Modern European*

This small, unshowy restaurant has made a name for itself with a short but perfectly formed menu and an easygoing conviviality. Dishes are seasonal and the kitchen produces lots of interesting but ungimmicky combinations – such as a special of halibut fillet with yellow beans, chilli and garlic, on a vivid romesco sauce. It's good value too. Tables are closely packed, and in the evening it can get noisy; bookings are taken for lunch but not dinner.

Bao £

53 Lexington Street, W1F 9AS (www.baolondon.com). Oxford Circus or Piccadilly Circus tube. Open noon-3.30pm, 5.30-10pm Mon-Thur; noon-10.30pm Fri, Sat. No reservations. Map p133 K7 ❷ *Taiwanese*

Bao

This slick Taiwanese operation has successfully made the journey from market pop-up to permanent Soho establishment. The tantalising menu is fresh and innovative, based on Taiwanese street food dishes, with *xiao chi* (small eats) and of course *bao* (fluffy white steamed buns) stuffed with braised pork, soy-milk-marinated chicken, or even Horlicks ice-cream. What lifts this diner from merely great to sublime is the drinks list. Sakés, artisanal ciders, well-matched beers and hot oolong teas vie for attention alongside creations such as foam tea – a chilled light oolong artistically topped with foamed cream. Arrive hungry, leave happy.

Burger & Lobster ££
36-38 Dean Street, W1D 4PS (7432 4800, www.burgerandlobster. com). Leicester Square tube. **Open** *noon-10.30pm Mon-Wed; noon-11pm Thur-Sat; noon-10pm Sun.* ***Map*** *p133 L7* **5** *American*
The Soho branch of this sleek surf 'n' turf eaterie – which now has branches across town – offers a choice of, you've guessed it: burger or lobster. Meals start at £14, an all-in price that includes a huge carton of thin-cut fries and a side salad. For ultimate value, choose the lobster: steamed or grilled with just a lick of smoke. And if you're

sensible enough to leave room for dessert, try one of the wicked desserts such as Snickers-in-a-tub pud: rich chocolate mousse layered on to a devilish peanut-studded salt caramel.

Ceviche ££
17 Frith Street, W1D 4RG (7292 2040, www.cevicheuk.com). Leicester Square tube. **Open** *noon-11.30pm Mon-Sat; noon-10.15pm Sun.* ***Map*** *p133 L7* **7** *Peruvian*
Ceviche showcases citrus-cured fish. It is available in half a dozen different forms, though the menu also includes everything from terrific chargrilled meat and fish skewers (*anticuchos*) to a simple but perfectly executed corn cake. Factor in the seating options (trendy at the steel counter-bar, more comfortable in the rear dining area), the charismatic, attentive staff and the party atmosphere, and it's no wonder this place has been such a huge hit.

Dean Street Townhouse £££
69-71 Dean Street, W1D 3SE (7434 1775, www.deanstreettownhouse. com). Piccadilly Circus or Tottenham Court Road tube. **Open** *7am-midnight Mon-Thur; 7am-1am Fri; 8am-1am Sat; 8am-11pm Sun.* ***Map*** *p133 L7* **9** *British*

All things to all people at all hours – whatever the Soho occasion, the chances are that Dean Street Townhouse will fit the bill. A leisurely breakfast, elevenses with the morning papers, a brisk business lunch, afternoon tea, pre-theatre snack, romantic dinner for two. Across a series of Georgian-era rooms, the restaurant buzzes from opening time until closing, which proves the simple, straightforward effectiveness of its menu of well-executed British classics.

Herman Ze German £

33 Old Compton Street, W1D 5JU (7734 0431, www. hermanzegerman.co.uk). Leicester Square tube. **Open** *11am-11pm Mon-Wed; 11am-11.30pm Thur; 11am-midnight Fri, Sat; 11am-10.30pm Sun.* **Map** *p133 L7* 12 *German*

Herman Ze German is a purveyor of German sausages, imported from a Schwarzwald (Black Forest) butcher called (we are not making this up) Fritz. They are *sehr gut*: the high-quality pork creates fat, juicy sausages. Our favourite – the bockwurst, made of smoked pork – has a delicate flavour, a springy middle and plenty of 'knack' when you bite into it. Just add ketchup and mustard for a cheap and delicious snack.

Hoppers £

49 Frith Street, W1D 4SG (www. hopperslondon.com). Tottenham Court Road or Leicester Square tube. **Open** *noon-2.30pm, 5.30-10.30pm Mon-Thur; noon-10.30pm Fri, Sat. No reservations.* **Map** *p133 L7* 14 *Sri Lankan*

For those not familiar with Sri Lankan cuisine, a hopper is a bowl-shaped savoury crepe, usually eaten at breakfast, and this small stylish joint has them down to a T. Decor is an effortless mix of old and new; exposed brick meets wood panelling; pretty patterned tiles meet carved-wood devil masks. The menu, likewise, gives traditional Sri Lankan street food a fashionable lift: slender breaded and deep-fried mutton rolls come with a ginger, garlic and chilli 'ketchup'; a dinky dish of roast bone marrow is treated to a fiery 'dry' sauce, and the guinea fowl curry is unapologetically spicy.

Hummus Bros £

88 Wardour Street, W1F 0TH (7734 1311, www.hbros.co.uk). Oxford Circus or Tottenham Court Road tube. **Open** *8.30am-10pm Mon-Fri; noon-10pm Sat, Sun.* **Map** *p133 L7* 15 *Café*

The humble chickpea paste is elevated to something altogether more delicious in the hands of Hummus Bros. Though the wraps aren't bad, go for the bowls of silky-smooth houmous sprinkled with paprika and olive oil. Mashed, cumin-scented fava beans is a good choice of topping, but our favourite is the chunky slow-cooked beef. Side dishes are heartily recommended, with deliciously smoky barbecued aubergine and zingy tabouleh particular highlights. Service is quick and casual.

Polpo Soho ££

41 Beak Street, W1F 9SB (7734 4479, www.polpo.co.uk). Piccadilly Circus tube. **Open** *11.30am-11pm Mon-Sat; 11.30am-10pm Sun.* **Map** *p133 K7* 19 *Italian*

With peeling paint and battered wooden panelling, the decor may not look like much but you won't find better Venetian food anywhere in W1. Brown paper menus and chunky tumblers for wine glasses underline the sense of squatter chic, as does sharing small plates of unfussy food. These stretch from humble plates of olives to tasty crab *arancini*, sirloin steak and calf's liver, or spinach and egg *pizzette*.

❤ Social Eating House £££

58 Poland Street, W1F 7NR (7993 3251, www.socialeatinghouse.com). Oxford Circus tube. **Open** *noon-2.30pm, 6-10.30pm Mon-Sat.* **Map** *p133 K7* ㉔ *British*

Chef-patron Jason Atherton, once sorcerer's apprentice to Gordon Ramsey, has the golden tough. In 2013, he opened his Little Social deluxe bistro opened right opposite his Michelin-starred Pollen Street Social in Mayfair. Just weeks later, chef role delegated to Paul Hood, Atherton opened Social Eating House – still our favourite of his stable. The ground-floor dining room has a mirrored ceiling to create the impression of space in a small room; upstairs is a smart cocktail bar, called the Blind Pig, which also has a separate entrance. But most of the action is in the dining room, with a kitchen brigade who are clearly at the top of their game: stunning presentation and amazing flavour combinations, with great service.

Swift

Pubs & bars

Bar Américain

Brasserie Zédel, 20 Sherwood Street, W1F 7ED (7734 4888, www.brasseriezedel.com). Piccadilly Circus tube. **Open** *4.30pm-midnight Mon-Wed; 4.30pm-1am Thur, Fri; 1pm-1am Sat; 4.30-11pm Sun.* **Map** *p133 K8* ②

We love the simplicity of the cocktail list here: around 20 drinks, most of them tried and tested classics. Expertly rendered martinis, manhattans and daiquiris sit alongside such rarities as the martinez (a vermouth- and gin-based concoction that was the precursor of the martini) and inventive house specialities like the Lindy Hop (vodka, apple, lychee liqueur, orgeat and lemon). Fancy a quiet drink in the West End without having to pay through the nose? You can't do much better than the Américain's beautiful art deco interior.

Bar Termini

7 Old Compton Street, W1D 5JE (07860 945018, www.bar-termini.com). Leicester Square or Tottenham Court Road tube. **Open** *10am-11.30pm Mon-Thur; 10am-1am Fri, Sat; 11am-10.30pm Sun. Note that for visits later than 5pm, you'll need to book. 60-minute time limit in evenings.* **Map** *p133 L7* ③

Part of cocktail-maestro Tony Conigliaro's mini-empire (his drinks lab is at 69 Colebrooke Row; *see p173*), Bar Termini does two things: coffee and cocktails, in a room for 25, with seated service only, though you may stand if you order a single 'espresso al bar' (£1) – then drink and run in the Italian style. The coffee list has three signature brews, all of them classics but with a twist. The alcohol list has four negronis, a selection of *aperitivi*, four wines and one bottled beer. There are also baked goods by day, and charcuterie and cheese in the evening.

The Lyric

37 Great Windmill Street, W1D 7LU (7434 0604, www.lyricsoho. co.uk). Piccadilly Circus tube. Open 11am-11.30pm Mon-Thur; 11am-midnight Sat, Sun; noon-10.30pm Sun. Food served noon-10pm daily. Map p133 L8 **7**

Small, slightly shambolic and with a jovial share-a-table vibe, the Lyric is a longstanding favourite, not least because of its location near a fantastically crowded part of London where disappointing, pricey tourist traps are the norm. The Victorian pub's 18 taps pour out reliable pints, including Camden Hells and Brooklyn Lager, as well as more unusual guests – perhaps the hyper-citrussy High Wire Grapefruit brew from Magic Rock.

❤ Swift

12 Old Compton Street, W1D 4TQ (7437 7820, www.barswift.com). Tottenham Court Road tube. Open 3pm-midnight Mon-Sat; 3-10.30pm Sun. Map p133 L7 **10**

From the couple who brought us cult faves Nightjar and Oriole, Swift is a buzzy, casual-yet-sparkling bar on the ground level and a dark, sophisticated lounge below. Upstairs, the look is faintly Italian, mirrored in a menu of affordable aperitivos. This includes an unmissable sgroppino – a thick and frothy prosecco-based drink with lemony sorbet floating on top. The minamalist basement is lit for romantic trysts. Attentive staff guide you through a menu of great originality that edges towards nightcaps, like the powerful Amber Cane, a manhattan reinvented with rum in place of the bourbon. The carefully considered snack menu includes delights such as oysters and Guinness Welsh rarebit.

Shops & services

You can shop in Soho for everything from cheap street fashion to upscale designer garb and stylish items from home-decor stores. Buzzy **Berwick Street** market is the place for street-food stalls, vintage shops and indie vinyl. **Denmark Street** has become a hub for music shops. **Carnaby Street** has long been a favourite among fans of music and fashion, while the three-tiered **Kingly Court** complex contains a funky mix of established chains and hip boutiques. Quaint **Cecil Court** is known for its antiquarian book, map and print dealers, housed in premises that haven't changed in a hundred years.

Algerian Coffee Stores

52 Old Compton Street, W1D 4PB (7437 2480, www.algcoffee.co.uk). Leicester Square tube. Open 9am-7pm Mon-Wed; 9am-9pm Thur, Fri; 9am-8pm Sat. Map p133 L7 **1** *Food & drink*

For more than 125 years, this unassuming little shop has been trading over the same wooden counter. The range of coffees is broad, with house blends sold alongside single-origin beans; some serious teas and brewing hardware are also available. If you're just passing, pick up an espresso or latte to go.

Axel Arigato

19-23 Broadwick Street, W1F 0DF (7494 1728, axelarigato.com). Piccadilly Circus tube. Open 11am-7pm Mon-Wed; 11am-8pm Thur-Sat; noon-6pm Sun. Map p133 K7 **2** *Shoes*

After successfully building a fan base online, Swedish footwear brand Alex Arigato opened its flagship store in 2016. The handcrafted designer trainers are meticulously displayed on marbled

Foyles

pedestals and stone podiums, while the white colour scheme, concrete and mirrored surfaces of the shop's interior reflect its minimalist aesthetic. There are accessories and clothing too, as well as a selection of Japanese literature and objects that inspired the collection.

Foyles

107 Charing Cross Road, WC2H 0EB (7437 5660, www.foyles.co.uk). Tottenham Court Road tube. Open 9.30am-9pm Mon-Sat; noon-6pm Sun (browsing from 11.30am). Map p133 L7 **8** *Books & music*

With 37,000sq ft of floorspace laid out around an impressive central atrium, Foyles' eight levels are packed with more than 200,000 books, as well as CDs and literary gifts. The shop's focus is on the social aspect of reading. A whole floor is dedicated to events, from readings by Michael Palin and Jarvis Cocker, to themed book groups or literary tours, and there's a space dedicated to contemporary art.

Gosh!

1 Berwick Street, W1F 0DR (7636 1011, www.goshlondon.com). Oxford Circus tube. Open 10.30am-7pm daily. Map p133 L7 **10** *Books & music*

There's nowhere better to bolster your comics collection. There's a huge selection of manga, but graphic novels take centre stage, from early classics such as Krazy Kat to Alan Moore's erotic Peter Pan adaptation *Lost Girls*. Classic children's books, of the This is London vein, are another strong point. First port of call? The central table, where you'll find new releases – sometimes even before official publication.

MAC Carnaby

30 Great Marlborough Street, W1F 7JA (0370 192 5555, www. maccosmetics.co.uk). Oxford Circus tube. Open 10am-9pm Mon-Fri; 10am-8pm Sat; 10am-6pm Sun. Map p133 K7 **15** *Cosmetics*

This impressive outpost of beauty heavyweight MAC features the brand's ever-popular collaborations and tongue-in-cheek limited edition lines – Haute Dogs, for instance, whose lipsticks were inspired by pedigree pooches. There are also nine kaleidoscopic make-up stations, for quick drop-in demos or longer, bookable lessons. Upstairs is dedicated to Mac's Pro line, beloved of make-up artists and drag queens alike. With an exhaustive selection of products, it's shopping nirvana for slaphappy amateurs and studious pros.

Machine-A

13 Brewer Street, W1F 0RH (7734 4334, www.machine-a. com). Oxford Circus tube. **Open** *11am-7pm Mon-Wed; 11am-8pm Thur-Sat; noon-6pm Sun.* **Map** *p133 L7* ⑯ *Fashion*

Hats off (make it an Alex Mattsson baseball cap) to Machine-A for championing London's most exciting emerging designers at this Soho concept store. It's the natural habitat for the young, bold and brave, a small space full of pieces that practically sizzle with energy. Outside, the neon signage is a cheeky nod to its massage-parlour neighbours on Brewer Street.

Monki

37 Carnaby Street , W1V 1PD (8018 7400, www.monki.com/gb). Oxford Circus tube. **Open** *10am-8pm Mon-Sat; noon-6pm Sun.* **Map** *p133 K7* ⑰ *Fashion*

Hailing from Sweden, Monki's aesthetic is a bold urban one featuring cute animal prints, oddly shaped sweater dresses and eccentric accessories – current hits include the animal-print backpacks, chunky leather ankle boots and cute woolly mittens emblazoned with big logos for less than a fiver.

Sounds of the Universe

7 Broadwick Street, W1F 0DA (7734 3430, www.soundsoftheuniverse. com). Tottenham Court Road tube. **Open** *11am-7.30pm Mon-Sat; 11.30am-5.30pm Sun.* **Map** *p133 L7* ㉓ *Music*

SOTU's remit is broad. This is especially true on the ground floor (new vinyl and CDs), where grime and dubstep 12-inches jostle for space alongside new wave cosmic disco, electro-indie re-rubs and Nigerian compilations. The second-hand vinyl basement is big on soul, jazz, Brazilian and alt-rock.

WAH Nails

4 Peter Street, W1F 0DN (07983 261672, wah-london.com). Leicester Square tube. **Open** *10am-8pm Mon-Wed, Fri; 10am-10pm Thur; 11am-7pm Sat.* **Map** *p133 L7* ㉕ *Nail salon*

Any self-respecting nail-art fanatic will have heard of WAH, whose fanzine kicked off the nail art craze in London a few years ago. Its two-floor flagship salon offers the usual manicures, but also has room for a 'play and discover' area with immersive virtual-reality experiences, nail-printing and a product-testing zone. The futuristic space, complete with industrial concrete walls and cool cocktail bar, feels more like a club than a salon.

Entertainment

Film premières are still regularly held in the monolithic **Odeon Leicester Square**, which once boasted the UK's largest screen and probably still has the UK's highest ticket prices; this is where the **London Film Festival** (*see p62*) kicks off every year. Get a price-conscious cinema fix just north of the square on Leicester Place at the excellent **Prince Charles** rep cinema. For details of Soho's gay scene, *see p45*.

100 Club

100 Oxford Street, Soho, W1D 1LL (7636 0933, www.the100club.co.uk). Oxford Circus or Tottenham Court Road tube. **Shows** *times vary. Tickets £10-£25.* **Map** *p133 K7* ① *Live music*

The 100 Club began life in 1942 hosting the Feldman Club, but over the decades jazz would give way to punk: one historic show, in September 1976, featured the Sex Pistols, the Clash and the Damned. These days the famous, 350-capacity basement room is more of a hub for pub rockers, blues rockers and, in a return to

Best of the West End

The show must go on...and on...

WEST END

Aladdin

*Prince Edward Theatre, 28 Old Compton Street, Soho, W1D 4HS (0871 716 7960, www. aladdinthemucical.co.uk). Victoria tube/rail. Box ofce 10am-7.45pm Mon-Sat. Tickets £25-£97.50. **Map** p133 L7* ⑰

Disney's big-hit London musical is a panto-like affair enlivened by a couple of jaw-dropping set pieces and the presence of US star Trevor Dion Nicholas, who is sensational as the Genie.

The Book of Mormon

*Prince of Wales Theatre, Coventry Street, Soho, W1D 6AS (0844 482 5110, www.bookofmormonlondon. com). Piccadilly Circus tube. Box ofce 10am-8pm Mon-Sat. Tickets £20-£150. **Map** p133 L8* ⑱

South Park creators Trey Parker and Matt Stone's smash musical about the absurdities of Mormonism is not as shocking as you might expect. There's lots of swearing and close-to-the-bone jokes, but this is a big-hearted affair about the spirit and sounds of Broadway's golden age. And it's very, very funny.

Hamilton

*Victoria Palace Theatre, Victoria Street, Victoria, SW1E 5EA (0844 248 5138, www.hamiltonthemusical. co.uk). Victoria tube. Box office 10am-7.45pm Mon-Sat. Tickets £37.50-£190. **Map** p83 J11.*

From the moment it opens in November 2017, the expectation is that Lin-Manuel Miranda's Broadway-devouring rap musical will be equally unstoppable here.

Harry Potter and the Cursed Child

*Palace Theatre, Shaftesbury Avenue, Soho, W1D 5AY (0844 412 4656, www. harrypottertheplaylondon.com). Leicester Square tube. Box ofce In person 10am-6pm Mon-Sat. Tickets £15-£65 (1 part); £30-£130 (both parts). **Map** p133 L7* ⑬

The final adventure in JK Rowling's Harry Potter series isn't a book or a film, but a monumentally ambitious two-part London stage play, written by Jack Thorne. The production is phenomenal and as close as you'll ever get to stepping into Harry's magical world – small wonder it won a record nine Olivier Awards in 2017. It's booked up well in advance but there's a weekly online sale at 1pm on Fridays and the returns queue is worth a shot.

Matilda the Musical

*Cambridge Theatre, 32-34 Earlham Street, Covent Garden, WC2H 9HU (0844 412 4652, www. matildathemusical.com). Covent Garden tube or Charing Cross tube/rail. **Box office** In person from 10am Mon-Sat. By phone 10am-6pm Mon-Sat. Tickets £20-£122.50. **Map** p133 M7* ③

Adapted from Roald Dahl's riotous children's novel, with songs by superstar Aussie comedian Tim Minchin, this RSC transfer received rapturous reviews on its first outing in Stratford-upon-Avon and has been going strong ever since, winning multiple Olivier awards.

its roots, trad jazzers. The space comes into its own for the odd secret gig by A-list bands such as Primal Scream and Oasis.

♥ Borderline

*Orange Yard, off Manette Street, Soho, W1D 4JB (information 3871 7777, tickets 0870 060 3777, borderline.london). Tottenham Court Road tube. **Open** gigs daily; club nights until 4am Wed-Sat. **Admission** £3-£20. **Map** p133 L7* ② *Live music*

The best venue in the West End? Surely. Reopened after a revamp in spring 2017, the Borderline is a 300-capacity dive bar and juke joint, perfectly placed on the fringe of Soho. It has long been a favoured stop-off for touring American bands of the country and blues varieties, though you'll also find a range of indie acts and singer-songwriters going through their repertoire. Be warned: it can get very cramped, but that's all to the good for intimacy and atmosphere.

♥ Comedy Store

*1A Oxendon Street, Soho, SW1Y 4EE (0844 871 7699, www. thecomedystore.co.uk/london). Leicester Square or Piccadilly Circus tube. Shows times vary. **Admission** £5-£23.50. **Map** p133 L8* ⑤ *Comedy*

The Comedy Store is still the daddy of all the laff clubs. Seemingly as old as London itself (it actually started in 1979, above a strip club), the Store has been instrumental in the growth of alternative comedy, and still to this day hosts stunning shows most nights of the week. The live room was created specifically for stand-up and it shows, with 400 chairs hugging the stage to keep each show intimate. Veteran improvisers the Comedy Store Players perform every Wednesday

Les Misérables

*Queen's Theatre, 51 Shaftesbury Avenue, Soho, W1D 6BA (0844 482 5160, www.lesmis.com). Leicester Square or Piccadilly Circus tube. Box ofce In person 10am-8pm Mon-Sat. By phone 24hrs daily. Tickets £12.50-£97.25. **Map** p133 L8* ⑲

The RSC's version of Boublil and Schönberg's musical first came to the London stage in 1985. It's not the freshest show in town, but the voices remain lush, the revolutionary sets are film-fabulous, and the lyrics and score (based on Victor Hugo's novel) will be considerably less trivial than whatever's on next door.

The Play that Goes Wrong

*Duchess Theatre, 3-5 Catherine Street, Covent Garden, WC2B 5LA (0844 482 9672, www. theplaythatgoeswrong.com). Charing Cross tube/rail. Tickets £20-£65. **Map** p133 N7* ⑧

It's impossible not to be delighted by the success of this play, which began life at the tiny Old Red Lion theatre pub and has now been sitting pretty in the West End since 2014. It even has its own seasonal spin-off, Peter Pan Goes Wrong.

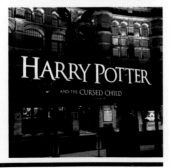

and Sunday. Don't miss the raucous King Gong new-act night on the last Monday of the month.

Curzon

99 Shaftesbury Avenue, W1D 5DY. Leicester Square tube. Screens 3. **Map** *p133 L7* 6 *Cinema*
Arthouse film fans have been known to go weak at the knees at the mention of the Soho Curzon, which has some of the best programming in London – a mix of arty new releases and documentaries, often introduced by the filmmakers themselves. Watching a film at the Curzon always feels special, surrounded by film lovers without it being pretentious. The coffee is good, the bar relaxed, and if you're watching a British film, you'll likely be seeing the finished product a stone's throw from where it was edited in Soho. Perfect for whiling away a rainy afternoon.

♥ Friendly Society

79 Wardour Street, Soho, W1D 6QB (7434 3804). Leciester Square tube. **Open** *5-11.30pm Mon-Thur; 5pm-midnight Fri, Sat; 4-10.30pm Sun.* **Map** *p133 L7* 9 *Gay bar*
Friendly Society benefits from the power of surprise: after entering through a bland back-alley doorway, you're greeted at the bottom of the stairs by Soho's most idiosyncratic drinking den. Barbie dolls hang from the ceiling, there's a big fishbowl in the middle and old movies are projected on to a back wall. Although the short cocktail menu has been the same for ever, the staff always seem perplexed when you order one, though that's definitely part of the charm. The crowd here is gay in the broadest sense – anyone with a sense of fun will feel at home, whatever their gender and sexuality. Come here when you fancy dancing to Donna Summer while sipping (relatively) inexpensive prosecco.

Leicester Square Theatre

6 Leicester Place, Leicester Square, WC2H 7BX (7734 2222, www. leicestersquaretheatre.com). Leicester Square tube. Shows times vary. **Admission** *£5-£50.* **Map** *p133 L8* 11 *Comedy*
Not strictly a comedy venue (it hosts music and theatre too), the Leicester Square Theatre's basement space is nonetheless home to enjoyable regular comedy nights and Edinburgh Fringe previews, while the 400-seat main house is a favourite room for big names (Stewart Lee, Jerry Sadowitz and Doug Stanhope often play long runs).

Odeon Leicester Square

Leicester Square, WC2H 7LQ (0333 006 7777, www.odeon.co.uk). Leicester Square tube. Tickets £14-£22; £7-£19.50 reductions. Screens 5. **Map** *p133 L8* 12 *Cinema*
London's number-one destination for red carpet premières. Not only do you get blockbuster bangs in the huge 1,683-seat auditorium, you get them in splendour: the Odeon Leicester Square has gorgeous 1930s art-deco nymph motifs on the walls and is one of the few remaining cinemas to retain its circle – from which the view (at extra cost) is pretty spectacular.

Picturehouse Central

Trocadero, Shaftesbury Avenue, Piccadilly, W1D 7DH (0871 902 5755, www.picturehouses.com). Piccadilly Circus tube. Tickets £13.50-£16.50; £7.50-£11.50 reductions. Screens 7. **Map** *p133 L8* 14 *Cinema*
On the corner of Shaftesbury Avenue, this central London cinema is an absolute gem. It's the antidote to Piccadilly Circus's rage-inducing pavements, with three floors of beautifully designed space. Before you even get anywhere near the plush

screening rooms, a hundred hanging lightbulbs lead you up a grand terracotta-tiled staircase past a mural inspired by a century of cinema.

Pizza Express Jazz Club

10 Dean Street, Soho, W1D 3RW (7439 4962, www.pizzaexpresslive. com). Tottenham Court Road tube. **Open** *7-10.30pm Mon-Thur; 7.30-9pm, 10pm-midnight Fri, Sat; 6.30-10pm Sun. Lunchtime shows 1.30-3.30pm.* **Admission** *£15-£25.* **Map** *p133 L7* **⑮** *Jazz*
The upstairs restaurant (7437 9595) is jazz-free, but the 120-capacity basement is one of the best mainstream jazz venues in town. Singers such as Kurt Elling and Lea DeLaria join instrumentalists from home and abroad on the nightly bills.

Prince Charles

7 Leicester Place, off Leicester Square, WC2H 7BY (7494 3654, www.princecharlescinema.com). Leicester Square tube. Tickets £8-£11.50. Screens 2. **Map** *p133 K8* **⑯** *Cinema*
This is the only time you'll spend in a cinema when no one's going to shush you. Singalong screenings at the Prince Charles are all about audience participation: whether your movie is *Frozen*, *Rocky Horror* or *The Sound of Music*. You can even settle in for a marathon all-night pyjama party. Having started life screening porn, the Prince Charles is central London's wildcard cinema, providing a fantastic blend of new-ish blockbusters and arthouse titles, with heaps of horror, sci-fi and teen-flick all-nighters, double bills and short seasons. It's comfy, cheap and cheerful.

❤ Ronnie Scott's

47 Frith Street, Soho, W1D 4HT (7439 0747, www.ronniescotts. co.uk). Leicester Square or Tottenham Court Road tube. Shows 6pm-3am Mon-Sat; noon-4pm, 6.30pm-midnight Sun. **Admission** *free-£50.* **Map** *p133 L7* **⑳** *Jazz*
Opened (on a different site) by the British saxophonist Ronnie Scott in 1959, this jazz institution – the setting for Jimi Hendrix's final UK performance, among many other distinctions – was completely refurbished in 2006. The capacity was expanded to 250, the food got better and the bookings became drearier. Happily, though, Ronnie's has got back on track, with jazz heavyweights dominating once more – from well-established talents such as Chick Corea to hotly tipped purists such as Kurt Elling to futuristic mavericks such as Robert Glasper. Perch by the rear bar, or get table service at the crammed side-seating or at the more spacious (but noisier) central tables in front of the stage.

SHE Soho

23A Old Compton Street, Soho, W1D 5JL (7437 4303, http://she-soho.com). Leicester Square tube. **Open** *4-11.30pm Mon-Thur; noon-midnight Fri, Sat; noon-10.30pm Sun.* **Map** *p133 L7* **㉓** *Lesbian venue*
Shockingly, this Soho basement bar is London's only exclusively lesbian venue, and takes this responsibility seriously. Run by the team behind Ku Bar, SHE has a comparable flair for laying on entertainment: as well as club nights, it regularly offers comedy, cabaret, karaoke and quiz evenings. BOi BOX, a monthly drag king talent contest hosted by scene heroes Adam All and Apple Derrières, is definitely worth popping in your Google Calendar.

Soho Theatre

21 Dean Street, Soho, W1D 3NE (7478 0100, www.sohotheatre. com). Tottenham Court Road tube. **Box office** *9am-9pm Mon-Fri; 1 hr before performance Sat . Tickets £9-£35.* **Map** *p133 L7* ㉔ *Theatre*

Since it opened in 2000, the Soho Theatre has built a terrific reputation – with excellence across three inter-related genres: cabaret, comedy and, yes, theatre. It attracts a younger, hipper crowd than most London spaces, and brings on aspiring writers and youth theatre companies. After a few years finding its feet, it has settled in as a producer of some of the best work to go to the Edinburgh Fringe, and has scored a notable success by launching the career of *Fleabag* creator Phoebe Waller-Bridge. In many ways the biggest draw is comedy: British and international talent has included Russell Brand, Michael McIntyre, Kristen Schaal and Doug Stanhope. The hard lines, low stage and packed table seating favour comedy over cabaret in the theatre's basement space, but the Soho consistently books outstanding talent from the international cabaret circuit for the room, from Meow Meow and Caroline Nin to London's own David Hoyle, Bourgeois & Maurice and the Tiger Lillies.

Covent Garden

Covent Garden is understandably popular with visitors. A traffic-free oasis in the heart of the city, replete with shops, cafés and bars – and the **London Transport Museum** – it centres on a restored 19th-century covered market. On the west side, the portico of **St Paul's Covent Garden** hosts jugglers and escapologists. And if you're looking for great vocal performances rather than street performances, the **Royal Opera House** is here too.

Sights & museums

Covent Garden Piazza

Covent Garden tube. **Map** *p133 M7/8.*

The Piazza offers a combination of gentrified shops, restaurants and cafés, and living statues and buskers. Most of the entertainment takes place under the portico of **St Paul's Covent Garden**, while tourists are drawn to the upmarket chain stores and sometimes quirky but often twee boutiques in the 180-year-old covered market. The architecture is handsome, though – it can be best appreciated from the terrace of the Amphitheatre Restaurant in the Royal Opera House (reopening 2018). Much classier shops have opened, led by the world's largest **Apple Store** (1-7 The Piazza, WC2E 8HB (7447 1400, www.apple.com/uk/retail), but the North Hall's **Apple Market** still has arts and crafts stalls (Tue-Sun) and antiques (Mon), while the **Jubilee Market** will exceed anyone's requirements for novelty T-shirts.

St Paul's Covent Garden

Bedford Street, WC2E 9ED (7836 5221, www.actorschurch. org). Covent Garden tube. **Open** *8.30am-5pm Mon-Fri; 9am-1pm Sun (5pm when there is Evensong). Times vary Sat; phone for details.* **Services** *1.10pm Tue, Wed; 11am Sun. Choral Evensong 4pm 2nd Sun of mth.* **Admission** *free; donations appreciated.* **Map** *p133 M8.*

Known as the Actors' Church for its long association with Covent Garden's theatres, this pleasingly spare building was designed by Inigo Jones in 1631. A lovely limewood wreath by the 17th-century master carver Grinling Gibbons hangs inside the front door as a reminder that he and his wife are interred in the crypt. But most visitors come to see the memorial plaques: many thespians are commemorated here,

💜 London Transport Museum

*Covent Garden Piazza, WC2E 7BB
(7379 6344, www.ltmuseum.co.uk).
Covent Garden tube.* **Open** *10am-
6pm Mon-Thur, Sat, Sun; 11am-
6pm Fri.* **Admission** *£17.50; £15
reductions; free under-18s.* **Map**
p133 M7.

Londoners and their transport, eh?
There's no need to keep banging
on about it, you might think. We
beg to differ. Most Londoners
spend more time commuting
than they do having lunch, and
their city's prodigious growth in
Victorian times into the biggest,
most flabbergastingly exciting and
frankly unpleasant city the world
had ever known was largely down
to transport infrastructure, which
supported an unprecedented
population explosion.

It is this story that the London
Transport Museum tells so well,
tracing the city's transport history
from the horse age to the present
day. The museum also raises
some interesting and important
questions about the future of
public transport in the city, even
offering a fanciful imagining
of London's travel network
in the years ahead.

Engaging and inspiring, the
Transport Museum's focus is on
social history and design, which
are illustrated by a superb array of
preserved buses, trams and trains.
The collections are in broadly
chronological order, beginning
with the Victorian gallery, where
a replica of Shillibeer's first horse-
drawn bus service from 1829 takes
pride of place. Along the way
there is a Northern line simulator

to drive, and train carriages and
buses to jump on and climb up.

A new permanent gallery,
London by Design, explores how,
under the leadership of Frank Pick
in the early 20th century, London
Transport developed one of the
most coherent brand identities
in the world. The gallery also
explores some of the network's
enduring industrial design and
arresting poster art from the
likes of Abram Games, Graham
Sutherland and Ivon Hitchens.

All in all, it's a great place for
families, with younger children
especially enjoying the small but
terrific play zone, All Aboard,
where they can repair a mini
Tube train, make passenger
announcements and operate the
Emirates Air Line cable car.

among them Vivien Leigh, Charlie Chaplin and Hattie Jacques of *Carry On* fame.

Restaurants

The Barbary ££

16 Neal's Yard, WC2H 9DP (thebarbary.co.uk). Covent Garden tube. **Open** *noon-3pm, 5-10pm Mon-Fri; noon-1pm Sat; noon-9.30pm Sun. No reservations.* **Map** *p133 M7* ❸ *North African*

The Barbary takes everything that's good about its sister restaurant Palomar and reinvents it. Seating is on 24 stools arranged at a horseshoe-shaped counter bar. Down one wall, there's a standing counter, where they'll feed you snacks like deep-fried pastry 'cigars' filled with cod, lemon and Moroccan spices while you wait for a seat. And the food – inspired by the eponymous Barbary coast, which stretches from Morocco to Egypt – is heady with smoke and North African spices. The signature *naan e beber*, made to an ancient recipe, emerges from the fiercely hot tandoor deliciously fluffy and blistered. Main courses such as slow-braised octopus with oranges cooked over a coal-fired *robata* are impossibly tender; while *knafeh* (filo pastry filled with goat's cheese and pan-fried until it's crispy on the outside, chewy on the inside, and sprinkled with roasted pistachio nuts) is dessert heaven.

Barrafina ££

10 Adelaide Street, WC2N 4HZ (7440 1456, www.barrafina.co.uk). Charing Cross or Leicester Square tube. **Open** *noon-3pm, 5-11pm Mon-Sat; 1-3.30pm, 5.30-10pm Sun. No reservations.* **Map** *p133 M8* ❹ *Tapas*

Like its predecessor in Soho, Barrafina Covent Garden takes no reservations, so arrive early – or late – if you don't want to queue at this perennially popular tapas

Covent Garden

restaurant. The menu is studded with tempting Mallorcan and Catalan dishes, but watch out if you're properly hungry: the bill adds up fast. Despite the fancy prices, remember that Barrafina is a modern Spanish tapas bar rather than a restaurant per se – this means that the list of sherries, cavas and other wines by the glass are as much a part of the appeal as the food, and perfect for experimenting with as you nibble.

Flesh & Buns ££

41 Earlham Street, WC2H 9LX (7632 9500, www.bonedaddies. com/flesh-and-buns). Covent Garden tube. **Open** *noon-3pm, 5-10.30pm Mon, Tue; noon-3pm, 5-11pm Wed-Fri; noon-11pm Sat; noon-9.30pm Sun.* **Map** *p133 M7* ❿ *Taiwanese*

Flesh & Buns is hidden in a capacious basement, with industrial-chic decor and young, pierced and tattooed staff setting the tone. It serves hirata buns – a US take on Taiwanese street food – with a side order of rock music. Sweet, fluffy dough is folded, then steamed and brought to table. Diners then stuff these pockets with their choice of 'flesh'. Mustard miso and a few slices of subtly pickled apple make a foil for tender pulled pork; crisp-skinned grilled sea bass is served with fresh tomato salsa.

❤ J Sheekey £££
28-32 St Martin's Court, WC2N 4AL (7240 2565, www.j-sheekey. co.uk). Leicester Square tube. **Open** *noon-3pm, 5pm-midnight Mon-Fri; noon-3pm, 5.15pm-midnight Sat; noon-3.30pm, 5.30-10.30pm Sun.* **Map** *p133 L8* 16 *Fish & seafood*
After well over a century of service, Sheekey's status as a West End institution is assured. With its monochrome photos of stars of stage and screen, wooden panelling and cream crackle walls, and array of silver dishes atop thick white tablecloths, it oozes old-fashioned glamour. The menu runs from super-fresh oysters and shellfish via old-fashioned snacks (herring roe on toast) to upmarket classics (dover sole, lobster thermidor). The fish pie – a rich, comforting treat – is acclaimed, but we feel the shrimp and scallop burger merits similar status.

Adjoining Sheekey restaurant, J Sheekey Oyster Bar (nos.33-35, www.jsheekeyatlanticbar.co.uk) serves a similar menu – with an expanded range of oysters – to customers sitting at the counter.

Kanada-Ya £
64 St Giles High Street, WC2H 8LE (7240 0232, www.kanada-ya. com). Tottenham Court Road tube. **Open** *noon-3pm, 5-10.30pm Mon-Fri; noon-3pm, 5-11pm Sat; noon-8.30pm Sun. No reservations.* **Map** *p133 L7* 17 *Japanese*
Small, brightly lit and minimal, this is not the place for a leisurely meal: there are always lengthy mealtime queues outside its

doors. But there's a reason for Kanada-Ya's already-large fan base: exceptional ramen. If you don't eat pork, forget it; but those pork bones are simmered for 18 hours to create the smooth, rich, seriously savoury *tonkotsu* broth – one of the best in London. If you don't have much time, the wait at Ippudo, just opposite, is always more bearable than that at Kanada-ya.

Tandoor Chop House ££
8 Adelaide Street, WC2N 4HZ (3096 0359, tandoorchophouse. com). Charing Cross tube. **Open** *11.30am-11.30pm Mon-Fri; noon-11pm Sat; 1-10pm Sun.* **Map** *p133 M8* 25 *Indian*
This slightly less hectic, more refined mini-me version of the original branch of **Dishoom** is by no means derivative. With cheerfully attentive service and a bustling Bombay vibe, it's a twist on what you'd get in an old-fashioned Brit 'chop house', only using Indo-Punjabi spices and swapping the grill for the tandoor. Plates are small and meant for sharing. Start with the pistachio-studded seekh kebab strewn with pomegranate seeds and coriander, or the 'beef dripping' keema naan. For mains, be sure to try the thickly marinated, fatty-edged lamb chops, all soot and spice, or the juice spice-rubbed rib-eye. But don't stop there: the malted kulfi ice cream is silky smooth and intense, served with chunks of caramelised banana and salted peanuts.

Pubs & bars
Beaufort Bar at the Savoy
The Savoy, 100 Strand, WC2R 0EW (7836 4343, www.fairmont. com/savoy-london). Charing Cross tube/rail or Embankment tube. **Open** *5pm-1am Mon-Sat.* **Map** *p133 M8* 4
Set in London's most famous hotel, the ultra-suave Beaufort Bar is

Neal's Yard

quite possibly the most attractive space to sip a drink in the city. Just off the busy lobby, it's a hideaway of supreme style and opulence, with jet-black walls, theatrical lighting and enough discreet touches of gold to remind you you're somewhere special. The drinks live up to the ambience, pushing the boundaries of mixology and incorporating fizz to great effect.

Cross Keys
31 Endell Street, WC2H 9BA (7836 5185, www.crosskeyscoventgarden. com). Covent Garden tube. **Open** *11am-11pm Mon-Sat; noon-10.30m Sun.* **Map** *p133 M7* ⑥
Central London pubs with a local vibe are the rarest of things, but the Cross Keys is precisely that. With its canopy of copper implements, garish carpet and walls covered in vintage beeraphernalia, it feels like it hasn't changed for 30 years. Despite the local competition, it makes zero effort to appeal to tourists, which is ironic, since sipping a pint in the failing sunlight amid wafts from the nearby chippie is one of the most perfectly London experiences you'll get in the West End.

Terroirs
5 William IV Street, WC2N 4DW (7036 0660, www.terroirswinebar. com). Charing Cross tube/rail. **Open** *noon-11pm Mon-Sat. Food served noon-3pm, 5.30-11pm Mon-Sat.* **Map** *p133 M8* ⑪
Terroirs – a wine bar with excellent food – is really two places under one roof. The always-crowded ground floor has a casual feel and a menu to match, focused on small plates for sharing. You can sample some of the same dishes in the atmospheric and surprisingly roomy basement, which feels more like a restaurant: the menu here, with its focus on rustic French dishes, seems designed to guide diners more towards a more traditional starter-main-dessert approach. The wine list is an encyclopaedia of organic and biodynamic bottles.

Shops & services

James Smith & Sons
Hazelwood House, 53 New Oxford Street, WC1A 1BL (7836 4731, www.james-smith.co.uk). Holborn or Tottenham Court Road tube. **Open** *10am-5.45pm Mon-Fri; 10am-5.15pm Sat.* **Map** *p133 M7* ⑫
Accessories

Nearly 190 years after it was established, this charming shop, with Victorian fittings still intact, is holding its own in the niche market of umbrellas and walking sticks. The stock here isn't the throwaway type of brolly that breaks at the first sign of a breeze. The lovingly crafted brollies – perhaps a classic City umbrella with a malacca cane handle at £175 – are built to last. A repair service is also offered.

Natural Selection

46 Monmouth Street, WC2H 9LE (7240 3506, naturalselectionlondon.com). Covent Garden tube. **Open** *10.30am-7pm Mon-Sat; 11am-5pm Sun.* **Map** *p133 M7* ⑱ *Menswear*

Originally a denim brand that took its name from Darwin's book *The Origin of Species by Means of Natural Selection*, Natural Selection has since branched out into a full ready-to-wear range of smart-casual essentials for men. Everything here is understated, but has a touch of sports luxe too. In the airy, stripped-back store, you can also get hold of a selection of fragrances, eyewear and accessories from brands like Thierry Lasry and No.288 footwear.

Neal's Yard Dairy

17 Shorts Gardens, WC2H 9AT (7240 5700, www.nealsyarddairy. co.uk). Covent Garden tube. **Open** *10am-7pm Mon-Sat.* **Map** *p133 M7* ⑲ *Food & drink*

Neal's Yard buys from small farms and creameries and matures the cheeses in its own cellars until they're ready to sell in peak condition. Names such as Stinking Bishop and Lincolnshire Poacher are as evocative as the aromas in the shop. It's best to walk in and ask what's good today: you'll be given tasters by the well-trained staff.

If you're gourmet shopping in **Borough Market** (*see p78*),

you'll find another branch of **Neal's Yard Dairy** (6 Park Street, Borough, SE1 9AB, 7367 0799, www.nealsyarddairy.co.uk).

Nigel Cabourn Army Gym

28 Henrietta Street, WC2E 8NA (7240 1005, www.cabourn. com). Covent Garden tube. **Open** *11am-6.30pm Mon-Wed, Fri, Sat; 11am-7pm Thur; noon-5pm Sun.* **Map** *p133 M8* ⑳ *Menswear*

This is the only Cabourn shop outside Japan, selling the hallowed designer's vintage-inspired collections, dreamed to life by consulting his vast personal archive of over 4,000 pieces. As the name might suggest, you're guaranteed to be able to get hold of some camo here, but there's also a solid amount of smart tailoring and shirting, all drawing on the best of British design.

Vintage Showroom

14 Earlham Street, Seven Dials, WC2H 9LN (7836 3964, www. thevintageshowroom.com). Covent Garden tube. **Open** *varies.* **Map** *p133 L7* ㉔ *Vintage menswear*

In the old FW Collins & Sons ironmongery, Roy Luckett and Doug Gunn show a tiny selection of their famous west London menswear archive, which they routinely loan out to big-name designers, denim brands and vintage obsessives. With stock sourced from around the world (Roy and Doug have some hair-raising stories of dealings with collectors and hoarders in obscure locations), it follows that the pair occasionally find it hard to part with an item, and they've been known to try to dissuade shoppers from buying the rarer pieces on display. But the shop has London's best men's vintage collection, with an emphasis on Americana (denim, sweats, a few choice tees) and classic military and British pieces.

Entertainment

English National Opera, Coliseum

St Martin's Lane, Covent Garden, WC2N 4ES (7845 9300, www.eno. org). Leicester Square tube or Charing Cross tube/rail. **Box office** *10am-6pm Mon-Sat. Tickets £12-£155.* **Map** *p133 M8* ❹ *Opera*
Built as a music hall in 1904, the home of the English National Opera (ENO) is in a rocky patch, with funding issues and a high turnover of directors. Despite this, theENO has offered some fascinating collaborations over the last few years: physical theatre troupe Complicité and former Python Terry Gilliam directing Berlioz's *Benvenuto Cellini*, for instance, and Bryn Terfel with Emma Thompson in Sondheim's *Sweeney Todd*. There have also been stagings of rare contemporary works (Ligeti's *Le Grand Macabre*, Glass's *Akhnaten*). But 2012 scheme 'Opera Undressed', encouraging new, younger audience members to attend some classic operas in their everyday clothes, have a drink and enjoy a pre-performance talk, may yet prove to be ENO's most important initiative. Meanwhile, ticket prices have been reduced to £20 and under on 60,000 seats.

Donmar Warehouse

41 Earlham Street, Covent Garden, WC2H 9LX (0844 871 7624, www. donmarwarehouse.com). Covent Garden or Leicester Square tube. **Box office** *10am-6pm Mon-Fri. Tickets £7.50-£35.* **Map** *p133 M7* ❼ *Theatre*
It may be central London's smallest major theatre, but the Donmar's influence outstrips its size many times over. Run by Sam Mendes then Michael Grandage, current boss Josie Rourke has made it her mission to steer the Donmar away from boutique productions of classics with big-name celebrities – though those are still here – and aim for a livelier, younger programme that is orientated more towards new writing.

Royal Opera, Royal Opera House

Bow Street, Covent Garden, WC2E 9DD (7304 4000, www.roh.org. uk). Covent Garden tube. **Box office** *10am-8pm Mon-Sat. Tickets £4-£200.* **Map** *p133 M7* ㉑ *Opera*
Thanks to a refurbishment at the start of the century, the Royal Opera House has once again taken its place among the ranks of the world's great opera houses – but it isn't enough: the £27m 'Open Up' redevelopment is making further infrastructural changes. Critics suggest that the programming at the Opera House can be a little spotty – especially so given the famously elevated ticket prices – but there is a solid spine to the programme: fine productions of the classics, often taking place under the assured baton of Sir Antonio Pappano. Productions take in favourite traditional operatic composers (Donizetti, Mozart, Verdi) and some modern (Mark-Anthony Turnage, Harrison Birtwistle), while the annual month-long Deloitte Ignite festival has filled the opera house with a wide range of free and ticketed events.

Coliseum

The City

The City's current role as the financial heart of London does no justice to its 2,000-year history. Here – on top of a much more ancient ritual landscape – the Romans founded the city they called Londinium. Within the defensive wall that defines what we now call the Square Mile were a forum-basilica, an amphitheatre and public baths.

Parts of the Roman city can still be seen – outside Tower Hill tube station or in the basement of the **Guildhall**, for example – yet today the area is dominated by the high-rise offices of legal and financial institutions. To understand the City properly, it's best to visit on a weekday when the commuter is king; at weekends many streets feel eerily quiet.

An exception to this is **St Paul's Cathedral**, whose vast stone interior echoes constantly with the voices of

Best sights
Sir Christopher Wren's masterpiece, St Paul's Cathedral (*p162*). Historic attraction par excellence, the Tower of London (*p165*).

Best restaurant
Sky-high breakfasts at Duck and Waffle (*p167*). Moorish food at Moro (*p159*). Fabulous fusion at Modern Pantry (*p159*).

Best art gallery
20th-century masters at the Courtauld Gallery (*p153*).

Best cultural venue
Barbican Centre (*p168*) for art, films, theatre and concerts.

Best nightlife venue
Fabric (*p161*), one of London's most famous clubs.

Best view
Take in the skyline from the Sky Garden (*p166*). Climb the steps up the Monument (*p164*).

Must-see museum
Sir John Soane's Museum (*p157*), packed with art, furniture and ornaments. Learn the history of the city at the Museum of London (*p164*).

Best bar
Zetter Townhouse (*p161*) for inventive cocktails. Asian-influenced confections at 7 Tales (*p160*).

worshippers and sightseers. Rising from the ashes of the Great Fire of 1666, Sir Christopher Wren's masterpiece lords it over the many pretty medieval churches dotted around the City.

To get a grasp of London's social history from prehistoric times to the present, don't miss the **Museum of London**. Here, reconstructions of interiors and street scenes, alongside artefacts found during the museum's archaeological digs offer a fascinating insight.

At the City's eastern edge, the **Tower of London** remains one of the best-preserved medieval fortresses in Europe. Tourists come from far and wide to get a glimpse of the Crown Jewels, Royal Armouries and 13th-century White Tower where traitors of the monarchy came to a sticky end.

→ Getting around
Tube and bus transport in the Square Mile is supplemented by commuter rail services through London Bridge and Blackfriars. Avoid travelling at peak times Monday to Friday when all transport options are filled to bursting.

Holborn and Clerkenwell

The City of London collides with the West End in Clerkenwell and Holborn. Bewigged barristers inhabit the picturesque Inns of Court, while city slickers head from their loft apartments to the latest restaurants in what is one of London's foodiest areas.

Sights & museums

Charles Dickens Museum

48 Doughty Street, WC1N 2LX (7405 2127, www.dickensmuseum. com). Chancery Lane or Russell Square tube. **Open** *10am-5pm Tue-Sat. Tours by arrangement.* **Admission** *£9; £4-£6 reductions; free under-6s.* **Map** *p154 N5.*

London is scattered with plaques marking addresses where Dickens lived, but this is the only one to have been preserved as a museum. He lived here from 1837 to 1840, writing *Nicholas Nickleby* and *Oliver Twist* while in residence. Ring the doorbell to gain access to four floors of Dickensiana, collected over the years from various former residences. Some rooms are arranged as they might have been when he lived here (especially atmospheric during the occasional candlelit openings); others deal with different aspects of his life, from struggling hack to famous performer. But the study has the key artefact: the chair and desk at which Dickens wrote *Great Expectations.*

❤ Courtauld Gallery

Somerset House, Strand, WC2R 0RN (7848 2777, www.courtauld. ac.uk/gallery). Temple tube. **Open** *10am-6pm daily.* **Admission** *£7; £6 reductions; students, unwaged & under-18s free.* **Map** *p154 N8.*

Located for the last two decades in the north wing of **Somerset House** (*see p157*), the Courtauld has one of Britain's greatest collections of paintings, including several works of world importance. Although there are some outstanding early works (Cranach's *Adam & Eve*, for one), the collection's strongest suit is in Impressionism and Post-Impressionism. Popular masterpieces here include Manet's *A Bar at the Folies-Bergère*, but there are also superb works by Monet and Cézanne, important Gauguins, and some Van Goghs and Seurats. On the top floor, there's a selection of gorgeous Fauvist pieces and a lovely room of Kandinskys.

Dr Johnson's House

17 Gough Square, off Fleet Street, EC4A 3DE (7353 3745, www. drjohnsonshouse.org). Chancery Lane tube or Blackfriars tube/rail. **Open** *May-Sept 11am-5.30pm Mon-Sat. Oct-Apr 11am-5pm Mon-Sat. Tours by arrangement; groups of 10 or more only.* **Admission** *£6; £2.50-£5 reductions; £12 family; free under-5s. Tours £5. No cards.* **Map** *p154 O7.*

Famed as the author of one of the first – as well as the most significant and unquestionably the wittiest – dictionaries of the English language, Dr Samuel Johnson (1709-84) also wrote poems, essays, literary criticism, a novel and an early travelogue, an acerbic account of a tour of the Western Isles with his biographer James Boswell. You can tour the stately Georgian townhouse where he came up with his inspired definitions – 'to make dictionaries is dull work' was his definition of the word 'dull' while 'oats' is a 'grain, which in England is generally given to horses, but in Scotland supports the people'.

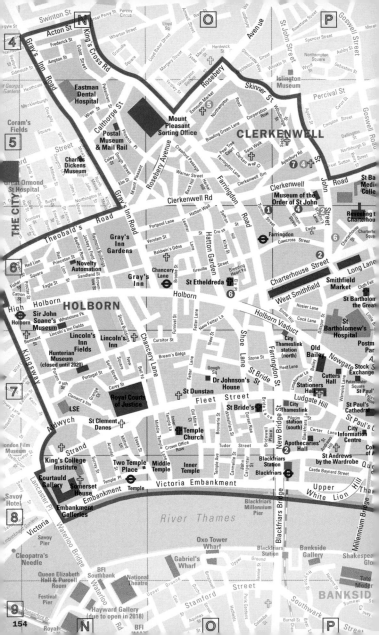

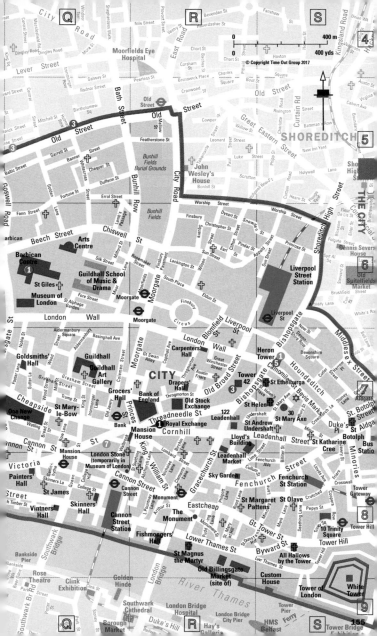

Fleet Street

Chancery Lane or Temple tube.
Map *p154 O7.*

The first printing press on this legendary street of newspapers was installed behind St Bride's Church (below) in 1500 by William Caxton's assistant, Wynkyn de Worde, but it wasn't until 1702 that the UK's first daily newspaper, the Daily Courant, rolled off the presses. By the end of World War II, half a dozen newspaper offices were churning out scoops, but they all moved away after Rupert Murdoch won his bitter war with the print unions in the 1980s, leaving only grand buildings including Reuters (no.85), the Daily Telegraph (no.135) and the jet-black art deco classic Daily Express (nos.121-128).

Postal Museum & Mail Rail

Phoenix Place, WC1X 0DA (www. postalmuseum.org). Russell Square tube or Farringdon tube/rail. **Open** *10am-5pm daily.* **Admission** *£16; £8 reductions (incl donation). Family play area (45min session) £5; £3.75 with Mail Rail ticket.* **Map** *p154 N5.*

Used to shuttle post across London, the Mail Rail opened in 1927 as one of the earliest driverless electric railways. Closed in 2003, it was mothballed for more than a decade. But now some of its disused tunnels have been revived as part of the new Postal Museum, where you can find out about what was effectively the first social network: the Royal Mail. Exhibits – many of them interactive – display such rare artefacts as a priceless sheet of Penny Black stamps and the original 1966 plastercast of the Queen, which remains on our stamps to this day. But the highlight for visitors will inevitably be hitching a subterranean ride on the refurbished Mail Rail.

Revealing the Charterhouse

Charterhouse Square, EC1M 6AN (3818 8873, www.thecharterhouse. org). Barbican tube. **Open** *11am-4.45pm Tue-Sun. 55min Standard tour 11.30am, 1.45pm, 2.45pm; 2hr Brother's tour 2.15pm Tue, Thur, Sat.* **Admission** *free. Tours £10-15.* **Map** *p154 P6.*

This tiny museum documents the history of the Charterhouse from the present day to the black death, from details of the lives of some of the Brothers who still live in these almshouses, past some neat artefacts – not least a sacred statue recut into the shape of a brick that was built into a wall after

Sir John Soane's Museum

the 16th-century Dissolution of the Monasteries – to the touchingly displayed skeleton of a victim of that most deadly mid 13th-century plague. Be sure to drop into the chapel (past a plaque dedicated the author William Thackeray), where an old wooden door – half burnt away – records how close the Charterhouse came to destruction in the Blitz. The tours last an hour (two hours if you opt for one led by a Brother) and are well worth the money: not only do you hear the whole history of the place, but you get access to private areas of the Charterhouse – such as the Great Hall and the solitary monks' cells, complete with hatch by the main door where food came in and, er, rubbish came out.

❤ Sir John Soane's Museum
*13 Lincoln's Inn Fields, WC2A 3BP (7405 2107, www.soane.org). Holborn tube. **Open** 10am-5pm Tue-Sat; also 6-9pm 1st Tue of mth. Tours 11am, noon Tue, Sat; noon Thur, Fri. **Admission** free; donations appreciated. Tours £10. **Map** p154 N6.*
When he wasn't designing notable buildings (among them the original Bank of England), Sir John Soane (1753-1837) obsessively collected art, furniture and architectural ornamentation. In the 19th century, he turned his house into a museum to which, he said, 'amateurs and students' should have access. The result is this perfectly amazing place.

The modest rooms were modified by Soane with ingenious devices to channel and direct daylight, and to expand space, including walls that fold out to display paintings by Canaletto, Turner and Hogarth. The Tivoli Recess – the city's first gallery of contemporary sculpture, with a stained-glass window and plaster sunbursts – has been restored, and further stained glass illuminates

a bust of Shakespeare. The Breakfast Room has a beautiful domed ceiling, inset with convex mirrors, while the Monument Court contains a sarcophagus of alabaster, so fine that it's almost translucent, that was carved for the pharaoh Seti I (1291-78 BC) and discovered in the Valley of the Kings. There are also numerous examples of Soane's eccentricity, not least the cell for his imaginary monk 'Padre Giovanni'.

A recent £7 million restoration project has opened up previously unseen parts of the building. The second floor contains the Model Room, open for the first time since 1850. It holds Britain's largest collection of historical architectural models.

Somerset House & the Embankment Galleries
*Strand, WC2R 1LA (7845 4600, www.somersethouse.org.uk). Temple tube. **Open** 10am-6pm Mon, Tue, Sat, Sun (last entry to galleries 5pm); 11am-8pm Wed-Fri (last entry to galleries 7pm). Tours Tue, Thur, Sat. **Admission** Courtyard & terrace free. Embankment Galleries prices vary. Tours free; check website for details. **Map** p154 N8.*
The original Somerset House was a Tudor palace commissioned by the Duke of Somerset. In 1775, it was demolished to make way for the first purpose-built office block in the world. Architect Sir William Chambers spent the last 20 years of his life working on this neoclassical edifice overlooking the Thames, built to accommodate learned societies such as the Royal Academy and government departments. The taxmen are still here, but the rest of the building is open to the public. Attractions include the **Courtauld Gallery**, the handsome fountain court and several eating options. Downstairs on the Thames side of the building,

the **Embankment Galleries** house exhibitions on a grander scale, and a Christmas market.

Temple Church

Off Fleet Street, EC4Y 7BB (7353 3470, www.templechurch.com). Chancery Lane or Temple tube. **Open** *varies.* **Admission** *£5; £3 reductions; free under 16s.* **Map** *p154 O7.*

Inspired by Jerusalem's Church of the Holy Sepulchre, the Temple Church was the chapel of the Knights Templar. The rounded apse contains the worn gravestones of several Crusader knights, but the church was refurbished by Wren and the Victorians, and was damaged in the Blitz. Not that that puts off the wild speculations of fans of Dan Brown's *The Da Vinci Code*. There are organ recitals most Wednesdays at 1.15pm.

Two Temple Place

2 Temple Place, WC2R 3BD (7836 3715, www.twotempleplace.org). Temple tube. **Open** *Exhibitions late Jan-mid Apr 10am-4.30pm Mon, Thur-Sat; 10am-9pm Wed; 11am-4.30pm Sun. Private tours only mid Apr-late Jan.* **Admission** *free. Tours free but must be booked in advance.* **Map** *p154 N8.*

The pale Portland-stone exterior and oriel windows here are handsome – but the interior is extraordinary. You get a hint about what's to come before you open the door: look right and there's a cherub holding an old-fashioned telephone to his ear. Built as an estate office in 1895 to the close specifications of William Waldorf Astor, Two Temple Place now opens to the public for three months a year with immensely popular exhibitions of 'publicly-owned art from around the UK', arranged by an up-and-coming curator. Ring the bell and you're warmly welcomed by volunteers into a house with decor that combines sublime, extravagant craftsmanship with a thorough lack of interest in coherence: above porphyry tiles, the Three Musketeers adorn the banisters of a staircase; intricately carved literary characters crowd the first floor, mixing Shakespeare with Fenimore Cooper; the medieval-style Great Hall, with lovely stained glass, crams together 54 random busts – Voltaire, Marlborough and Anne Boleyn enjoying the company of Mary Queen of Scots.

Restaurants

Foxlow ££

69-73 St John Street, EC1M 4AN (7014 8070, www.foxlow.co.uk). Farringdon tube/rail. **Open** *noon-3pm, 5.30-10.30pm Mon-Fri; 11am-3.30pm, 5.30-10pm Sat; 11am-3.30pm Sun.* **Map** *p154 P6* ❷ *International*

Will Beckett and Huw Gott, the duo behind the very popular Hawksmoor steakhouses, scored again at Foxlow. It has a cosily masculine vibe (warm woods, low lighting, comfy retro-themed furniture) and a compact menu of meaty dishes to comfort and soothe, plus impeccably sourced steaks. 'Smokehouse rillettes' sees a smoky mound of beef, turkey, pork and lardo knocked into shape by a tart jumble of cucumber, pickles and capers. The youthful staff are an absolute marvel, with bags of personality, beaming smiles and a nothing's-too-much-trouble attitude.

Look Mum No Hands £

49 Old Street, EC1V 9HX (7253 1025, www.lookmumnohands. com). Barbican tube or Old Street tube/rail. **Open** *7.30am-10pm Mon-Fri; 8.30am-10pm Sat; 9am-10pm Sun. Food served noon-9pm Mon-Fri; 2.30-9pm Sat, Sun.* **Map** *p154 Q5* ❸ *Café*

Look Mum No Hands

Look Mum is a cycle-friendly café-bar with cycle parking in a courtyard, a small workshop and plenty of space to hang out, snack, use the Wi-Fi and – in the evenings – drink bottled beer or well-priced wine. Live afternoon screenings of cycle races take place in the big main room. The food is simple: expect cured meat platters, baked tarts, pastries and cakes.

♥ Modern Pantry £££
47-48 St John's Square, EC1V 4JJ (7553 9210, www. themodernpantry.co.uk). Farringdon tube/rail. **Open** *Café 8-11am, noon-10pm Mon; 8-11am, noon-10.30pm Tue-Fri; 9am-4pm, 6-10.30pm Sat; 10am-4pm, 6-10pm Sun. Restaurant noon-3pm, 6-10.30pm Tue-Fri; 9am-4pm, 6-10.30pm Sat; 10am-4pm Sun.* **Map** *p154 P5* 4 *International*
Chef Anna Hansen creates enticing fusion dishes that make the most of unusual ingredients sourced from around the globe. Antipodean and Asian flavours (yuzu, tamarind) pop up frequently, alongside plenty of seasonal British fare (wild garlic, purple sprouting broccoli); the combinations can seem bewildering on the page, but rarely falter in execution, and the signature dish of sugar-cured prawn omelette with chilli, coriander and spring onion is always a winner. The stylish ground-floor café is quite feminine in feel, with soothing white and grey paintwork, white furniture and burnished copper light fittings; there's a more formal restaurant upstairs.

♥ Moro ££
34-36 Exmouth Market, EC1R 4QE (7833 8336, www.moro.co.uk). Farringdon tube/rail or bus 19, 38, 341. **Open** *Restaurant noon-2.30pm, 6-10.30pm Mon-Sat; 12.30-2.45pm Sun. Tapas available noon-3.30pm, 4.30-10.30pm Mon-Sat from the bar.* **Map** *p154 O5* 5 *North African/Spanish*
Back in 1997, in a former supermarket on Exmouth Market, Sam(antha) and Sam Clarks set the benchmark for a distinctly British style of Mediterranean cooking that puts a North African twist on Iberian food. Their restaurant (and beautifully produced cookbooks) is still in London's culinary front rank some 20 years later. Moro provides a spectacular showcase for modern Spanish and Portuguese wines, and vibrantly fresh food that throws out surprising and pleasurable flavours at every turn.

Next door to Moro is its offshoot Morito (no.32, EC1R 4QE, 7278 7007, www.morito.co.uk), a fine no-bookings tapas bar.

St John £££
26 St John Street, EC1M 4AY (7251 0848, www.stjohngroup.uk.com). Barbican tube or Farringdon tube/rail. **Open** *Restaurant noon-3pm, 6-11pm Mon-Fri; 6-11pm Sat; 12.30-4pm Sun. Bar 11am-11pm Mon-Fri; 6-11pm Sat; noon-5pm Sun.* **Map** *p154 P6* 6 *British*
Fergus Henderson and Trevor Gulliver's restaurant has

been praised to the skies for reacquainting the British with the full possibilities of native produce, and especially anything gutsy and offal-ish. Perhaps as influential, however, has been its almost defiantly casual style. The mezzanine dining room in the former Smithfield smokehouse has bare white walls, battered floorboards and tables lined up canteen-style. St John's cooking is famously full-on, but also sophisticated, concocting flavours that are delicate as well as rich, as in black cuttlefish and onions, with a deep-flavoured ink-based sauce with a hint of mint. The airy bar here is a great place for a drink and a no-fuss snack.

Pubs & bars

♥ 7 Tales
*Sosharu, 64 Turnmill Street, EC1M 5RR (3805 2304, sosharulondon. com/seventales-board). Farringdon tube/rail. **Open** noon-2.15pm, 5.30-10pm Mon-Thur; noon-2.15pm, 5.30-10.30pm Fri, Sat. **Map** p154 O6* ❶
In the basement of Jason Atherton's restaurant (for more on Atherton, *see p136*), 7 Tales is a wonderfully cool cocktail bar with a playful tone. In homage to Tokyo, the walls are plastered with black-and-white images of the city's street signage, picked out in the glow from a cheeky neon sign that says 'drink sake stay soba'. It's not pure silliness, though – the creative cocktails are absolutely flawless, the music selection is slick-as-hell hip hop and staff are just plain charming.

Black Friar
*174 Queen Victoria Street, EC4V 4EG (7236 5474, www. nicholsonspubs.co.uk). Blackfriars tube/rail. **Open** 9am-11pm Mon-Sat; noon-10.30pm Sun. **Map** p154 P7* ❷

Built in 1875 on the site of a medieval Dominican friary, the Black Friar had its interior completely remodelled in the Arts and Crafts style. It is now part of the Nicholson's stable – the group runs most of the trad pubs in the City, serving moderate food but decent real ales – so you'll come here for the intricate friezes and carved slogans ('Industry is Ale', 'Haste is Slow') of the main saloon bar. You're basically sinking an ale in the middle of a stunning work of art. Admittedly, there's a far more prosaic bar adjoining it, but this remains one of London's most interesting pub interiors.

Jerusalem Tavern
*55 Britton Street, EC1M 5UQ (7490 4281, www.stpetersbrewery.co.uk/london-pub). Farringdon tube/rail. **Open** 11am-11pm Mon-Fri. **Map** p154 P6* ❹
Despite the carefully scuffed wooden floors, peeling paint and tables that look like they've had centuries-worth of pints spilled on them, the Jerusalem Tavern has actually only been a pub since 1990 – it was originally a coffeehouse. Still, the place feels embedded in the history of the area, notwithstanding nods to modernity from the poshed-up bar snacks, taxidermy cabinets and beer from the excellent St Peter's Brewery in Suffolk that includes premium-strength IPAs and whisky-accented ale. Crowds frequently spill out onto the side streets.

Ye Olde Mitre
*1 Ely Court, EC1N 6SJ (7405 4751, www.yeoldemitreholborn.co.uk). Farringdon tube/rail. **Open** 11am-11pm Mon-Fri. Food served 11.30am-9.30pm Mon-Fri. **Map** p154 O6* ❻
Largely due to its location – down a barely marked alley between Hatton Garden's jewellers and Ely Place – this little traditional pub,

the foundation of which dates to 1546, is a favourite of 'secret London' lists. There's always a good range of ales on offer at the tiny central bar, but people come for the atmosphere: lots of cosy dark wood and some overlooked curiosities, such as the tree in the front bar. It's a cherry tree that Good Queen Bess is said to have danced around, but now supports a corner of the bar.

❤ Zetter Townhouse

49-50 St John's Square, EC1V 4JJ (7324 4545, www.thezettertownhouse.com). Farringdon tube/rail. **Open** *7am-midnight Mon-Wed, Sun; 7am-1am Thur-Sat.* **Map** *p154 P5* ❼

The decor at Townhouse embodies a 'more is more' philosophy: every square inch of surface area is occupied by something lovely. The result: one of the most beautiful bars in London. The cocktail list is high quality, devised by Tony Conigliaro, the man behind the brilliant 69 Colebrooke Row (*see p173*), among others. Even though Conigliaro is known as a techno-wizard, the original drinks here are fairly simple and restrained, as well as being typically wonderful. Among the house cocktails, check out the Köln Martini, Lime Blossom Fizz and the White Mrytle Kir. Service is friendly and helpful.

Entertainment

❤ Fabric

77A Charterhouse Street, Clerkenwell, EC1M 6HJ (7336 8898, www.fabriclondon.com). Farringdon tube/rail. **Open** *11pm-6am Fri, Sun; 11pm-8am Sat.* **Admission** *£21-£27.* **Map** *p154 P6* ❷ *Nightclub*

Fabric is the club that most party people come to see in London – no wonder there was a major campaign to keep it open when two drug-related deaths led to Fabric being temporarily shut down in autumn 2016. Located in a former meatpacking warehouse, it has a well-deserved reputation as the capital's biggest and best club. Line-ups across the three rooms are legendary, with the world's most famous DJs bringing the finest low-frequencies and the deepest grooves, as the hip crowds that pack out the dancefloors testify.

The City

Fewer than 10,000 souls are resident within the Square Mile (1.21 square miles, in fact), but every working day the population increases tenfold, as bankers, brokers, lawyers and traders storm into their towering office blocks. The City still holds to boundaries set by the second-century walls of Roman Londinium (a few sections of which remain), although it then had six times more inhabitants than it does now. The streets are full of historic gems, but the real crowd-pullers are **St Paul's** and the **Tower of London**.

In the know
Get the gen

Newcomers to the City are advised to head straight to **St Paul's** (*see p162*), not just for the beauty of the architecture, but because the spiky-roofed **City of London Information Centre** (7332 3456, www.cityoflondon.gov.uk) is there, on the river side of the cathedral. Open daily (9.30am-5.30pm Mon-Sat; 10am-4pm Sun), it has information on sights, events, walks and talks, as well as offering tours with specialist guides, and has free Wi-Fi.

💙 St Paul's Cathedral

*St Paul's Churchyard, EC4M 8AD
(7246 8348, www.stpauls.co.uk).
St Paul's tube. **Open** 8.30am-
4.30pm Mon-Sat. Galleries, crypt
& ambulatory 9.30am-4.15pm
Mon-Sat. Special events may cause
closure; check before visiting. Tours
of cathedral & crypt 10am, 11am,
1pm, 2pm Mon-Sat. **Admission**
Cathedral, crypt & gallery (incl
tour) £18; £8-£16 reductions; £44
family; free under-6s. Book online
for reductions. **Map** p154 P7.*

St Paul's Cathedral hasn't
been lucky through most of its
history, but it has been at the
centre of some of London's most
momentous events. The first
cathedral to St Paul was built
on this site in 604, but fell to
Viking marauders. Its Norman
replacement, a magnificent
Gothic structure with a 490ft
spire (taller than any London
building until the 1960s), burned
in the Great Fire. The current
church was commissioned in
1673 from Sir Christopher Wren,
as the centrepiece of London's
resurgence from the ashes, and
though modern buildings now
encroach on the cathedral from
all sides, the passing of three
centuries has done nothing to
diminish the appeal of the master
architect's finest work.

After £40m-worth of restoration
removed most of the Victorian
grime from the outside walls,
the extravagant main façade
looks as brilliant today as it must
have when the last stone was
placed in 1708. The vast open
spaces of the interior contain
memorials to national heroes
such as Wellington and Lawrence
of Arabia. The statue of John
Donne, metaphysical poet and
former Dean of St Paul's, is often
overlooked, but it's the only
monument to have been saved
from Old St Paul's. There are also
more modern works, including a
Henry Moore sculpture and Bill
Viola's video installation *Martyrs
(Earth, Air, Fire, Water)*. The
Whispering Gallery, inside the
dome, is reached by 259 steps from
the main hall; the acoustics here
are so good that a whisper can be
bounced clearly to the other side

of the dome. Steps continue up to first the Stone Gallery (119 tighter, steeper steps), with its high external balustrades, then outside to the Golden Gallery (152 steps), with its giddying views.

Before leaving, head down to the maze-like crypt, where, alongside memorials to such dignitaries as Alexander Fleming, William Blake and Admiral Nelson, you'll find the small, plain tomb of Christopher Wren himself. At their request, Millais and Turner were buried nearby.

Bank of England Museum

Entrance on Bartholomew Lane, EC2R 8AH (7601 5545, www. bankofengland.co.uk/museum). Bank tube/DLR. **Open** *10am-5pm Mon-Fri.* **Admission** *free.* **Map** *p154 R7.*
Housed inside the former Stock Offices of the Bank of England (there's a full-size recreation of Sir John Soane's Bank Stock Office from 1693), this surprisingly lively museum explores the history of the national bank. As well as ancient coins and original artwork for British banknotes, the museum offers a rare chance to lift nearly 30lbs of gold bar (you reach into a secure box, closely monitored by CCTV) and displays Kenneth Grahame's resignation letter – the *Wind in the Willows* author worked here for three decades.

Guildhall Art Gallery

Guildhall Yard, off Gresham Street, EC2V 5AE (7332 3700, www. cityoflondon.org.uk). St Paul's tube or Bank tube/DLR. **Open** *10am-5pm Mon-Sat; noon-4pm Sun.* **Admission** *free. Temporary exhibitions vary.* **Map** *p154 Q7.*
The City of London's gallery had always been a favourite of ours, even before a comprehensive rehang in 2014, which saw dull portraits of royalty and long-gone mayors replaced by the entertaining and informative thematic display of the Victorian Collection. Here, you'll find lushly romantic and superbly camp Pre-Raphaelite works by Frederic Leighton, Dante Gabriel Rossetti and John Everett Millais; you wouldn't mess with Clytemnestra, as painted by John Collier in 1832. A few steps down from the entrance, a mezzanine gallery holds sun-filled abstracts by Matthew Smith; continuing to the Undercroft you'll find various

London-themed pieces, some of historical and sociological more than artistic merit, but fascinating nonetheless. There are also neat heritage displays of Roman artefacts and medieval charters that explain the background to Dick Whittington, Gog and Magog and various other topics. Still towering over the temporary exhibition spaces on this floor is John Singleton Copley's *Defeat of the Floating Batteries at Gibraltar*, all two storeys of it.

❤ Monument

*Monument Street, EC3R 8AH (7626 2717, www.themonument. info). Monument tube. **Open** Apr-Sept 9.30am-6pm daily. Oct-Mar 9.30am-5.30pm daily. **Admission** £4.50; £2.30-£3 reductions; free under-5s. **Map** p154 R8.*

One of 17th-century London's most important landmarks, the Monument is a magnificent Portland stone column, topped by a landmark golden orb with more than 30,000 fiery leaves of gold. The Monument was designed by Sir Christopher Wren and his (often overlooked) associate Robert Hooke as a memorial to the Great Fire. The world's tallest free-standing stone column, it measures 202ft from the ground to the tip of its golden flames, exactly the distance east to Farriner's bakery in Pudding Lane, where the fire is supposed to have begun on 2 September 1666. The

viewing platform is surrounded by a lightweight mesh cage, but the views are great – you have to walk 311 steps up the internal spiral staircase to enjoy them, though.

❤ Museum of London

*150 London Wall, EC2Y 5HN (7001 9844, www.museumoflondon.org. uk). Barbican or St Paul's tube. **Open** 10am-6pm daily. **Admission** free; suggested donation £5. **Map** p154 Q6.*

One of the original settlements established by the Romans after their first invasion in 43AD, Londinium – as it was known then – has survived war, plague and fire to become the bustling metropolis it is today. This journey, from ancient marshland to one of the greatest cities on earth, is documented through a mind-boggling array of exhibits alongside innovative interactive displays.

On the entrance floor, the social history of London is told in chronological displays that begin with 'London Before London', where artefacts include flint axes from 300,000 BC, found near Piccadilly. 'Roman London' includes an impressive reconstructed dining room complete with mosaic floor. Sound effects and audio-visual displays illustrate the medieval, Elizabethan and Jacobean city, with particular focus on the plague and the Great Fire, which marked 400-year anniversaries in 2016.

Downstairs, the lower-ground-floor gallery tells the story of the city from 1666 to the present day. This newer space features everything from an unexploded World War II bomb to the impressive golden Lord Mayor's coach (it dates from 1757). There are displays and brilliant interactives on poverty (an actual debtor's cell has been reconstructed, complete with graffiti), finance, shopping and 20th-century fashion,

---

In the know
Street-wise museum

The **Museum of London** and sister-museum the **Museum of London Docklands** (*see p186*) have issued a number of excellent free apps, including Streetmuseum and Streetmuseum Londinium. They offer archive images and /or information about historic sites, geolocated to where you're standing.

💙 Tower of London

*Tower Hill, EC3N 4AB (3166 6000, www.hrp.org.uk /tower-of-london). Tower Hill tube or Tower Gateway DLR. **Open** Mar-Oct 10am-5.30pm Mon, Sun; 9am-5.30pm Tue-Sat. Nov-Feb 10am-4.30pm Mon, Sun; 9am-4.30pm Tue-Sat. **Admission** £25; £12-£19.50 reductions; £45-63 family; free under-5s. Book online for reductions. **Map** p154 S8.*

If you haven't been to the Tower of London before, you should go now. Despite the exhausting crowds, this is one of Britain's finest historical attractions. Who wouldn't be fascinated by a close-up look at the crown of Queen Victoria or the armour (and prodigious codpiece) of King Henry VIII? The buildings of the Tower span 900 years of – mostly violent – history, and the bastions and battlements house a series of interactive displays on the lives of British monarchs, and the often excruciatingly painful deaths of traitors. There's easily enough to do here to fill a whole day, and it's worth joining one of the entertaining free tours led by the Yeoman Warders (or Beefeaters).

Make the Crown Jewels your first stop. Beyond satisfyingly solid vault doors are such treasures of state as the Monarch's Sceptre, mounted with the Cullinan I diamond, and the Imperial State Crown, which is worn by the Queen each year for the opening of Parliament.

The other big draw is the Royal Armoury in the central White Tower, with its swords, armour, poleaxes, morning stars (spiky maces) and other gruesome tools for separating human beings from their body parts. Kids are entertained by swordsmanship games, coin-minting activities and even a child-sized longbow. The garderobes (medieval toilets) also seem to appeal.

Back outside is Tower Green, where executions of prisoners of noble birth were carried out (the last execution, of World War II German spy Joseph Jakobs, was in 1941). Overlooking the green, Beauchamp Tower, dating from 1280, has intriguing graffiti by the prisoners who were held here. The Tower only ceased functioning as a prison in 1952 and over the years counted Anne Boleyn, Rudolf Hess and the Krays among its inmates.

Towards the entrance, the 13th-century Bloody Tower is another must-see. The ground floor is a reconstruction of Sir Walter Raleigh's study, the upper floor details the fate of the Princes in the Tower.

Sky Garden

including a recreated Georgian pleasure garden.

The museum's biggest obstacle had always been its location: the entrance is two floors above street level, and hidden behind a dark and rather featureless brick wall. With visitor numbers higher than ever, the museum is set to move half a mile from its current location to take up residence in the abandoned Victorian market at Smithfield in 2021.

💙 Sky Garden

20 Fenchurch Street (entrance via Philpot Lane), EC3M 8AF (7337 2344, http://skygarden. london). Monument tube. **Open** *10am-6pm Mon-Fri; 11am-9pm Sat, Sun. Advance booking required.* **Admission** *free. Photo ID required.* **Map** *p154 R8.*

The distinctive but not widely admired skyscraper, 20 Fenchurch Street (better known as the Walkie Talkie), has a major calling card: a free public space with spectacular views of London. After passing through airport-style security, a lift zips you up 35 floors to the soaring space on the top floors. Flights of steps rise through lush, leafy plants to a series of terraces and an open-air piazza.

Tower Bridge Exhibition

Tower Bridge Road, SE1 2UP (7403 3761, www.towerbridge.org.uk). Tower Hill tube or Tower Gateway DLR. **Open** *Apr-Sept 10am-5.30pm daily. Oct-Mar 9.30am-5pm daily.* **Admission** *£9; £3.90-£6.30 reductions; £14.10-£22.50 family; free under-5s.* **Map** *p154 S9.*

Opened in 1894, this is the 'London Bridge' that wasn't sold to America. Originally powered by steam, the drawbridge is now opened by electric rams when big ships need to venture upstream (check when the bridge is next due to be raised on the bridge's website or follow the Twitter feed). An entertaining exhibition on its history is displayed in the old

In the know
Getting yourself in

Visitors must book a 90-minute timeslot on the **Sky Garden** website at least three days in advance. If no slots are available, try booking a table at the **Sky Pod Bar** (cocktails there cost around a tenner) or at one of the two restaurants (the **Darwin Brasserie** is cheaper than the **Fenchurch Restaurant**): all three also give access to the viewing floors.

steamrooms and the west walkway, which provides a crow's-nest view along the Thames. Since 2014, when glass panels were placed in the walkways, you've also been able to look directly down past your own feet at the river below – assuming you're not prone to vertigo.

Restaurants

♥ Duck & Waffle £££

Floor 40, Heron Tower, 110 Bishopsgate, EC2N 4AY (3640 7310, http://duckandwaffle. com). Liverpool Street tube/rail. **Open** *24hrs daily. Food served 6-11am, 11.30am-4pm, 5-11pm, 11.30pm-5am Mon-Fri; 6am-4pm, 5-11pm, 11.30pm-5am Sat, Sun.* **Map** *p154 S7* ❶ *Modern European*
There's a dedicated entrance in Heron Tower from which a glass lift whizzes you up to Duck & Waffle on the 40th floor, or its glitzier sibling Sushisamba (*see p168*) below. The views are stunning – if you're pointed the right way and, preferably, sitting at a window table (many of which are for couples). Food is an on-trend mix of pricey small plates, raw offerings (oysters, ceviche) and a few main courses (including the namesake duck confit and waffle), as well as sensational barbecue-spiced crispy pigs' ears. Service wavers between keen and offhand, and the acoustics are terrible. But Duck & Waffle is open 24/7 – even though the menu is limited between midnight and 5am, all-night dining is pretty much unheard of in London.

Sweetings ££££

39 Queen Victoria Street, EC4N 4SA (7248 3062, www. sweetingsrestaurant.co.uk). Mansion House tube. **Open** *11.30am-3pm Mon-Fri.* **Map** *p154 Q7* ❼ *Fish & seafood*

Things don't change much at this enduring City classic, and that's the way everyone likes it. The walls remain covered with photos of old sports teams, and many of the staff have been here for years. Lobster and crab bisques preface a choice of fish and seafood dishes that read and taste like upmarket versions of a pub-side stall – smoked fish, whitebait, trout and so forth. Top-quality fish are then served fried, grilled or poached to order. The handful of more elaborate dishes includes an excellent fish pie.

Pubs & bars

City Social Bar

Tower 42, 25 Old Broad Street, EC2N 1HQ (7877 7703, http:// citysociallondon.com). Liverpool Street tube/Overground/rail. **Open** *noon-late Mon-Fri; 4pm-late Sat.* **Map** *p154 R7* ❸
Chef-about-town Jason Atherton (*see p136*) took over what had been a pretty run-of-the-mill City restaurant on the 24th floor of what used to be the NatWest Tower – and made it pretty terrific. It is mighty expensive, however, so we recommend the attached bar, which anyone can just show up to – having negotiated two lots of security, an escalator and at least one lift. Still, the bar food and drink is of a far higher standard than you might expect. The cocktails are great, with just enough invention to make them worth the lofty prices: the Oh My Gourd!, for example, comprises pumpkin-infused Tapatío Blanco tequila, lychee, lime, agave – and a pumpkin crisp. Bar snacks aren't so decently priced, but are characteristically Atherton: a 'ploughman's basket' (£15) came with cheese, bread and things in little jars, picnic-style on a checked cloth.

Sushisamba

*Floors 38 & 39, Heron Tower, 110 Bishopsgate, EC2N 4AY (3640 7330, www.sushisamba.com). Liverpool Street tube/rail. **Open** 11.30am-1.30am Mon, Tue, Sun; 11.30am-2am Wed-Sat.* **Map** p154 S7 ❺

Duck & Waffle (*see opposite*) is a floor higher and has 24-hour opening, but Sushisamba's two small bars and outdoor roof terrace bar have the edge for views; tell the door staff you don't have a meal reservation but are going to the bar, then take the lift to the 39th floor to avoid another volley of questions, and walk on in. The few cocktails are a little unimaginative – try the saké list instead. But this is a classic destination bar: views, a blinged-up crowd, and relatively easy access. If you do want to eat, the restaurant serves a fusion of Japanese, Brazilian and Peruvian cuisines, with a highlight being the sushi. That's not an eye-opener these days, but then your eyes are bound to be elsewhere.

Shops & services

For a roof-level view of St Paul's Cathedral, take the glass elevator to the top floor of the sprawling **One New Change mall** (New Change Road, EC4M 9AF, 7002 8900, www.onenewchange. com), where you can enjoy it for free, or accompanied by a pricey drink or tapas.

Entertainment

❤ Barbican Centre

Silk Street, EC2Y 8DS (information 7638 4141, tickets 7638 8891, www. barbican.org.uk). Barbican tube or Moorgate tube/rail. **Box office** *10am-8pm Mon-Sat; 11am-8pm Sun. Tickets £10-£70.* **Map** p154 Q6 ❶ *Concert hall*

Europe's largest multi-arts centre is easier to navigate after a renovation – although 'easier' still isn't quite the same as 'with ease', so allow a little extra time to get to your seat. The programming remains as rich as ever, and the London Symphony Orchestra, with Sir Simon Rattle its new music director from September 2017, remains in residence. The BBC Symphony Orchestra also performs an annual series of concerts, including the weekend composer portrait Total Immersion, and there's a laudable amount of contemporary classical music, not least an ambitious ENO production in 2015 covering the events of 9/11. Beyond classical, programming falls into a wide range of genres from Sufi music to New York rock legends.

LSO St Luke's

UBS & LSO Music Education Centre, 161 Old Street, EC1V 9NG (information 7490 3939, tickets 7638 8891, www.lso.co.uk/ lsostlukes). Old Street tube/rail. **Box office** *(at the Barbican Centre) 10am-8pm Mon-Sat; 11am-8pm Sun. Tickets free-£40.* **Map** p154 Q5 ❸ *Concert hall*

Built by Nicholas Hawksmoor in the 18th century, this Grade I-listed church was beautifully converted into a performance and rehearsal space by the LSO several years ago. The orchestra occasionally welcomes the public for open rehearsals (book ahead); the more formal side of the programme takes in global sounds alongside classical music, including lunchtime concerts every Thursday that are broadcast on BBC Radio 3.

North London

North London's list of famous former residents gives a good idea of the scope of the area – from Amy Winehouse and Noel Gallagher to Karl Marx, John Keats and Charles Dickens, a huge variety of people have been drawn to its mix of pretty, sleepy retreats and buzzing, creative party zones. First stop is normally **Camden Town**, with its markets, indie pubs and general alternative vibe, but there's further joy to be found in the leafy squares of **Islington**. Further to the north, **Hampstead** and **Highgate** offer genteel village life and a glorious public space: **Hampstead Heath**.

Best for kids
Don't miss the penguins at ZSL
London Zoo (*p171*).

Best for teens
Camden Market (*p173*) is heaven
for teens, hell for their parents,
and an experience for everyone.

Best for culture and calm
At Kenwood House (*p170*) you can
see a Rembrandt, have a
café lunch and stroll on the Heath.

Best cocktails
Drink beneath the laboratory of a
cocktail magician at 69 Colebrook
Row (*p173*).

Best night out
Watch ground-breaking theatre at
the Almeida (*p174*). The Forum,
the Roundhouse and the Union
Chapel (*p176*) are among many
legendary music venues in
Camden Town.

Sights & museums

Highgate Cemetery

*Swains Lane, N6 6PJ (8340
1834, www.highgate-cemetery.
org). Archway tube.* **Open** *East
Cemetery Mar-Oct 10am-5pm
Mon-Fri; 11am-5pm Sat, Sun.
Nov-Feb 10am-4pm Mon-Fri;
11am-4pm Sat, Sun. Tours 2pm
Sat. West Cemetery by tour only,
check website for times.* **Admission**
*£4; free under-18s. Tours East
Cemetery £8, £4 reductions. West
Cemetery £12; £6 reductions.*
The final resting place of some
very famous Londoners, Highgate
Cemetery is a wonderfully overgrown
maze of ivy-cloaked Victorian tombs
and time-shattered urns. Visitors
can wander at their own pace
through the East Cemetery, with its
memorials to Karl Marx, George Eliot
and Douglas Adams, but the most
atmospheric part of the cemetery is
the foliage-shrouded West Cemetery,
laid out in 1839. Only accessible on
an organised tour (book ahead, dress
respectfully and arrive 30 minutes
early), the shady paths wind past
gloomy catacombs, grand Victorian
pharaonic tombs, and the graves
of notables such as poet Christina
Rossetti, scientist Michael Faraday
and poisoned Russian dissident
Alexander Litvinenko.

♥ Kenwood House/Iveagh Bequest

*Hampstead Lane, NW3 7JR (8348
1286, www.english-heritage.org.
uk). Hampstead tube, or Golders
Green tube then bus 210.* **Open**
10am-4pm daily. **Admission** *free.*
Set in lovely grounds at the top of
Hampstead Heath, Kenwood House
is every inch the country manor
house. Built in 1616, the mansion
was remodelled in the 18th century
for William Murray, who made the
vital court ruling in 1772 that made
it illegal to own slaves in England.
The house was purchased by brewing
magnate Edward Guinness, who
was kind enough to donate his art
collection to the nation in 1927. After

ZSL London Zoo

extensive, splendid renovations, it reopened in 2014. The interiors have been returned to a state that enhances such highlights of the collection as Vermeer's *The Guitar Player*, Gainsborough's *Countess Howe*, and one of Rembrandt's finest self-portraits (dating to c1663). There's a terrific kids' room with games and activities too.

💜 ZSL London Zoo
Regent's Park, NW1 4RY (7722 3333, www.zsl.org/london-zoo). Baker Street or Camden Town tube then bus 274, C2. **Open** *daily, times vary; check website for details.* **Admission** *£29.75; £22-£26.80 reductions; free under-3s. Book online for reductions.*
London Zoo has been open in one form or another since 1826. Spread over 36 acres and containing more than 600 species, it cares for many of the endangered variety – part of the entry price (pretty steep at nearly £30 in peak season) goes towards the ZSL's projects around the world. Regular events include 'animals in action' and keeper talks. Exhibits are entertaining: look out, for example, for the re-creation of a kitchen overrun with large cockroaches. In the fabulous 'In with the Lemurs' exhibit, you get to walk through jungle habitat with the long-tailed primates leaping over your head. Other major attractions are 'Tiger Territory', where Sumatran tigers can be watched through floor-to-ceiling windows, and 'Gorilla Kingdom'. The relaunched 'Rainforest Life' biodome and the 'Meet the Monkeys' attractions allow visitors to walk through enclosures that recreate the natural habitat of, respectively, tree anteaters and sloths, and black-capped Bolivian squirrel monkeys. Personal encounters of the avian kind can be had in the Victorian Blackburn Pavilion – as well as at Penguin Beach, where the black-and-white favourites are plainly visible as they swim underwater; responses to the snakes and crocodiles in the reptile house tend to involve a good proportion of shudders. Bring a picnic and you could easily spend the day here.

Restaurants

Bull & Last ££
168 Highgate Road, NW5 1QS (7267 3641, www.thebullandlast.co.uk). Kentish Town tube/rail then bus 214, C2, or Gospel Oak Overground then bus C11. **Open** *Bar noon-11pm Mon-Thur; noon-midnight Fri, Sat; noon-10.30pm Sun. Restaurant breakfast 9-11am Sat, Sun; other hours vary.* Gastropub
For a place with such a good reputation for its food, the Bull & Last is refreshingly pubby: heavy wooden furniture, velvet drapes, stuffed animals and old prints decorate both the bar and the upstairs dining room. The latter is a calmer and cooler place to eat than the ground-floor bar, and allows diners to focus on dishes such as pig's cheek with watermelon pickle, basil and sesame. There are (big) roasts at weekends, a changing selection of beers and ciders from small breweries and a decent wine list.

Ottolenghi ££
287 Upper Street, N1 2TZ (7288 1454, www.ottolenghi.co.uk). Angel tube or Highbury & Islington tube/Overground. **Open** *8am-10.30pm Mon-Sat; 9am-7pm Sun.* Café
Hit cookbooks have made this flagship branch of the burgeoning Ottolenghi empire a point of pilgrimage for foodies the world over. French toast made from brioche and served with crème fraîche and a thin berry and muscat compote makes a heady start to the day. Or there's welsh rarebit, scrambled eggs with smoked salmon or a lively chorizo-spiked

Sporting Success

Sports fans will want to make a pilgrimage to one of London's iconic sporting venues

In northwest London, **Lord's Cricket Ground** (St John's Wood, NW8 8QN, 7616 8500, www.lords. org) is the headquarters of the Marylebone Cricket Club (MCC), the official guardian of the sport. The MCC Museum has the famous and unfeasibly tiny Ashes urn and plenty of player memorabilia, while the tour takes in the Dressing Rooms, the Long Room, the Victorian Pavilion and the Media Centre. Further out of town, an arch on the horizon marks **Wembley Stadium** (Empire Way, Wembley, HA9 0WS, 0844 980 8001, www.wembleystadium.com). Wembley has been hosting the nation's biggest sporting spectacles since 1923, but its legendary status was secured when England won the World Cup Final here in 1966. The Wembley Tour is led by enthusiastic guides and includes the changing rooms, the players' tunnel and the chance to climb the steps up to where the winners collect their medals. In southwest London the **Wimbledon Lawn Tennis Museum** (All England Lawn Tennis Club, Church Road, Wimbledon, SW19 5AE, 8946 6131, www.wimbledon. com/museum) covers the history of tennis, with interactive exhibits and a behind-the-scenes tour. Finally, in East London, don't miss the multiple attractions and distractions of the **Queen Elizabeth Olympic Park** (see p187).

(see p187)

take on baked beans served with sourdough, fried egg and black pudding. In the evening (when bookings are taken), the cool white interior works a double shift as a smart and comparatively pricey restaurant serving elegant fusion dishes for sharing.

Salut! ££

412 Essex Road, N1 3PJ (3441 8808, salut-london.co.uk). Essex Road rail. **Open** *6-11pm Mon-Wed; noon-3pm, 6-10pm Thur-Sat; noon-3pm, 6-10pm Sun. Modern European*
Salut offers a relaxed take on modern European haute cuisine. The menu is understated but everything on it demonstrates exquisite attention to detail: on one recent visit, king crab and watercress came with unexpected crab roe foam and micro herb pesto; the 'selection of onions' with a juicy pork belly was three colourful piles of alliums that were in turn pickled, caramelised and

charred to perfection; poached pear was perfectly complemented by fermented berries, rich fruit jelly, hazelnut crumble and white chocolate foam. These beautiful plates of food taste as good as they look – without breaking the bank.

Trullo ££

300-302 St Paul's Road, N1 2LH (7226 2733, www.trullorestaurant. com). Highbury & Islington tube/ Overground. **Open** *12.30-2.45pm, 6-10pm Mon-Sat; 12.30-3pm Sun. Italian*
While evenings are still busy-to-frantic in this two-floored contemporary trattoria, lunchtime finds Trullo calm and the cooking relaxed and assured. Grills and roasts from the carte might include Black Hampshire pork chop and cod with cannellini beans and mussels, while pappardelle with beef shin ragù has been a staple since Trullo's early days and remains a silky, substantial delight.

Pubs & bars

❤ 69 Colebrooke Row

69 Colebrooke Row, N1 8AA (07540 528 593, www.69colebrookerow. com). Angel tube. **Open** *5pm-midnight Mon-Wed, Sun; 5pm-1am Thur; 5pm-2am Fri, Sat.*
It's not easy to get a seat in the flagship of bar supremo Tony Conigliaro without booking. Punters come for the outstanding cocktails – some of which may push the boundaries of what can be put in a glass, but they always maintain the drinkability of the classics. Take the Terroir, for instance, which lists as its ingredients 'distilled clay, flint and lichen', and tastes wonderfully like a chilled, earthy, minerally vodka. It's made in Conigliaro's upstairs laboratory, which also produces bespoke cocktail ingredients such as Guinness reduction, paprika bitters, rhubarb cordial and pine-infused gin. There's a subtle jazz-age vibe in the small, tight, low-lit room and – on certain nights – a pianist belts out swinging standards.

Earl of Essex

25 Danbury Street, N1 8LE (7424 5828, www.earlofessex.net). Angel tube. **Open** *noon-11.30pm Mon-Thur; noon-midnight Fri, Sat; noon-11pm Sun.*
The first thing you notice on entering this backstreet Georgian pub is the beautiful island back-bar with a 1960s 'Watney Red Barrel' sign; the second is the vast list of beers on offer. There are 11 on keg, five on cask, plus a couple of quality ciders. The range covers Britain (including a pouring from the on-site Earl's Brewery), Europe and the USA. Staff are happy to offer tastings and know their stuff. On the menu, dishes are all listed with beer recommendations. Whether you really need a suggested beer match for a fishfinger sandwich is a matter of opinion, but it's a nice touch.

Shops & services

Aria

Barnsbury Hall, Barnsbury Street, N1 1PN (7704 1999, www.ariashop. co.uk). Angel tube or Highbury & Islington tube/Overground. **Open** *10am-6.30pm Mon-Sat; noon-5pm Sun. Homewares*
Housed in an impressive Victorian-era former concert hall, Aria is one of London's best design destinations. As well as mid-range contemporary designed kitchenware, clocks and lighting by Alessi, Marimekko and Kartell, there are quirkier international treasures, including vintage Indian trestle market tables and Finnish folklore cushions from Klaus Haapaniemi.

❤ Camden Market

Camden Lock Market *Camden Lock Place, off Chalk Farm Road, NW1 8AF (7485 7963, www. camdenlockmarket.com).* **Open** *10am-6pm daily (note: there are fewer stalls Mon-Fri).*
Camden (Buck Street) Market *Camden High Street, NW1 (www. camdenmarket.com).* **Open** *9.30am-5.30pm daily.*
Inverness Street Market *Inverness Street, NW1 7HJ (www.camdenlock. net/inverness).* **Open** *8.30am-5pm daily.*
Stables Market *off Chalk Farm Road, opposite Hartland Road, NW1 8AH (7485 5511).* **Open** *10.30am-6pm Mon-Fri (reduced stalls); 10am-6pm Sat, Sun. All Camden Town or Chalk Farm tube.*
Camden's sprawling collection of markets is a smörgåsbord of street culture. Wander past loitering goths and punks to join the throng of tourists, locals and random celebs fighting it out at the vast and varied selection of shops and stalls. Saturdays are not for the faint-hearted or the middle-aged – crowds craving

Camden Lock Market

cocktail bar *(see p173)*, houses a dazzling array of art materials. Everything is here, from sable brushes and oil paints to Winsor & Newton inks and artists' mannequins. You'll find all you need for crafting too, with full accessories for screen printing, calligraphy and découpage. It's absolutely brilliant for kids, with stickers, origami and paper-doll sets from hip French brand Djeco, art toys like Etch-a-Sketch and more felt-tip pens and glitter pots than you can shake a glue stick at.

lava lamps, skull rings, fashion, interiors, music and vintage swarm about. Teenagers are likely to be in seventh heaven. Camden Market proper (on the junction with Buck Street) is the place for cheapo jeans, T-shirts and accessories, and the same goes for Canal Market. Down the road, a multimillion-pound redevelopment project is in the midst of transforming the once boho Stables Market into something a little more sterile. However, vintage threads can still be found here alongside crafts, antiques and the now-sprawling Proud gallery and bar. Next door, the pleasant, waterside Camden Lock Market suffered a terrible fire in summer 2017 – when it's back up and running, you'll be able to find everything from corsets and children's clothes to Japanese tableware and multicultural street food.

Cass Art
*66-67 Colebrooke Row, N1 8AB (7619 2601, www.cassart.co.uk). Angel tube. **Open** 10am-7pm Mon-Wed, Fri, Sat; 10am-8pm Thur; 11.30am-5.30pm Sun, open for browsing from 11am. Art supplies* This cavernous store, hidden down a back street by Tony Conigliaro's

Entertainment

♥ Almeida
*Almeida Street, Islington, N1 1TA (information 7288 4900, tickets 7359 4404, www.almeida.co.uk). Angel tube. **Box office** 10am-7pm Mon-Sat. Tickets £10-£38. Theatre* Since Rupert Goold took over as artistic director in 2013, the Almeida has been reinvented from something rather chintzy to London's hippest theatre, the leftfield programming doing nothing to staunch a seemingly endless stream of acclaimed shows that headed into the West End: *Chimerica*, *1984*, *King Charles III*, *Oresteia* and *Hamlet* are all recent transfer hits. The secrets of the Almeida's success are many: Goold's sheer audacity ranks up there, while associate director Robert Icke is probably the most exciting director of his generation. A dud is incredibly rare here: if you can bag a ticket, you should go.

Everyman & Screen Cinemas
Everyman Belsize Park *203 Haverstock Hill, NW3 4QC.* **Tickets** *£12.50-£26.50; £10.50-£13.50 reductions. Screens 1.* **Everyman Hampstead** *5 Hollybush Vale, NW3 6TX. Hampstead tube.* **Tickets** *£13-£19.50; £11-£17.50 reductions. Screens 2.*

Screen on the Green *83 Upper Street, Islington, N1 0NP. Angel tube.* **Tickets** *£15.40-£25.50; £10.60-£12.80 reductions. Screens 1.* **Tickets** *0871 906 9060, www.everymancinema.com. Cinema*
Do you like the smell of expensive leather? Everyman has half a dozen venues across London, each with plush seats, posh food and carpets you could lick without getting a stomach bug. It all started with the Everyman Hampstead, which has a glamorous bar and two-seaters (£39) in its 'screening lounges', complete with foot stools and wine coolers, but the Belsize Park is our favourite – a flagship for the luxe-ing of the chain, it has good food and drink, and seats so comfy you might find yourself nodding off. It was one of three former Screen cinemas, of which Screen on the Green retains its name. It's another beauty, having lost seats to make space for the more comfortable kind, gained a bar and a stage for gigs, but kept its classic neon sign.

Jazz Café

5 Parkway, Camden, NW1 7PG (7485 6834, thejazzcafelondon.com. Camden Town tube. Shows from 7pm. **Restaurant** *7pm-11pm daily. Club nights Fri, Sat 10pm-3am. Tickets £5-£30. Jazz*
In 2015 the Jazz Café celebrated 25 years in business, having brought some of the most respected names in the jazz and soul world – D'Angelo, Roy Ayers, Bobby Womack – as well as Amy Winehouse and Adele to Camden Town. Then, in 2016, it was relaunched with a new look, a technical upgrade and revamped food and drink. The programming still focuses on funk, soul, R&B and electronic music, but there are more new and rising acts. With a capacity of 440, it's an intimate space, but the two-level layout offers you a choice: get sweaty in the downstairs standing area, or book an upstairs table for a bit of luxury and guaranteed good view.

Koko

1A Camden High Street, Camden, NW1 7JE (information 7388 3222, tickets 0844 477 1000, www.koko.uk.com). Mornington Crescent tube. **Box office** *In person noon-5pm Mon-Fri (performance days only). By phone 24hrs daily. Tickets £10-£40. Rock & pop*
Koko has had a hand in the gestation of numerous styles over the decades. As the Music Machine, it hosted a four-night residency with the Clash in 1978; the venue changed its name to Camden Palace in the '80s, whereupon it became home to the emergent New Romantic movement and saw Madonna's UK debut. Later, it was one of the first 'official' venues to host acid-house events. Since a spruce-up in the early noughties, it has hosted acts as diametrically opposed as Joss Stone and Queens of the Stone Age, not to mention one of Prince's electrifying 'secret' gigs in 2014. Nonetheless, the 1,500-capacity hall majors on weekend club nights – Annie Mac Presents and Club NME – and gigs by indie rockers, from the small and cultish to those on the up.

Lexington

96-98 Pentonville Road, Islington, N1 9JB (7837 5371, www.thelexington.co.uk). Angel tube. **Open** *noon-2am Mon-Wed, Sun; noon-3am Thur; noon-4am Fri, Sat. Tickets free-£15. Rock & pop*
Effectively the common room for the music industry's perennial sixth form, this 200-capacity venue has a superb sound system in place for the leftfield indie bands that dominate the programme. It's where the hottest US exports often make

their London debut: indie greats such as the Drums and Sleigh Bells have cut their teeth here in front of London's most receptive crowds. Downstairs, there's a lounge bar with a vast array of US beers and bourbons, above-par bar food and a Rough Trade music quiz (every Monday).

❤ O2 Forum Kentish Town

9-17 Highgate Road, Kentish Town, NW5 1JY (information 7428 4080, tickets 0844 877 2000, www.academymusicgroup.com/ o2forumkentishtown). Kentish Town tube/rail. Box office In person 90mins before doors open on show days. By phone 24hrs daily. Tickets £10-£40. Rock & pop

Originally constructed as part of a chain of art deco cinemas with a spurious Roman theme (hence the name, the incongruous bas relief battle scenes and imperial eagles flanking the stage), the 2,000-capacity Forum became a music venue back in the early 1980s. Since then, it's been vital to generations of gig-goers, whether they cut their teeth on Ian Dury & the Blockheads, The Pogues, Duran Duran, Killing Joke or the Wu-Tang Clan, all of whom have played memorable shows here.

❤ Roundhouse

Chalk Farm Road, Camden, NW1 8EH (tickets 0300 678 9222, www.roundhouse.org.uk). Chalk Farm tube. Box office In person 9.30am-5pm Mon, Sat, Sun; 9.30am-9pm Tue-Fri. By phone 9am-7pm Mon-Fri; 9am-4pm Sat; 9.30am-4pm Sun. Tickets £5-£25. Music & performance

The main auditorium's supporting pillars mean there are some poor sightlines at the Roundhouse, but this one-time railway turntable shed (hence the name), which was used for hippie happenings in the 1960s before becoming a

famous rock (and punk) venue in the '70s, has been a fine addition to London's music venues since its reopening in 2006. Expect a mix of arty rock gigs (the briefly re-formed Led Zeppelin played here), dance performances, theatre and multimedia events.

Sadler's Wells

Rosebery Avenue, Finsbury, EC1R 4TN (7863 8000, www.sadlerswells. com). Angel tube. Box office 10am-8pm Mon-Sat. Tickets £10-£65. Dance

Built in 1998 on the site of a 17th-century theatre of the same name, this dazzling complex is home to impressive local and international performances of contemporary dance in all its guises. The Lilian Baylis Studio offers smaller-scale new works and works-in-progress; the Peacock Theatre (on Portugal Street in Holborn) operates as a satellite venue.

❤ Union Chapel

Compton Terrace, off Upper Street, Islington, N1 2UN (7226 1686 , www.unionchapel.org. uk). Highbury & Islington tube/ Overground/rail. Open varies. Tickets free-£40. Rock & pop

Readers of *Time Out* magazine have three times voted Union Chapel their top music venue – and it's easy to see why. The Grade I-listed Victorian Gothic church, which still holds services and also runs a homeless centre, is a wonderfully atmospheric gig venue. It made its name hosting acoustic events and occasional jazz shows, becoming a magnet for thinking bands and their fans. These days, you'll also find classy intimate shows from bigger artists such as Paloma Faith. Watch out for the Daylight Music free afternoon concerts.

East London

Browse Instagram today, and it's hard to believe how recently east London was notorious for slums and smelly industries. How things change. East London now comprises much of what is most vibrant about the capital. On the doorstep of the City, **Spitalfields** and neighbouring **Brick Lane** mix upmarket shopping and dining with Bangladeshi cafés and boho boutiques. North of Spitalfields, **Shoreditch** and **Hoxton** retain some lively bars and clubs, although local hipsters have moved north to once unheralded **Dalston**, now shorthand for cool London, with a cluster of fine music and arts venues. Further east, **Bethnal Green** has the **Museum of Childhood** and Sunday's **Columbia Road Market**.

London's **Docklands**, once the busiest in the world, became the flagship of finance-led urban redevelopment in the 1990s. Now the Isle of Dogs is all shiny megabanks,

Unmissable World Heritage Site
History, architecture and a
Thames-side setting come
together in Maritime Greenwich
(*p188*).

Best small museum
Visit the bijou and beautiful
Geffrye Museum (*p178*).

Best attraction
Slide down the ArcelorMittal Orbit
(*p187*).

Best market
Find Sunday blooms at Columbia
Road (*p183*) or a cool crowd at
Broadway (*p182*).

Coolest food & drink combos
Happiness Forgets (*p181*) and
Sager+Wilde serve both creative
cocktails and fab food (*p182*).

Best nightlife
Join the polysexual party fun at
Dalston Superstore (*p185*).

with the landmark 'Canary Wharf Tower' almost lost
between them. Follow the River Lea upstream to the
north to reach the **Queen Elizabeth Olympic Park**, or
cross the Thames south to **Greenwich**.

East End and around

Sights & museums

Dennis Severs' House
*18 Folgate Street, E1 6BX (7247
4013, www.dennissevershouse.
co.uk). Liverpool Street tube/
rail or Shoreditch High Street
Overground. **Open** noon-2pm,
5-9pm Mon; 5-9pm Wed, Fri; noon-
4pm Sun. **Admission** daytime
visits £10; £5 reductions; evening
visits £15-£50. **Map** p179 S6.*
The ten rooms of this original
Huguenot house have been decked
out to recreate vivid snapshots of
daily life in Spitalfields between
1724 and 1914. A tour through the
compelling 'still-life drama', as
American creator Dennis Severs
dubbed it, takes you through
the cellar, kitchen, dining room,
smoking room and upstairs to
the bedrooms. With hearth and
candles burning, smells lingering
and objects scattered apparently
haphazardly, it feels as though

the inhabitants have deserted the
building only moments before
you arrived.

❤ Geffrye Museum
*136 Kingsland Road, E2 8EA (7739
9893, www.geffrye-museum.org.
uk). Hoxton Overground. **Open**
10am-5pm Tue-Sun. Almshouse
tours 1st Sat, 1st & 3rd Tue, Wed of
mth. **Admission** free; donations
appreciated. Almshouse tours £4;
free under-16s. **Map** p179 S4.*
Housed in a set of 18th-century
almshouses, the Geffrye Museum
has for more than a century offered
a vivid physical history of the
English interior. Displaying original
furniture, paintings, textiles and
decorative arts, the museum
recreates a sequence of typical
middle-class living rooms from
1600 to the present. It's an oddly
interesting way to take in domestic
history, with any number of
intriguing details to catch your eye
– from a bell jar of stuffed birds to
a particular decorative flourish on
a chair. There's an airy restaurant

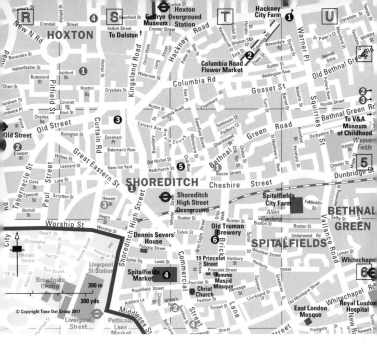

overlooking the lovely gardens, which include a walled plot for herbs and a chronological series in different historical styles.

V&A Museum of Childhood
Cambridge Heath Road, E2 9PA (8983 5200, www.vam.ac.uk/moc). Bethnal Green tube/Overground or Cambridge Heath Overground. **Open** *10am-5.45pm daily.* **Admission** *free; donations appreciated.*

Home to one of the world's finest collections of children's toys, dolls' houses, games and costumes, the Museum of Childhood is part of the Victoria & Albert Museum (*see p100*). It has been amassing childhood-related objects since 1872 and continues to do so, with *Incredibles* figures complementing bonkers 1970s puppets, Barbie dolls and Victorian praxinoscopes.

The museum has lots of hands-on stuff for kids dotted about the many cases of historic artefacts, including dressing-up boxes and soft play areas, though the cases themselves might be of more interest to nostalgic adults than their spawn. Regular small exhibitions are held upstairs, while the café in the central space helps to revive flagging spirits.

Whitechapel Gallery
77-82 Whitechapel High Street, E1 7QX (7522 7888, www.whitechapelgallery.org). Aldgate East tube. **Open** *10am-6pm Tue, Wed, Fri-Sun; 11am-9pm Thur.* **Admission** *free. Temporary exhibitions vary.*

This East End stalwart, a perennial favourite of avant-garde aficionados and art students, continues to build on a stellar

Geffrye Museum

reputation as a contemporary art pioneer that began with exhibitions of Picasso – *Guernica* was shown here in 1939 – Jackson Pollock, Mark Rothko and Frida Kahlo. The Grade II-listed building underwent a 21st-century refurb that saw it expand into the similarly historic former library next door – rather brilliantly, the architects left the two buildings stylistically distinct rather than trying to smooth out their differences. As well as nearly tripling its exhibition space, the Whitechapel gave itself a research centre and archives, plus a café/bar. With no permanent collection, there's a rolling programme of temporary shows, but an increasing number of artists have contributed permanently to the fabric of the building: a few years back, Rachel Whiteread added gold vine leaves to the gallery's frontage.

Restaurants

Despite Brick Lane's global reputation for quality curries, most of the food on offer there is disappointing. Try nearby **Gunpowder** instead or opt for Bengali sweets from the **Madhubon Sweet Centre** at 42 Brick Lane.

Brick Lane Beigel Bake £

*159 Brick Lane, E1 6SB (7729 0616). Shoreditch High Street Overground. **Open** 24hrs daily. **Map** p179 T5* ❶ *Jewish*
This little East End institution rolls out perfect bagels (egg, cream cheese, salt beef, at seriously low prices), good bread and moreish cakes. Even at 3am, fresh-baked goods are pulled from the ovens at the back; no wonder the queue for bagels trails out the door when the local bars and clubs close. Note: this is essentially a takeaway operation – don't expect to be able to linger.

Gunpowder ££

11 Whites Row, E1 7NF (7426 0542, www.gunpowderlondon.com). Aldgate East tube or Liverpool Street tube/rail. **Open** *noon-3pm, 5.30-10.30pm Mon-Sat.* **Map** *p179 T6* ❷ *Indian*

Despite its 'Curry Mile' reputation, it's still surprisingly hard to find a good Indian restaurant in the Brick Lane area. This tiny family-run restaurant – with a kitchen headed by Nirmal Save, once a chef at Mayfair's storied Tamarind – aims to bring quality small-plate eating to Indian food, ditching stomach-bursting breads and creamy sauces for delights such as *rasam ke bomb*, chilli cheese toast and Chettinad pulled duck served with homemade *oothappam*. The place oozes passion without a hint of pretension; at weekends it positively buzzes.

Rök Smokehouse & Bar ££

26 Curtain Road, EC2A 3NY (7377 2152, roklondon.co.uk). Old Street tube/rail or Shoreditch High Street Overground. **Open** *5-11pm Mon-Thur; 5pm-1am Fri, Sat.* **Map** *p179 S5* ❸ *Modern European*

Habitually filled with pristine 30-year-olds, not a beard hair out of place, the narrow, low-lit dining room has white walls, dark-wood tables, a small open kitchen with a custom-made charcoal grill, and jars of homemade pickles adorning the bar. The food, with its powerfully flavoured meat cures, pickles and jams, is vaguely Nordic, but centres on British produce, with the odd wild-card southern European ingredient: witness the single scallop, served sizzling in the chilli-hot oil from Italian 'nduja sausage, or the pot of juicy mussels steamed in east-London wheat beer ('It's Cockney marinière,' joked our waiter). Although meat – including two huge fennel-cured lamb chops, cooked *sous-vide* then finished over

the coals – is the star, the sides are equally impressive. In fact, our only bugbear is the teeny size of the tables for two.

Som Saa £££

43a Commercial Street, E1 6BD (7324 7790, www.somsaa. com). Shoreditch High Street Overground. **Open** *6-10.30pm daily.* **Map** *p179 T6* ❹ *Thai*

Taking up this permanent site last year after a monstrously successful crowdfunding campaign, Som Saa isn't somewhere you come for a cheeky green curry and a plate of pad thai – this is authentic, red-hot food from Thailand's north-eastern provinces. Take the deep-fried seabass with Isaan (north-eastern) herbs, for instance. The delicate flesh comes loose easily, leaving a cartoon fish skeleton and crunchy roasted-rice-battered skin, herbs (mint, coriander, Thai basil), mandolin-thin shallots and a puddle of sweet-sour-salt-fire sauce. The effect is thrilling: like setting off ooh-aahh fireworks of taste and texture.

Pubs & bars

❤ Happiness Forgets

8-9 Hoxton Square, N1 6NU (7613 0325, www.happinessforgets.com). Old Street tube/rail or Shoreditch High Street Overground. **Open** *5-11pm daily.* **Map** *p179 S4* ❶

From the moment you walk in, the staff will know how to make you happy. The short list of original cocktails is unfailingly good: lots of nice twists on classic ideas but never departing from the essential cocktail principles of balance, harmony and drinkability. Star turns: Mr McRae, Perfect Storm and Tokyo Collins. But the classics are brilliantly handled too, the food is fabulous and so is the service. This is a very special place but not very large: booking is a good idea.

❤ Sager + Wilde Paradise Row

250 Paradise Row, E2 9LE (7613 0478, www.sagerandwilde.com). Bethnal Green tube/Overground. **Open** *6pm-midnight Tue-Fri; noon-midnight Sat, Sun.* **Map** *p179 V4* ❷

This bar-restaurant lies in a railway arch, low lit in the evenings, with a cathedral-like vaulted ceiling the colour of Carrara marble and a spacious courtyard which faces the traffic-free street. The wine list is intimidatingly vast, but, thankfully, the staff know it well and adroitly help you navigate it. Abundant beverages aside, the food is excellent, having enlisted the talents of Sebastian Myers (formerly of Chiltern Firehouse, *see p115*) to produce British dishes with European flourishes.

Satan's Whiskers

343 Cambridge Heath Road, E2 9RA (7739 8362). Bethnal Green tube/Overground or Cambridge Heath Overground. **Open** *5pm-midnight daily.* **Map** *p179 V4* ❸

Satan's Whiskers might sound like a Captain Haddock curse, but it refers to a classic cocktail containing gin, orange and vermouth topped with Grand Marnier and orange bitters. It's a staple on the otherwise daily changing menu here, along with seductive alternatives – this tiny bar was set up by three bartenders, and they really know their stuff. Leather booths, an illuminated ice box and taxidermy for decor all add to the atmosphere.

Super Lyan

155 Hoxton Street, N1 6PJ (3011 1153, www.superlyan.com). Hoxton Overground. **Open** *5-11.45pm Tue; 5pm-midnight Wed, Thur, Sun; 5pm-1am Fri, Sat.* **Map** *p179 S4* ❹

Comparing Super Lyan to your local boozer is like comparing Heston Blumenthal's Fat Duck to a greasy spoon. The latest venture from mixologist Ryan Chetiyawardana ('Mr Lyan') is in the basement of his former experimental cocktail bar White Lyan, which gained a reputation for eschewing the usual cocktail components (such as ice, citrus, sugar and fruit) and distilling its own spirits. Following in its footsteps, Super Lyan will focus on classic cocktails using unconventional ingredients and intriguing techniques. The secluded setting – plain dark walls, dim lighting and worn leather upholstery – is deliberately low-key so all attention is focused on the main event: the artistry of the cocktails.

Shops & services

Once a shabby Shoreditch cut-through, **Redchurch Street** has become a strong contender for London's best shopping street.

❤ Broadway Market

Broadway Market, E8 4QL (www. broadwaymarket.co.uk). London Fields Overground or bus 394. **Open** *9am-5pm Sat.* **Map** *p179 U3* ❶ *Market*

The coolest and most ridiculous of east London's young trendies can be found at this endearing market, where fruit-and-veg sellers trade alongside vintage clothes 'specialists'. It's as busy as a beehive, but the slew of cafés, pubs, restaurants and boutiques along the street – plus the market itself, plus the nearby Netil Market for further streetfood, plus Saturday's School Yard Market, plus the overspill of drunks and slumming may-do-wells on London Fields when there's even a whiff of sunshine – is a fine education in new London.

Columbia Road Market

🖤 Columbia Road Market

*Columbia Road, E2 7RG (www. columbiaroad.info). Hoxton Overground or Bethnal Green tube/ Overground. **Open** 8am-3.30pm Sun. **Map** p179 T4* ❷ *Market*

On Sunday mornings, this unassuming East End street is transformed into a delightful swathe of fabulous plant life and the air is fragrant with blooms and the shouts of old-school Cockney stallholders (most offering deals for 'a fiver'). But a visit here isn't only about flowers and pot plants: alongside the market is a growing number of shops selling everything from pottery and arty prints to cupcakes and perfume; don't miss **Ryantown's** delicate paper cut-outs at no.126 (7613 1510 robryanstudio.com/ ryantown). Refuel at **Jones Dairy** (23 Ezra Street, 7739 5372, www. jonesdairy.co.uk).

House of Hackney

*131 Shoreditch High Street, E1 6JE (7739 3901, www. houseofhackney.com). Old Street tube/rail or Shoreditch High Street Overground. **Open** 10am-7pm Mon-Sat; 11am-5pm Sun. **Map** p179 S5* ❸ *Homewares*

House of Hackney has the makings of a new Liberty (*see p122*): buy your future design classics now, we say. This is one of the most gorgeous retail establishments to land in London in years – bedecked in the deliberately over-the-top juxtapositions of print-on-print-on-print that have made the brand's name, and with the entrance full of flowers. Upstairs, you'll find rolls of gorgeous paper, fabric, trays, mugs, fashion and collaborative designs with brands such as Puma; downstairs are generously proportioned sofas and plump armchairs in more-is-more combinations of print and texture.

Old Spitalfields Market

*Brushfield Street, E1 6AA (www.oldspitalfieldsmarket. com). Liverpool Street tube/ rail or Shoreditch High Street Overground. **Open** 10am-5pm Mon-Fri, Sun; 11am-5pm Sat. **Map** p179 S6* ❹ *Market*

Operating from these premises since 1887, the market at Spitalfields had since 1682 sold fruit and veg wholesale. When that function moved out to Leyton in 1991, battles began over redevelopment of a site toothsomely placed next to the

House of Hackney

vast wealth of the City. Fortunately, the most aesthetic part of the market was saved, where you'll find fashion, crafts and plenty to eat. The cooler (and cheaper) purchases are found around Brick Lane, but it's still a pleasant venue.

Redchurch Street

Redchurch Street, E2 7DJ. Shoreditch High Street rail. **Map** *p179 S5* ⑤ *High street*
Come here for civilised, imaginative, independent-minded shopping – driven by art and fashion. As one of Redchurch Street's first new residents, Caravan (no.3) helped redefine the street with its eccentric vintage-style homewares and gifts. Aussie botanical beauty shop Aesop (no.5A) and classic menswear brand Sunspel (no.7) can be found at one end. Further up are darkly lit menswear store Hostem (nos.41-43), vintage-style up-dos and manicures at the Painted Lady (no.65) and eminently wearable clothes at Modern Society (no.33). Expansive Labour & Wait (no.85)

is an absolute highlight, selling aesthetically pleasing mops, enamel bread bins, stylish ladles and other simple essentials.

Rough Trade East

Dray Walk, Old Truman Brewery, 91 Brick Lane, E1 6QL (7392 7788, www.roughtrade.com). Shoreditch High Street Overground. **Open** *9am-9pm Mon-Thur; 9am-8pm Fri; 10am-8pm Sat; 11am-7pm Sun.* **Map** *p179 T6* ⑥ *Music*
The indie music label Rough Trade – perhaps most famous for signing the Smiths in the early 1980s – set up this 5,000sq ft record store, café and gig space in the noughties when the death of music shops in the face of internet price-cutting was widely accepted as inevitable. Perversely, Rough Trade instead offered a physical space where music-lovers could browse a dizzying range of vinyl and CDs, spanning punk, indie, dub, soul, electronica and more, providing them with 16 listening posts and a stage for live sets. Now its triumph seems like it was always certain.

Entertainment

💜 Dalston Superstore

117 Kingland High Street, Dalston, E8 2PB (7254 2273, dalstonsuperstore.com). Dalston Kingsland Overground. **Open** *noon-midnight Mon; noon-2.30am Tue-Thur; noon-3am Fri; 10am-3am Sat; 10am-2.30am Sun.* **Admission** *varies. Club*

This Kingsland High Street hangout is a bit of a face on the east London party scene. In true Dalston style it's home to all sorts: popular with a large and diverse LGBT crowd, but welcoming to everyone. A café during the day, at night you can expect queues for a hugely impressive roster of guest DJs spinning a typically east London mix of of pop and dance tunes to a floor that's pitch-black and intense. Regular dates, such as Sunday's Disco Brunch (soul, disco and funk with all-day breakfast and cocktails), are well worth putting in the diary. Upstairs, alt-cabaret drag stars whip revellers into shape with sharp one-liners.

Oval Space

29-32 The Oval, Bethnal Green, E2 9DT (7183 4422, www. ovalspace.co.uk). Bethnal Green tube/Overground or Cambridge Heath overground. **Open** *varies.* **Admission** *varies. Club*

Located at the base of a disused gasworks off Hackney Road, this hangar-style space is 6,000sq ft of fun, and one of the most impressive and exciting recent additions to London nightlife. A mix of ace one-off parties and regular events mark Oval Space out as one of the most innovative venues around: DJs regularly play spacey techno, twisted electronica, alt hip hop and glitchy house, while on-point events such as Secretsundaze are regulars.

Village Underground

54 Holywell Lane, Shoreditch, EC2A 3PQ (7422 7505, www. villageunderground.co.uk). Shoreditch High Street Overground. **Open** *varies.* **Admission** *varies.* **Map** *p179 S5* ❶ *Club*

Rough Trade East

You can't miss Village Underground: four graffiti-covered tube carriages are perched on its roof. These and a series of shipping containers accommodate artists, writers, designers, film-makers and musicians, while a Victorian warehouse space hosts exhibitions, concerts, plays, live art and club nights.

XOYO

32-37 Cowper Street, Shoreditch, EC2A 4AP (7608 2878, www. xoyo.co.uk). Old Street tube/rail. ***Open/admission*** *varies.* ***Map** p179 R5* **2** *Club*

There's live music during the week at this 800-capacity venue, but XOYO is first and foremost a club. The former printworks is a bare concrete shell, defiantly taking the 'chic' out of 'shabby chic', but the open space means the atmosphere is always buzzing, as the only place to escape immersion in the music is the small smoking courtyard outside. The Victorian loft-style space provides effortlessly cool programming and high-profile DJs, while the longer residencies – a 12-week stint for Erol Alkan in summer 2017, for instance – is the best kind of old-school.

Docklands and beyond

Sights & museums

Museum of London Docklands

No.1 Warehouse, West India Quay, Hertsmere Road, E14 4AL (7001 9844, www.museumoflondon.org. uk/museum-london-docklands). Canary Wharf tube/DLR or West India Quay DLR. ***Open*** *10am-6pm daily.* ***Admission*** *free. Temporary exhibitions vary.*

Housed in a 19th-century warehouse (itself a Grade I-listed building), this museum explores the complex history of London's

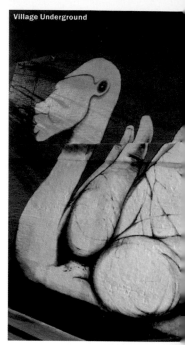

Village Underground

docklands and the river over two millennia. Displays spreading over three storeys take you from the arrival of the Romans all the way to the docks' 1980s closure and the area's subsequent redevelopment. The Docklands at War section is very moving, while a haunting new permanent exhibition sheds light on the dark side of London's rise as a centre for finance and commerce, exploring its involvement in the slave trade. You can also walk through full-scale mock-ups of a quayside and a dingy riverfront alley. Temporary exhibitions are set up on the ground floor, where you'll also find a café and a docks-themed play area. Just like its elder sibling, the Museum of London (*see p164*), the MoLD has a great programme of special events.

Emirates Air Line
North terminal *27 Western Gateway, E16 4FA. Royal Victoria DLR.*
South terminal *Edmund Halley Way, SE10 0FR (www.tfl.gov.uk/modes/emirates-air-line). North Greenwich tube.*
Open *Apr-Sept 7am-9pm Mon-Fri; 8am-9pm Sat; 9am-9pm Sun. Oct-Mar 7am-8pm Mon-Fri; 8am-8pm Sat; 9am-8pm Sun.* **Tickets** *£4.50 single; £2.30 reductions, free under-5s.*

Arguments for a cable car across the Thames as a solution to any of London's many transport problems are, at best, moot, but its value as a tourist thrill is huge. The comfy pods zoom 295ft up elegant stanchions at a gratifying pace. Suddenly there are brilliant views of the expanses of water that make up the Royal Docks, the ships on the Thames, Docklands and the Thames Barrier. Good fun and good value – but note that the cable car may not run in high winds.

❤ Queen Elizabeth Olympic Park
www.queenelizabetholympicpark. co.uk. Stratford tube/rail/DLR, Hackney Wick Overground
The site of London's 2012 Olympic Games, the park comprises immaculate landscaping to the north, laced by a network of paths and waterways. By the Timber Lodge café are the Tumbling Bay Playground and the **Lee Valley VeloPark** with a velodrome, BMX track and 8km of mountain bike trails. The 7,500-seat **Copper Box Arena** is now a flexible indoor venue for sports and concerts. In the southern part of the park are the handsome Zaha Hadid-designed **Aquatics Centre** (www. londonaquaticscentre.org) and the landmark **ArcelorMittal Orbit** (0333 800 8099, arcelormittalorbit. com). The Orbit was designed by sculptor Anish Kapoor and

engineer Cecil Balmond, with the addition of a spiral slide by Belgian artist Carsten Höller in 2016. At 274ft, this is the world's longest and tallest tunnel slide, taking a dozen turns around the Orbit in 40 seconds. The **Olympic Stadium** is the home ground of West Ham Football Club, which took up residence for the 2016/17 season, but it continues to host other major sporting events.

Entertainment

O2 Arena & IndigO2
Peninsula Square, North Greenwich, SE10 0DX (information 8463 2000, tickets 0844 856 0202, www.theo2.co.uk). North Greenwich tube. **Box office** *In person noon-7pm daily. By phone 8am-8pm daily. Tickets £15-£70. Music & sport*
The national embarrassment that was the Millennium Dome has been transformed into the city's de facto home of the mega-gig. This 20,000-seater has outstanding sound, unobstructed sightlines and the potential for artists to perform 'in the round'. Shows from even the world's biggest acts (U2, Beyoncé, the reformed Led Zep, the mostly reformed Monty Python) don't feel too far away, and the venue seems to handle music, comedy and even sport (international tennis, boxing, basketball) with equal aplomb.

On the same site, IndigO2 is the Arena's little sister – but 'little' only by comparison. It has an impressive capacity of 2,350, arranged as part-standing room, part-amphitheatre seating and, sometimes, part-table seating. IndigO2's niche roster of MOR (middle-of-the-road) acts is dominated by soul, funk, pop-jazz and old pop acts, but it does also host after-show parties for headliners from the Arena.

♥ Maritime Greenwich

Greenwich is an irresistible mixture of maritime, royal and horological history, a combination that earned it recognition as a UNESCO World Heritage Site in 1997 and a Royal Borough in 2012. Indeed, royalty has haunted Greenwich since 1300, when Edward I stayed here. Henry VIII was born in Greenwich Palace, which was later redeveloped as the Royal Naval Hospital, now the **Old Royal Naval College** (www. ornc.org.uk). Designed by Wren in 1694, and completed with the help of Hawksmoor and Vanbrugh, the college complex is now a very handy first port of call. Its Pepys Building contains the Greenwich Tourist Information Centre (0870 608 2000, www.visitgreenwich. org.uk), and is the home of Discover Greenwich, which provides a great overview of the area's numerous attractions. The public are also allowed into the college's rococo chapel and the Painted Hall, which took Sir James Thornhill 19 years to complete. Walk south between Wren's grand colonnades, which were deliberately placed to frame the **Queen's House** (www.rmg. co.uk/queens-house) – begun by Inigo Jones in 1616 and the first building in Britain to be designed on Classical principles. West of the Queen's House is the **National Maritime Museum** (www. rmg.co.uk/national-maritime-museum), the world's largest such museum, which contains a huge store of creatively organised maritime art, cartography, models, interactives and regalia.

Beyond lies **Greenwich Park**, laid out by André Le Nôtre (1613-

GREENWICH

1700), the chief gardener of French King Louis XIV. It's a ten-minute walk (or shorter shuttle-bus trip) south up the park's steep slopes to the **Royal Observatory** (www.rmg.co.uk/royal-observatory) – a collaboration between Wren and the scientist Robert Hooke (1635-1703). It also marks the work of astronomer John Flamsteed (1646-1719), who predicted solar eclipses and laid the groundwork for later advances in navigation. There are superb views out over the Royal Naval College to Canary Wharf, and, at night, the bright green Meridian Line Laser illuminates the path of the Prime Meridian across the London sky.

Elsewhere, shoppers swarm to **Greenwich Market**, a handsome 19th-century building sheltering a mixture of shops and stalls.

Nearby, close to Greenwich Pier, is the 19th-century tea clipper, the **Cutty Sark** (King William Walk, www.rmg.co.uk/cuttysark), as well as the domed entrance to a Victorian pedestrian tunnel that emerges on the far side of the Thames in Island Gardens. The tunnel is rather dingy, due to incomplete repair work, but it's still fun to walk beneath the river.

The best way to travel to or from Greenwich, however, is on board the popular and speedy **Thames Clipper** boats (7001 2200, www.thamesclippers.com), which shuttle passengers to and from central London. Seeing the vistas change as you approach this most historic area of London is an unparalleled joy – redolent of the long period when the city was utterly dependent on its river.

Old Royal Naval Coll

PLANNING A TRIP TO NEW YORK?

From budget to boutique, the best hotels in New York uncovered.

London
Essentials

Accommodation

Even at the height of the recession, London's hoteliers seemed to think it was boomtime. Whether the country's faltering steps towards Brexit cools their ardour remains to be seen, but so far the pace of deluxe openings has hardly slowed, with the **Beaumont** and **Mondrian at Sea Containers** two of the more notable additions over the last few years. They are, of course, overlooked – if not overshadowed – by the lofty **Shangri-La** at the Shard. The price of rooms in London is pretty shocking, but it's not all top-dollar activity. The pioneering **Hoxton** has opened an even better sister-hotel – the **Hoxton Holborn** – and the excellent Dutch **citizenM** chain is expanding its properties over here. **Qbic** and the **Z** hotels are other relative bargain favourites.

Staying in London

Always research the location before you part with your money. Greater London is pretty huge and few people have a vision of their holiday that involves spending an hour on public transport to get to the heart of things. That said, there's no need to focus exclusively on the **West End**. Get somewhere to stay on the **South Bank** and you certainly won't regret it, and the **City** has plenty of business hotels offering great deals, particularly at weekends. **East London** retains some of its art-and-fashion coolness and is ideal if you're planning on some hard nights of clubbing. Or, if you can afford it,

In the know
Price categories

Our price categories are based on hotels' standard prices (not including seasonal offers or discounts) for one night in a double room with en suite shower/bath.

Luxury	£350+
Expensive	£250-£350
Moderate	£130-£250
Budget	up to £130

a stay in one of the grand old **Mayfair** hotels such as **Claridges** (www.claridges.co.uk) or the **Dorchester** (www.dorchestercollection.com) is a holiday without even having to step out of the door.

Money matters

As a rule, it's best to book as far ahead as possible, and always try hotels' own websites first: many offer special online deals; pretty much every business hotel will offer steep reductions for a Sunday night stay. Be aware that a few hotels – particularly at the top of the price range – don't include VAT (a 20 per cent sales tax) in the rates they quote. And watch out for added extras. Some hotels charge for Wi-Fi, some do not. Few central hotels offer parking and those that do charge steeply for it. It's also worth looking at hotel booking websites such as **uk.hotels.com**. If you're feeling more adventurous – especially if you fancy a stay in one of the thriving neighbourhoods outside central London – have a look on **www.airbnb.co.uk**.

Luxury
Beaumont
Brown Hart Gardens, Mayfair, W1K 6TF (7499 1001, www.thebeaumont.com). Bond Street tube. **Map** *p113 H7.*
Oddly, the Grade II-listed façade is the least impressive part of this hotel. The first new Mayfair hotel for a decade is set in the vast 1926 garage where Selfridges' shoppers used to get their jalopies tuned up, but it is in the painstakingly and totally rebuilt interiors – bland hire-car offices in 2011 – that this art deco fantasia sings. There's smooth service and a lovely private bar/drawing room off the foyer. The staff gets the marriage of glamorous formality and approachability just right, and the owners' personal travel bugbears have created some really thoughtful touches, from the sliding screens that isolate beds from bathrooms to the free soft drinks, movies and shoeshines.

Towering over the handsome square in front of the Beaumont is the Antony Gormley-designed **ROOM**: on the outside it's a striking Cubist-influenced sculpture; on the inside it's a two-storey suite in immaculate art deco style, leading through to a low-lit, almost womb-like bedroom right inside the sculpture.

Covent Garden Hotel
10 Monmouth Street, Covent Garden, WC2H 9HB (7806 1000, www. firmdalehotels.com). Covent Garden or Leicester Square tube. **Map** *p133 M7.*
This hotel's excellent location – in the heart of London's theatre district – continues to attract starry customers, with anyone needing a bit of privacy able to retreat upstairs to the lovely panelled private library and drawing room. In the guest rooms, Kit Kemp's distinctive style mixes

pinstriped wallpaper, pristine white quilts and floral upholstery with bold, contemporary elements; each room is unique, but each has the Kemp trademark upholstered mannequin and granite and oak bathroom. On the ground floor, the 1920s Paris-style Brasserie Max and the retro zinc bar retain their buzz – outdoor tables give a perfect viewpoint on Covent Garden boutique life in summer.

Mondrian at Sea Containers

20 Upper Ground, South Bank, SE1 9PD (3747 1000, www.morganshotelgroup. com/mondrian/mondrian-london). Blackfriars tube. Map p68 O8.
Location's everything here: this Mondrian is right on the Thames, with the views on the bank side of the building among the best in London – low enough to feel part of the city, high enough to feel exclusive. The rooms are nicely furnished by Tom Dixon in a kind of postmodern deco style, minimalist without leaving you feeling the sharp edges. Public spaces are terrific and playfully ship-themed (not least the prow that encases the reception desks) and there are plenty of areas for meetings. There's a connoisseurs' bar (Dandylyan, *see p77*) and less accomplished restaurant on the ground floor, as well as a blingier bar in a glass cube on the roof (the Rumpus Room, closed Mon, Sun) and a cosy Curzon cinema.

Shangri-La at the Shard

31 St Thomas Street, Southwark, SE1 9QU (7234 8000, www.shangri-la.com/ london). London Bridge tube/rail. Map p68 R9.
The Shangri-La is unusual in many ways. The hotel proper starts on floor 35 with a spacious foyer and restaurant. The building's pyramid shape means every room is different, with most floor space and hence the poshest suites on 36 and 37, not at the top. And the rooms are priced by view: the most expensive look north, offering 180º Thames vistas. Those views are amazing, as you'd expect: absorbing as dusk falls

and the city lights come on, especially from the lobby and restaurant. The Skypool, fitness room and bar feel a bit remote, way up on floor 52. The decor is cosmopolitan Asian neutral, with some unimpressive bits of design offset by imaginative touches (binoculars for you to enjoy the view, torches to ease jetlagged room navigation in bedside drawers).

Expensive

Boundary

2-4 Boundary Street, Shoreditch, E2 7DD (7729 1051, www.theboundary. co.uk). Liverpool Street tube/rail or Shoreditch High Street Overground. Map p179 S5
Design mogul Sir Terence Conran's Boundary Project warehouse conversion was a labour of love. Its restaurants – which include Albion, Tratra, a French restaurant by best-selling cookery book writer Stéphane Reynaud, and a rooftop bar – are high quality but relaxed places, and all 17 bedrooms are beautifully designed. Each has a handmade bed, but all are otherwise individually furnished with classic furniture and original art. The five studios, lofts and suites range in style from the bright and sea-salt fresh Beach to modern Chinoiserie by Sir David Tang, while the remaining bedrooms (the slightly larger corner bedrooms have windows along both external walls) are themed by design style: Mies van der Rohe, Eames, Shaker.

Great Northern Hotel

King's Cross St Pancras Station, Pancras Road, King's Cross, N1C 4TB (3388 0800, www.gnhlondon.com). King's Cross tube/rail. Map p125 M3.
Designed by Lewis Cubitt, the city's first railway hotel opened in 1854, part of the Victorian railway explosion. It has had plenty of rough times since then, not least the 12 years it was dark, but almost £40m of renovation has recreated the place as a classic. The furniture is by artisans and, in many cases, bespoke: witness the Couchette

rooms, each with a double bed snugly fitted into the window to playfully echo sleeper carriages; the neatly upholstered bedside cabinets; or the ceiling lights raised and lowered by fabulously steampunk pulleys. You're not expected to suffer the privations of a Victorian traveller, though: fast Wi-Fi, film and music libraries on the large TV, Egyptian cotton sheets and walk-in showers are all standard. There's no room service but each floor has a simply charming pantry, full of jars of vintage sweets, a stand of fresh cakes, tea and coffee, newspapers and books – even a USB printer. There's also Plum + Spilt Milk, a grand restaurant with a quiet bar, on the first floor, while the busy ground-floor GNH Bar has direct access to King's Cross station.

London Edition
10 Berners Street, Fitzrovia, W1T 3NP (7781 0000, www.editionhotels.com/london). Oxford Circus or Tottenham Court Road tube. **Map** *p113 K6.*
The London Edition makes a big impact as you walk into its grand hall of a lobby, complete with double-height rococo ceilings, floor-to-ceiling windows and marble pillars. And there's more to the space: it's the setting for the lobby bar, with an eclectic mix of comfortable, snazzy seating – sofas with faux-fur throws and wing-backed chairs – plus a snooker table, a blackened steel bar, a real fire and a colossal silver egg-shaped object hanging where you might expect a chandelier. Off on one side is the equally opulent Berners Tavern, where Jason Atherton is executive chef. With banquette seating and many paintings, it has the vibe of a grand café and a brasserie-style menu to match. Hidden away at the back of the public area is the clubby, wood-panelled Punch Room bar, where the speciality is – you've guessed it – punch. Bedrooms are a contrast: akin to lodges or dachas, with matte oak floors, wood-panelled walls and more faux-fur throws tossed on luxurious beds. Larger rooms come with sofas, some have large furnished terraces,

and all have rainforest showers, Le Labo toiletries (with the hotel's woody signature scent) and iPod docks.

Portobello Hotel
22 Stanley Gardens, Notting Hill, W11 2NG (7727 2777, www.portobellohotel.com). Holland Park or Notting Hill Gate tube.
The Portobello is a hotel with nearly half a century of celebrity status, having hosted the likes of Johnny Depp, Kate Moss and Alice Cooper, who used his tub to house a boa constrictor. It remains a pleasingly unpretentious place, with a more civilised demeanour than its legend might suggest. There is now a lift to help rockers who are feeling their age up the five floors, but there's still a 24-hour guest-only bar downstairs for those who don't yet feel past it. The rooms are themed – the superb basement Japanese Water Garden, for example, has an elaborate spa bath, its own private grotto and a small private garden – but all are stylishly equipped with a large fan, tall house plants and round-the-clock room service.

Rookery
12 Peter's Lane, Cowcross Street, Clerkenwell, EC1M 6DS (7336 0931, www.rookeryhotel.com). Farringdon tube/rail. **Map** *p154 P6.*
The Rookery has long been something of a celebrity hideaway deep in the heart of Clerkenwell. Its front door is satisfyingly hard to find; when Fabric (see p161) devotees are about the front rooms can be noisy, but the place is otherwise as creakily calm as a country manor. Once inside, guests enjoy an atmospheric warren of rooms, each individually decorated in the style of a Georgian townhouse: huge clawfoot baths, elegant four-posters, antique desks, old paintings and brass shower fittings. While the decor is dialled to 18th-century glamour, modernity is definitely not forgotten. There's an honesty bar in the bright and airy drawing room at the back, which opens on to a sweet little patio.

W London Leicester Square

*10 Wardour Street, Leicester Square, W1D 6QF (7758 1000, www.wlondon. co.uk). Leicester Square tube. **Map** p133 L8.*

Where the old Swiss Centre used to be in the north-west corner of Leicester Square is the UK's first W Hotel, the entire building veiled in translucent glass that is lit in different colours through the day. The brand made its name with hip hotels around the world that offer glamorous bars, upmarket food and functional but spacious rooms. The London W is no exception: Room 913 is a large nightclub/bar space with possibly the largest glitterball in town; while the W lounge offers classy cocktails and a Sunday brunch party. There's also a branch of the deathlessly popular concept restaurant Burger & Lobster (*see p134*). The rooms – across ten storeys – are well equipped, with their own munchie boxes. FIT (the hotel's state-of-the-art fitness facility), placed next to the pale and serene Away Spa on the sixth floor, offers fine views over Soho. Oh, and there's a private 3D cinema.

Moderate
Bermondsey Square Hotel

*Bermondsey Square, Tower Bridge Road, Bermondsey, SE1 3UN (7378 2450, www.bermondseysquarehotel. co.uk). Borough tube or London Bridge tube/rail. **Map** p68 R11.*

This is a deliberately kitsch new-build hotel on a redeveloped square. Loft suites are named after the heroines of psychedelic rock classics (Lucy, Lily, Jude, Ruby and Eleanor); some have private terraces or a hammock, or Japanese baths. Rooms have classic discs on the walls, and you can kick your heels from the suspended Bubble Chair at reception. But, although occupants of the Lucy suite get a multi-person jacuzzi (with a great terrace view), the real draw isn't the gimmicks – it's well-designed rooms for competitive prices.

Hoxton Holborn

*199-206 High Holborn, Holborn, WC1V 7BD (7661 3000, thehoxton.com). Holborn tube. **Map** p125 M6.*

Shoebox, Snug, Cosy and Roomy. That's the choice you get when you stay at the Hoxton's trendy Holborn outpost, but who cares about room size when you're just about as close to the centre of London as it's possible to be. In truth, the rooms are so well designed you barely notice their size. Clever use of mirrors helps to enlarge the space, reflecting the room's dark walls, soft lighting and casually hip vibe. Add to that a snazzy TV and a lovely walk-in shower. The West End's bars and restaurants are right on your doorstep but the hotel bar, decked out in 1970s furniture, does a mean negroni to get you started.

La Suite West

41-51 Inverness Terrace, Bayswater, W2 3JN (7313 8484, www.lasuitewest.com). Bayswater or Queensway tube.

A typical row of west London townhouses on the outside, La Suite has been transformed on the inside by designer Anouska Hempel, with sleek lines and a black and white palette. A discreet side entrance leads into a long, minimalist reception area with an open fire and a zen-like feel. An Asian influence persists in the rooms, with slatted sliding screens for windows, wardrobe and bathrooms helping to make good use of space (which is limited in the cheaper rooms). Thoughtfully designed white marble bathrooms, with rainforest shower and bath, give a feeling of luxury despite not being huge. The large terrace running along the front of the building, with trees planted for an arbour-like effect, is a big summer asset for drinks, lunch or dinner, and the Raw vegetarian restaurant is an unusual take on hotel dining. A great hotel for this price range. Highly recommended.

Shoreditch Rooms

Ebor Street, Shoreditch House, Shoreditch, E1 6AW (7739 5040, www.shoreditchhouse.com/hotel). Shoreditch High Street Overground. Map p179 U5.

Shoreditch Rooms perfectly catches the local atmosphere, with its unfussy slightly retro design. The rooms are a bit like urban beach huts, with pastel-coloured tongue-and-groove shutters and swing doors to the en suite showers. They feel fresh, bright and comfortable, even though they're furnished with little more than a bed, an old-fashioned phone and DAB radio, and a big, solid dresser (minibar, hairdryer and treats within, flatscreen TV on top). Guests get access to the fine eating, drinking and fitness facilities (including a gym and an excellent rooftop pool) in the members' club next door. Everything's put together with a light touch, from the 'Borrow Me' bookshelf by the lifts (jelly beans, umbrellas, boardgames) to the room grades: Tiny (from just £125), Small or Small+ (with little rooftop balconies from which to survey the grey horizon).

Zetter Hotel

86-88 Clerkenwell Road, EC1M 5RJ (7324 4567, www.thezetter.com). Farringdon tube/rail. Map p154 P5.

Zetter is a fun, laid-back, modern hotel with some interesting design notes. There's a refreshing lack of attitude and a forward-looking approach, with friendly staff and firm eco-credentials (such as free Brompton bikes for guests' use). The rooms, stacked up on five galleried storeys around an impressive atrium, look into an intimate and recently refreshed bar area. They are smoothly functional, but cosied up with choice home comforts such as hot-water bottles and old Penguin paperbacks, as well as having walk-in showers with REN smellies. The downstairs is home to Club Zetter, while the fabulous sister-hotel Zetter Townhouse, in a historic building just across the square, has a fantastic cocktail bar with a hip vintage feel.

Budget

citizenM London Bankside

20 Lavington Street, Southwark, SE1 0NZ (3519 1680, www.citizenm.com). Southwark tube. Map p68 P9.

This casually stylish new build is a superbly well-designed – and well-located – addition to London's affordably chic hotels. The ground floor is a slick yet cosy café-bar and reception area: self-check-in, but with staff on hand to help and, where better rooms are available, offer upgrades. The rooms themselves are tiny but well thought through: there are blackout blinds, drench showers with removable sideheads, storage under the bed and free movies. The rooms are also fun: those blinds are automatic, controlled – as are the movies, air-con and funky coloured lighting – from a touch-sensitive tablet. While the Bankside branch gets our nod for its location right behind Tate Modern, the two more recent London citizenMs – one in Shoreditch (6 Holywell Lane, EC2A 3ET), the other near the Tower of London (40 Trinity Square, EC3N 4DJ) – are also very handy for holidaymakers.

Dictionary Hostel

10-20 Kingsland Road, Shoreditch, E2 8DA (7613 2784, thedictionaryhostel. com/en). Old Street tube/rail or Shoreditch High Street Overground. Map p179 S4.

Club kids, you've found your home: right at the axis of Kingsland Road and Old Street and so walking – or crawling – distance from Hoxton's best dance spots. There's a bar downstairs, Translate, and also a laundrette, a café, a cute, plant-covered interior courtyard and an intimate roof terrace. There are dorm beds and private rooms starting at £17 (with TVs, kettle and coffee). Jam-jar lighting, swings in the dorms and fairy-lit communal areas are quirky touches, which make for an enjoyable stay. Breakfast is free and includes the highly prized bagels from nearby Brick Lane.

Jenkins

45 Cartwright Gardens, Bloomsbury, WC1H 9EH (7383 9210, www. juddhotelbloomsbury.com). Russell Square tube or Euston tube/rail. **Map** *p125 L4.*

This well-to-do Georgian beauty has been a hotel since the 1920s. It still has an atmospheric, antique air, although the rooms have mod cons enough – TVs, mini-fridges, tea and coffee, and free Wi-Fi. Its looks have earned it a role in Agatha Christie's *Poirot*, but it's not chintzy, just floral. The breakfast room is handsome, with snowy cotton tablecloths and Windsor chairs, and the buffet breakfast – which includes hot options – is free.

Qbic London City Hotel

42 Adler Street, Whitechapel, E1 1EE (3021 2644, www.qbichotels.com). Aldgate East or Whitechapel tube.

The Dutch invasion of stylish budget hotels continues with this Brick Lane offering, created by the incredibly rapid fit-out of a former office building using modular 'Cubi' bedrooms. The hotel also works with local cycling charity Bikeworks and with Food Cycle, which provides free soup every afternoon. The rooms are sold at four levels – starting

at £69 a night for no view. Prices are pegged by keeping down the numbers of staff, which means self check-in and no cash accepted – even vending machines are card only. Still, the essentials are covered: TVs in each room, Wi-Fi throughout, free snack breakfast (or £13 for a continental) in the natty social space downstairs. The location is gritty but great: minutes from Brick Lane.

Z Hotel Soho

17 Moor Street, Soho, W1D 5AP (3551 3700, www.thezhotels.com/soho). Leicester Square tube. **Map** *p133 L7.*

For the money, the Z is an absolute bargain. First, the location is superb: it really means Soho, not a short bus-ride away – the breakfast room/bar exits on to Old Compton Street. Then there's the hotel itself, which is surprisingly chic – especially the unexpected interior courtyard – and very cheerfully run, down to free wine and nibbles of an evening. The rooms are quite handsome, and have everything you need, from a little desk to free Wi-Fi, but not much more. Expect beds (perhaps a bit short for anyone over 6ft tall) to take up most of the room, a feeble shower, and no wardrobes or phones. A great little hotel – in both senses.

Getting Around

ARRIVING & LEAVING

By air

Gatwick Airport *0844 892 0322, www.gatwickairport.com. About 30 miles south of London, off the M23.*
The quickest link to London is the **Gatwick Express** (0345 850 1530, www.gatwickexpress.com) to Victoria; it takes 30mins and runs 4.30am-12.30am daily. Tickets cost £19.90 single or £35.50 for an open return.

Southern (0345 127 2920, www.southernrailway.com) also runs a rail service between Gatwick and Victoria, every 5-10mins (hourly 2-4am and every 15-30mins midnight-2am, 4-6am). It takes about 35mins, and costs from £12 for a single, £15.80 for a day return (after 9.30am) and £31.40 for an open return.

Thameslink Great Northern (www.thameslinkrailway.com) costs from £19.90 single and from £27.20 day return (after 9.30am).

A **taxi** to the centre costs from £90 and takes a bit over an hour.

Heathrow Airport *0844 335 1801, www.heathrowairport.com. About 15 miles west of London, off the M4.*
The **Heathrow Express** train (0845 600 1515, www.heathrowexpress.co.uk) runs to Paddington every 15mins (5.10am-11.25pm daily) and takes 15-20mins. Tickets cost £22-£25 single and £37 return

The journey by **tube** is longer but cheaper. The 50-60min Piccadilly line ride into central London costs £6 one way. Trains run every few minutes from about 6am to 12.30am daily (7am-11.30pm Sun).

The **Heathrow Connect** (0345 604 1515, www.heathrow connect.com) rail service offers direct access to stations including Ealing Broadway and Paddington. The trains run every 15-30mins, from 4.42am to 11.05pm, terminating at Heathrow Central (Terminals 2 and 3). From there, take a free shuttle to Terminal 4; between Central and Terminal 5, there's free use of the Heathrow Express. A single from Paddington is £10.30; an open return is £20.70.

National Express (0871 781 8171, www.nationalexpress.com) runs daily coach services to London Victoria (35-60mins, 4.20am-10.05pm daily), leaving Heathrow Central bus terminal every 20-30mins. It's £10 for a single and £16 for a return.

A **taxi** into town will cost £45-£70 and take 30-60mins.

London City Airport *7646 0088, www.londoncityairport.com. About 9 miles east of central London.*
The **Docklands Light Railway** (DLR) includes a stop for London City Airport and runs every 8-15mins. The journey to Bank station in the City takes around 20mins, and trains run 5.36am-12.16am Mon-Sat, 7.06am-11.16pm Sun. Tickets cost £4.90; £2.45 11-15s.

A **taxi** costs around £40 to central London.

Luton Airport *01582 405100, www.london-luton.com. About 30 miles north of London, J10 off the M1.*
A short bus ride links the airport to Luton Airport Parkway station, from which **Thameslink Great Northern trains** depart for stations including St Pancras and City, 35-45mins. Trains leave every 15mins (hourly through the night) and cost £14.20 one-way, £22.80 return.

By coach, the Luton to Victoria journey takes 60-90mins. **Green Line** (0844 801 7261, www.green line.co.uk) runs a 24hr service. Tickets are £10 single, £17 return.

A **taxi** to London costs from £80.

Stansted Airport *0844 335 1803, www.stanstedairport.com. About 35 miles north-east of London, J8 off the M11.*

The **Stansted Express** train, www.stanstedexpress.com) runs to and from Liverpool Street Station; taking 40-45minss and leaving every 15 mins. Tickets are £16.50 single, £28 return.

National Express (0871 781 8171, www.nationalexpress.com) is one of several coach services running to Victoria Coach Station; the journey takes 1hr 45mins with coaches roughly every 20mins (24hrs daily). A single is £13, an open return is £19.

A **taxi** into the centre of London costs from £60.

By coach

Coaches run by **National Express** (0871 781 8171, www.nationalexpress.com) and **Eurolines** (0871 781 8177, www.eurolines.co.uk) arrive at **Victoria Coach Station** (164 Buckingham Palace Road, SW1W 9TP, 0343 222 1234, www.tfl.gov.uk), a good 10min walk from Victoria tube station.

By rail

Trains from mainland Europe run by **Eurostar** (0343 218 6186, www.eurostar.com) arrive at **St Pancras International** (Pancras Road, Euston Road, N1C 4QP, 7843 7688, www.stpancras.com).

PUBLIC TRANSPORT

Timetables and other travel information are provided by **Transport for London** (0343 222 1234, www.tfl.gov.uk).

In the know
Routemaster buses

London's original hop-on/hop-off double-decker buses still run on Route 15 (between Trafalgar Square and Tower Hill; head to stop F on the Strand) every 15 minutes from 9.30am. You must have a ticket or valid card before boarding.

Travel Information Centres

These offer help with the tube, buses and DLR. Call 0343 222 1234 for more information.

Euston *opposite Platform 8, 8am-6pm Mon-Sat, 8.30am-6pm Sun.*
Gatwick Airport *North Terminal arrivals hall, 9.15am-4pm daily. South Terminal arrivals hall 9.15am-4pm daily.*
Heathrow Airport *Terminals 1, 2, 3 underground station concourse, 7.30am-8.30pm daily.*
King's Cross *Western Ticket Hall, near St Pancras, 8am-6pm Mon-Sat, 8.30am-6pm Sun.*
Liverpool Street tube/rail *9am-5pm daily.*
Piccadilly Circus tube *9.30am-4pm daily.*
Victoria (main station) *opposite Platform 8 8am-6pm daily.*

Fares & tickets

London transport is becoming increasingly cash-free. Paper tickets for buses and trains are still available from ticket machines but it's far easier (and cheaper) to use a pre-paid Oyster card or contactless debit/credit card (*see below*).

Tube and DLR fares are based on a system of six zones, which stretch 12 miles out from from central London. The single adult fare is £4.90 for journeys within zones 1-3; £6 for zones 1-6; £7.40 for zones 1-7; £8.50 for zones 1-9. Using Oyster pay-as-you-go or a contactless card, journeys within zone 1 cost £2.40; zones 1-3 costs £2.80 (off peak)/£3.30 (peak); zones 1-6 costs £3.10 (off peak)/£5.10 (peak). Peak hours are 6.30-9.30am, 4-7pm Mon-Fri.

Oyster cards & contactless payments

You can buy and charge Oyster cards at Travel Information Centres (*see above*), tube stations, and some newsagents and rail stations. Cards are also available from www.tfl.gov.uk/oyster. A £5 refundable deposit is payable on new cards.

If you have a credit or debit card with the contactless symbol you can use it instead of getting an Oyster card – and you will pay the same fare.

Travelcards

If you're only using the tube, DLR and buses, using Oyster to pay-as-you-go will always be capped at the same price as or slightly lower than an equivalent Day Travelcard. However, if you're also using certain National Rail services, Oyster may not be accepted: opt, instead, for a Day Travelcard, a ticket that allows travel across all networks.

Anytime Day Travelcards can be used all day. They cost £12.30 for zones 1-2, £17.50 for zones 1-6. Tickets are valid for journeys begun by 4.30am the next day. The **Off-Peak Day Travelcard** allows travel after 9.30am Mon-Fri (all day at weekends and public holidays). It costs £12.30 for zones 1-6.

Travelling with children

The single tube fare for children aged 5-15 is 75p (off peak)/85p (peak) for any journey in zones 1-6. Under-5s travel free without the need to provide any proof of identity. Five-to 10-year-olds can also travel free, but need to obtain a 5-10 Zip Oyster photocard. An 11-15 Zip Oyster photocard is needed by 11- to 15-year-olds to pay as they go on the tube/DLR and to buy 7-day, monthly or longer period Travelcards. Photocards can be obtained in advance from www.tfl.gov.uk/tickets.

London Underground

Trains are hot and crowded in rush hour (8-9.30am, 4.30-7pm Mon-Fri). Even so, the 12 colour-coded lines of the Underground ('the tube') are the quickest way to get about. For fares, *see p200*.

Paper single or day tickets can be bought from self-service ticket machines in tube stations. To enter using a paper ticket, place it in the slot with the black magnetic strip facing down, then pull it out of the top to open the gates. Exit in the same way; tickets for single journeys will be retained by the gate on final exit.

To enter and exit the tube using an Oyster or contactless card, touch it to the yellow reader, which opens the gate. You must also touch the card to the reader when you exit, or you'll be charged a higher fare when you next use your card. On certain lines, you'll see a pink reader (the 'validator') – touch it in addition to the yellow entry/exit readers and on some routes it will reduce your fare.

Timetables

Tube trains run daily from around 5.30am (except Sunday, when they start an hour or so later, and Christmas Day, when there's no service). You shouldn't have to wait more than 10mins for a train; during peak times, services should run every 2-3mins. Times of last trains vary; they're usually around 12.30am (11.30pm on Sun). The Night Tube, offering a limited 24hr service, runs Fri/Sat on the Victoria, Jubilee, and most of the Central, Northern and Piccadilly lines. Tubes also run all night on New Year's Eve. Otherwise, you're limited to night buses (*see p202*).

Night Tube

The all-night tube service started in 2016. Now almost all of the Central, Northern and Piccadilly lines, and the entire Jubilee and Victoria lines, have services through Fri/Sat and Sat/Sun. They are fast, frequent (roughly every 10mins) and you can continue to use your Day Travelcard (or capped pay-as-you-go card) until 4.30am in the morning after the day covered by that card.

In the know
Travelling fines

Anyone caught travelling witho[ut] ticket, Oyster or contactless [is] subject to an £80 on the s[pot] (reduced to £40 if you p[ay] three weeks).

Docklands Light Railway

DLR trains (0343 222 1234, www.tfl. gov. uk/modes/dlr) run from Bank station (where they connect with the Central, Northern and Waterloo & City lines) or Tower Gateway, close to Tower Hill tube (Circle and District lines). Stations are shown on the Underground map. Trains run 5.30am-12.40am daily, and there are lots of good views of Docklands to be enjoyed. Fares are the same as the tube.

Overground

The **Overground** (0343 222 1234) is a patchwork of different rail services, some tracing a complex orbital route roughly following the boundary of zones 2 and 3 (the orange-and-white line on the tube map) and providing a useful service for areas with poor Underground coverage. From December 2017, the **Night Tube** will begin Overground services, with a very useful link between New Cross Gate and Dalston Junction; from 2018 it will head as far north as Highbury & Islington. Fares are the same as the tube.

National Rail services

Independently run commuter services co-ordinated by **National Rail** (03457 48 49 50, www.national rail.co.uk) leave from the city's main rail stations. Visitors heading to south London, or to more remote destinations such as Hampton Court Palace, use these services.

Fares

Travelcards are valid on these services within the right zones, but not all routes accept Oyster pay-as-you-go or contactless payments.

rail

untingly massive infrastructure
as been burrowing under the
nsive parts of London since
2018, the central sections
ration; from 2019, sleeper-
will be whisked into
and west at great

speed. See www.crossrail.co.uk for details.

Buses

Buses are now cash-free, so you must have a ticket, Travelcard pass or Oyster card/contactless card (for both, *see p200*). You can buy a ticket from machines in tube and rail stations. All buses are now low-floor vehicles that are accessible to wheelchair-users and passengers with buggies. The only exception is Heritage route 15, which is served by the historic and world-famous open-platform Routemaster buses.

Using an Oyster card costs £1.50 per trip; your total daily payment, regardless of how many journeys you take, will be capped at £4.50. Under-16s travel for free (using an Under-11 or 11-15 Oyster photocard, as appropriate; *see p201*). You can take a second busjourney for free if you board within an hour of touching in on your first bus.

Night buses

Many bus routes operate 24hrs a day, seven days a week. There are also night buses with an 'N' prefx, which run from about 11pm to 7am. Most night services run every 15-30mins, but busier routes run every 10mins or so. Fares are the same as for daytime buses; Bus Passes and Travelcards can be used at no extra fare until 4.30am of the morning after they expire, with Oyster day-capping in effect until then too.

Water transport

Most river services operate every 20-60mins from 7am-9pm, more often and later in summer; see www.tfl.gov. uk. For commuters, **Thames Clippers** (www.thamesclippers.com) runs a service between Embankment Pier and Royal Arsenal Woolwich Pier boarded at Blackfriars, Bankside, London Bridge, Canary Wharf and Greenwich. A standard day roamer ticket (valid 9am-9pm) costs £18.50, £9.25 for a child (5-15s), while a single from Embankment to Greenwich is £8, £4 under-16s, or

£6.30 for Oyster cardholders. Book online for reductions.

Thames River Services (7930 4097, www.thamesriverservices.co.uk) operates from Westminster pier, with trips to Greenwich and Tower Pier, and the Thames Barrier from May to Oct. A trip to Greenwich costs £12.50. Travelcard holders get a third off. Book online for reductions.

TAXIS & MINICABS

If a **black cab**'s orange 'For Hire' sign is lit, it can be hailed. If it stops, the cabbie must take you to your destination if it's within seven miles. Fares rise after 8pm, on weekdays and at weekends. You can book black cabs using the very handy free **Hailo app** (for a list of apps visit tfl.gov.uk/modes/taxisand-minicabs/taxi-and-minicab-apps), or from **Radio Taxis** (7272 0272) and **Dial-a-Cab** (7253 5000; cards only).

Minicabs (saloon cars) are generally cheaper than black cabs, but can be less reliable. Only use licensed firms (look for a disc in the front and rear windows) and avoid drivers who illegally tout for business in the street: such drivers may be uninsured and dangerous. Check the price when booking, and with the driver before getting in. If you text HOME to 60835 ('60TFL'), Transport for London will reply with the numbers of the two nearest licensed minicab operators and the number for **Radio Taxis**, which provides licensed black taxis in London (35p plus standard call rate). You can also use the **Uber** app to hail – and pay for – a minicab.

DRIVING

Congestion charge

Drivers into central London 7am-6pm Mon-Fri costs £11.50. You'll know when you're about to drive into the charging zone from the red 'C' signs on the road. The restricted area is shown at www.tfl.gov.uk/modes/congestioncharging. You can pay at some newsagents, garages, NCP car parks or at www.tfl.

gov.uk/modes/congestion charging, by phone on 0343 222 2222 or by SMS. You can pay any time during the day or, for £2.50 more, until midnight on the next day. Expect a fine of £130 for non-payment (reduced to £65 if you pay within 14 days).

Parking

Parking on a single or double yellow line, a red line or in residents' parking areas during the day is illegal, and you may be fined, clamped or towed. In the evening (from 6pm or 7pm in much of central London) and at various times at weekends, parking on single yellow lines is legal and free; look for a sign giving the local regulations. During the day meters cost upwards of £1 for 15mins, limited to two hours, but they are free at certain times during evenings and weekends. Parking on double yellows and red routes is always illegal. Use an app like **AppyParking** to help you find the nearest free car parking; otherwise, there are many **NCP** car parks (www.ncp.co.uk), open 24hrs a day.

Vehicle removal

If your car has disappeared, it's either been stolen or, if it was parked illegally, towed to a car pound by the local authorities. A release fee of £200 is levied for removal, plus upwards of £40 per day from the first midnight after removal. You'll also probably get a parking ticket, typically £130 (reduced by 50% if paid within 14 days). Contact **Trace Information Service** (0845 206 8602, trace.london).

CYCLING

London isn't the friendliest town for cyclists, but the **London Cycle Network** (www.londoncyclenetwork. org.uk) and **London Cycling Campaign** (7234 9310, www.lcc.org.uk) help to keep things improving.

Cycling tips are available at tfl.gov.uk/modes/cycling. TfL also runs the **Santander Cycles** scheme (0343

222 6666, tfl.gov.uk/modes/cycling/santander-cycles), nicknamed 'Boris Bikes' and recognisable by their red Santander sponsorship branding. These can be found at various 24hr docking stations. Touch the 'Hire a cycle' icon and insert a credit or debit card. The machine will print out a five-digit code, which you then tap into the docking point of a bike, releasing the cycle. A £2 fee buys 24hr access to the bikes; the first 30 minutes are free.

WALKING

The best way to see London is on foot, but the street layout is complicated. There's route advice at www.tfl.gov.uk/modes/walking (the map of walking times between stations, which can be downloaded from content.tfl.gov.uk/walking-tube-map.pdf, is particularly useful). Look out too for the yellowtopped 'Legible London' information posts (www.tfl.gov.uk/microsites/legible-london), which are oriented to the direction you're heading, rather than with north at the top.

Resources A-Z

ACCIDENT & EMERGENCY

In the event of a serious accident, fire or other incident, call 999 – free from any phone, including payphones – and ask for an ambulance, the fire service or police. If no one is in immediate danger, call 101.

Emergency departments

Listed below are most of the central London hospitals that have Accident & Emergency (A&E) departments which are open 24 hours daily.

Charing Cross Hospital *Fulham Palace Road, Hammersmith, W6 8RF (3311 1234, www.imperial.nhs.uk). Hammersmith tube.*

Chelsea & Westminster Hospital *369 Fulham Road, Chelsea, SW10 9NH (3315 8000, www.chelwest. nhs.uk). South Kensington tube.*

Royal Free Hospital *Pond Street, Hampstead, NW3 2QG (7794 0500, www.royalfree.nhs.uk). Belsize Park tube or Hampstead Heath Overground.*

Royal London Hospital *Whitechapel Road, Whitechapel, E1 1BB (7377 7000, www.bartshealth.nhs.uk). Whitechapel tube/Overground.*

St Mary's Hospital *Praed Street, Paddington, W2 1NY (3312 6666, www. imperial.nhs.uk). Paddington tube/rail.*

St Thomas' Hospital *Westminster Bridge Road, South Bank, SE1 7EH (7188 7188, www.guysandstthomas.nhs. uk). Westminster tube or Waterloo tube/ rail.* **Map** *p68 M10.*

University College Hospital *235 Euston Road, NW1 2BU (3456 7890, www.uclh.nhs.uk). Euston Square or Warren Street tube.* **Map** *p113 K5*

Dental emergencies

Guy's Hospital *floors 17-28, Tower Wing, Great Maze Pond, SE1 9RT (7188 8006, www.guysandstthomas.nhs.uk/ our-services/dental). London Bridge tube/rail.* **Open** *9am-12.30pm, 1.30-3pm Mon-Fri.* **Map** *p68 Q9.*
Queues start forming at 8am; arrive by 10am if you're to be seen at all.

Pharmacies

Also called 'chemists' in the UK. Branches of **Boots** (www.boots.com) and larger supermarkets will have a pharmacy. Most keep shop hours (9am-6pm Mon-Sat) but the Boots store

Travel Advice

For up-to-date information on travel to a specific country – including the latest on safety and security, health issues, local laws and customs – contact your home country government's department of foreign affairs. Most have websites with useful advice for would-be travellers

Australia
www.smartraveller.gov.au

Canada
www.voyage.gc.ca

New Zealand
www.safetravel.govt.nz

Republic of Ireland
www.dfa.ie

UK
www.fco.gov.uk/travel

USA
www.state.gov/travel

at 44-46 Regent Street, Mayfair, W1B 5RA (7734 6126), opens until 11.30pm (6.30pm Sun).

Useful websites

www.alcoholics-anonymous.org.uk
www.citizensadvice.org.uk
www.missingpeople.org.uk
www.nhsdirect.nhs.uk
www.rapecrisis.org.uk
www.samaritans.org
www.victimsupport.org.uk

AGE RESTRICTIONS

Buying/drinking alcohol 18
Driving 17
Sex 16
Smoking 18

CUSTOMS

Citizens entering the UK from outside the EU must adhere to duty-free import limits:

• 200 cigarettes or 100 cigarillos or 50 cigars or 250g of tobacco
• 4 litres still table wine plus either 1 litre spirits or strong liqueurs (above 22% abv) or 2 litres fortified wine (under 22% abv), sparkling wine or other liqueurs
• other goods to the value of no more than £390

The import of meat, poultry, fruit, plants, flowers and protected animals is restricted or forbidden; there are no restrictions on the import or export of currency if travelling from another EU country. If you are travelling from outside the EU, amounts over €10,000 must be declared on arrival.

People over the age of 17 arriving from an EU country are able to import unlimited goods for their own personal use, if bought tax-paid (so not duty-free). Quite what the arrangements will be post-Brexit, it seems not even the government yet knows – but the likelihood of any rapid change is

Climate

Average temperatures and monthly rainfall in London

	Temp High (°C/°F)	Temp Low (°C/°F)	Rainfall (mm/in)
January	6/ 43	2/36	54 /2.1
February	7/44	2/36	40 / 1.6
March	10/50	3/37	37 / 1.5
April	13/55	6/43	37 / 1.5
May	17/63	8/46	46 / 1.8
June	20/68	12/54	45 / 1.8
...ly	22/72	14/57	57 / 2.2
...st	21/70	13/55	59 / 2.3
...ber	19/66	11/52	49 / 1.9
	14/57	8/46	57 / 2.2
	10/50	5/41	64 / 2.5
	7/44	4/39	48 / 1.9

remote. For the current details, see www.gov.uk.

DISABLED

As a city that evolved long before the needs of disabled people were considered, London is difficult for wheelchair users, though facilities are slowly improving. The bus fleet is now low-floor for easier wheelchair access and all DLR stations have either lifts or ramp access. However, most tube stations still have escalator-only access; those with lifts are marked with a blue wheelchair symbol on tube maps. The *Step-free Tube Guide* map is free; call 0343 222 1234 or download it from tfl.gov.uk/accessguides.

Most major attractions and hotels have good accessibility, though provisions for the hearing- and sight-disabled are patchier. *Access in London* is an invaluable reference book for disabled travellers (£10 donation) from **Access Project** (39 Bradley Gardens,W13 8HE, www.accessinlondon.org).

Useful websites
www.artsline.org.uk
www.canbedone.co.uk
www.disabilityrightsuk.org
www.tourismforall.org.uk
www.wheelchair-travel.co.uk

DRUGS

Illegal drug use remains higher in London than the UK as a whole, though it's becoming less visible on the streets and in clubs. Despite fierce debate, cannabis has been reclassified from Class C to Class B (where it rejoins amphetamines), but possession of a small amount might attract no more than a warning for a first offence. More serious Class B and A drugs (ecstasy, LSD, heroin, cocaine and the like) carry stiffer penalties, with a maximum of seven years in prison for possession plus a fine.

ELECTRICITY

The UK uses 220-240V, 50-cycle AC voltage and three-pin plugs.

EMBASSIES & CONSULATES

American Embassy *24 Grosvenor Square, Mayfair, W1A 2LQ (7499 9000, www.london.usembassy.gov). Bond Street or Marble Arch tube.* **Open** *8.30am-5.30pm Mon-Fri.* **Map** *p113 H8.*

Australian High Commission *Australia House, Strand, Holborn, WC2B 4LA (7379 4334, www. uk.embassy.gov.au). Holborn or Temple tube.* **Open** *9am-5pm Mon-Fri.* **Map** *p154 N7.*

Canadian High Commission *Canada House, Trafalgar Square, Westminster, SW1Y 5BJ (7004 6000, www.canada. org.uk). Charing Cross tube/rail.* **Open** *9.30am-12.30pm Mon-Fri.* **Map** *p83 L8.*

Embassy of Ireland *17 Grosvenor Place, Belgravia, SW1X 7HR (7235 2171, 7373 4339 passports & visas, www.dfa.ie/irish-embassy/great-britain). Hyde Park Corner tube.* **Open** *9.30am-12.30pm, 2.30-4.30pm Mon-Fri.* **Map** *p96 H10.*

New Zealand High Commission *New Zealand House, 80 Haymarket, St James's, SW1Y 4TQ (7930 8422, www. mfat.govt.nz/en/embassies). Piccadilly Circus tube.* **Open** *9am-5pm Mon-Fri.* **Map** *p133 L8.*

HEALTH

It's advisable that all travellers take out insurance before leaving home. EU residents travelling in the UK require a European National Health Insurance Card (EHIC). This allows them to benefit from free or reduced-cost medical care. For further information, refer to www.dh.gov.uk/travellers and *p205*, Accident & Emergency.

LEFT LUGGAGE

Airports
Gatwick Airport *01293 569 900.*
Heathrow Airport *8759 3344.*
London City Airport *7646 0088.*
Luton Airport *01582 405100.*
Stansted Airport *0330 223 0893.*

Rail & bus stations
London stations tend to have left-luggage desks rather than lockers. Call 0845 748 4950 for details.

Charing Cross *7930 5444. **Open** 7am-11pm daily.*
Euston *7387 1499. **Open** 7am-11pm daily.*
King's Cross *7837 4334. **Open** 7am-11pm daily.*
Paddington *7262 0344. **Open** 7am-11pm daily.*
Victoria *7963 0957. **Open** 7am-midnight daily.*

LGBT

London Friend *86 Caledonian Road, N1 9DN (7833 1674, londonfriend.org. uk). **Open** 7.30-9.30pm Mon-Wed.*
London Lesbian & Gay Switchboard *0300 330 0630, www. llgs.org.uk. **Open** 10am-11pm daily.*

LOST PROPERTY

Always inform the police if you lose anything, if only to validate insurance claims. Only dial 999 if violence has occurred; use 101 for non-emergencies. Report lost passports both to the police and to your embassy (*see p207*).

Airports
For items left on the plane, contact the relevant airline. Otherwise, phone:

Gatwick Airport *01293 223 457.*
Heathrow Airport *0844 824 3115.*
London City Airport *7646 0000.*
Luton Airport *01582 809174.*
Stansted Airport *0844 824 3109.*

Public transport
Transport for London *Lost Property Office, 200 Baker Street, Marylebone, NW1 5RZ (0343 222 1234, www.tfl.gov. uk/lostproperty). Baker Street tube.* **Open** *8.30am-4pm Mon-Fri.* **Map** *p113 H5.*
Allow two to ten working days from the time of loss. If you lose something on a bus, call 0343 222 1234 and ask for the numbers of the depots at either end of the route. For tube losses, pick up a lost-property form from any station. There is a fee to cover costs.

Taxis
The Transport for London office (*see above*) deals with property found in registered black cabs. Allow two to ten days from the time of loss. For items lost in a minicab or Über, contact the relevant company.

MONEY

Britain's currency is the pound sterling (£).

ATMs
Cash machines are found at banks, supermarkets and in larger larger stations. You should be able to withdraw cash from ATMs using any credit or debit card. Generally this is the cheapest form of currency exchange.

Credit cards
Credit cards, especially Visa, are accepted in most shops (except small corner shops) and restaurants. American Express and Diners Club tend to be accepted only at more expensive outlets. You will usually have to have a PIN number to make a purchase.

If you lose your card, call the relevant 24hr number:

American Express *01273 696 933, www.americanexpress.com.*
Diners Club *0845 862 2935, www. dinersclub.co.uk.*

MasterCard *0800 964767, www. mastercard.com.*
Visa *0800 891725, www.visa.co.uk.*

Tax

Value Added Tax (VAT) of 20% is a sales tax added to most goods and services in the UK. This will be included in the prices quoted in shops, although it may not be included in hotel rates. Foreign visitors from outside the EU may be able to claim back VAT paid on goods via a scheme called 'Tax Free Shopping'. Fill in a refund form at the time of purchase (till receipts are not sufficient) and get verified by customs staff at the airport. You can then apply for your refund by posting the form back to the retailer or to a commercial refund company, or by taking your form to a refund booth to get immediate payment.

OPENING HOURS

Banks *9am-4.30pm (some close at 3.30pm, some 5.30pm) Mon-Fri; some also Sat mornings.*
Businesses *9am-5pm Mon-Fri.*
Post offices *9am-5.30pm Mon-Fri; 9am-noon Sat.*
Pubs & bars *11am-11pm Mon-Sat; noon-10.30pm Sun; many pubs and bars, particularly in central London, stay open later.*
Shops *10am-6pm Mon-Sat, some to 8pm. Many also open on Sun, usually 11am-5pm or noon-6pm.*

POLICE

For emergencies, call **999**. The non-emergency number is **101**.
London's police are used to helping visitors. If you've been robbed, assaulted or a victim of crime, go to your nearest police station.

Belgravia Police Station *202-206 Buckingham Palace Road, Pimlico, SW1W 9SX. Victoria tube/rail.*
Charing Cross Police Station *Agar Street, Covent Garden, WC2N 4JP.*

Charing Cross tube/rail. **Map** *p133 M8.*
Holborn Police Station *10 Lambs Conduit Street, Bloomsbury, WC1N 3NR. Holborn tube.* **Map** *p125 N6.*
Islington Police Station *2 Tolpuddle Street, Islington, N1 0YY. Angel tube.*
Kensington Police Station *72 Earls Court Road, W8 6EQ. High Street Kensington tube.*
West End Central Police Station *27 Savile Row, Mayfair, W1S 2EX. Oxford Circus tube.* **Map** *p113 K8.*

POSTAL SERVICES

The UK has a reliable postal service. Some central post offices are listed below; for others, check the Royal Mail website www.royalmail.com.

Baker Street *no.111, Marylebone, W1U 6SG. Baker Street tube.* **Map** *p113 H6.*
Great Portland Street *nos.54-56, Fitzrovia, W1W 7NE. Oxford Circus tube.* **Map** *p125 K6.*
High Holborn *no.181, Holborn, WC1V 7RL. Holborn tube.* **Map** *p133 M7.*

PUBLIC HOLIDAYS

On public holidays (bank holidays), many shops remain open, but public-transport services generally run to a Sunday timetable. On Christmas Day, almost everything, including public transport, closes down.

Good Friday *Fri 30 Mar 2018, Fri 19 Apr 2019*
Easter Monday *Mon 2 Apr 2018, Mon 22 Apr 2019*
May Day Holiday *Mon 7 May 2018, Mon 6 May 2019*
Spring Bank Holiday *Mon 28 May 2018, Mon 27 May 2019*
Summer Bank Holiday *Mon 27 Au 2018, Mon 26 Aug 2019*
Christmas Day *Mon 25 Dec 201 25 Dec 2018, Wed 25 Dec 2019*
Boxing Day *Tue 28 Dec 201 Dec 2018, Thur 26 Dec 2019*
New Year's Day *Mon 1 J 1 Jan 2019*

SMOKING

Smoking is banned in enclosed public spaces, such as pubs, clubs, shops, restaurants and public transport.

TELEPHONES

London's **dialling code** is 020; standard landlines have eight digits after that. If you're calling from outside the UK, dial your international access code code (Australia 61, Canada 1, New Zealand 64, Republic of Ireland 353, South Africa 27, USA 1), then the UK code, 44, then the full London number, omitting the first 0.

Mobile phones in the UK operate on the 900 MHz and 1800 MHz GSM frequencies. US cellphone users need a tri- or quad-band handset.

Public payphones take coins and/ or credit cards, but aren't widely distributed. International calling cards are widely available.

TIME

London operates on Greenwich Mean Time (GMT), five hours ahead of the US's Eastern Standard Time. In spring (25 March 2018) the UK puts its clocks forward by one hour to British Summer Time. In autumn (28 October 2018), the clocks go back to GMT.

TIPPING

In Britain, it's accepted that you tip in taxis, minicabs, restaurants (some waiting staff rely heavily on tips), hotels, hairdressers and some bars (not pubs). Around 10% is normal, but some restaurants add as much as 15%.

Always check whether service has been included in your bill: some restaurants include an automatic service charge, but also give the opportunity for a gratuity when paying with a card.

TOURIST INFORMATION

See also Travel Information Centres, *p200*

City of London Information Centre *St Paul's Churchyard, City, EC4M 8BX (7332 3456, www.cityoflondon.gov.uk).* **Open** *9.30am-5.30pm Mon-Sat; 10am-4pm Sun.* **Map** *p154 P7.*

Greenwich Tourist Information Centre *Old Royal Naval College, 2 Cutty Sark Gardens, Greenwich, SE10 0LW (0870 608 2000, www.visitgreenwich.org.uk). Cutty Sark DLR.* **Open** *10am-5pm daily.*

Holborn Information Kiosk *89-94 Kingsway, outside Holborn tube, WC2B 6AA (no phone).* **Open** *8am-6pm Mon-Fri.* **Map** *p125 M6.*

Twickenham Visitor Information Centre *Civic Centre, 44 York Street, Twickenham, Middx, TW1 3BZ (8891 1441, www.visitrichmond.co.uk). Twickenham rail.* **Open** *9am-5.15pm Mon-Thur; 9am-5pm Fri.*

WEIGHTS & MEASURES

The UK is moving slowly and reluctantly towards full metrication. Distances are still measured in miles but all goods are officially sold in metric quantities. Nonetheless, imperial measurements are still more commonly used, so we use them in this guide.

Index

Picture credits

Credits

Crimson credits

Editors Simon Coppock, Nicola Gibbs
Contributors Miriam Bouteba, Simon Coppock, Nicola Gibbs, Jonathan Lennie, Andrzej Lukowski, Laura Richards, Peter Watts
Proofreader Ros Sales
Layouts Emilie Crabb, Patrick Dawson
Cartography John Scott

Series Editor Sophie Blacksell Jones
Production Manager Kate Michell
Production Assistant Courtney Lawrence
Design Mytton Williams

Chairman David Lester
Managing Director Andy Riddle

Advertising Media Sales House
Marketing Lyndsey Mayhew
Sales Joel James

Acknowledgements

The editor thanks: the staff at Time Out London for their help, especially Tania Ballantine, Oliver Keens, James Manning and Ben Rowe for assistance way beyond the call of duty; Liz Gibbons, Florence and Esther; and all contributors to previous editions of *Time Out London* whose work forms the basis of this guide.

Photography credits

Front cover iStock.com/Westersoe
Back cover lJose Luis Vega/Shutterstock.com
Interior photography credits, see *p215*.

Publishing information

Time Out London Shortlist 10th edition
© TIME OUT ENGLAND LIMITED 2017
October 2017

ISBN 978 1 780592 57 2
CIP DATA: A catalogue record for this book is available from the British Library

Published by Crimson Publishing
19-21c Charles Street, Bath, BA1 1HX
(01225 584 950, www.crimsonpublishing.co.uk) on behalf of Time Out England.

Distributed by Grantham Book Services
Distributed in the US and Canada by Publishers Group West (1-510-809-3700)

Printed by Grafostil